POWER AND INFLUENCE

A Source Book for Nurses

POWER AND INFLUENCE

A Source Book for Nurses

Edited by

Kathleen R. Stevens, R.N., M.S., Ed.D.

Clinical Nurse Specialist
Nursing Research Section
The University of Texas System Cancer Center
M. D. Anderson Hospital and Tumor Institute
Houston, Texas

WY
16
P887
1983

1 0 2 0 1

A WILEY MEDICAL PUBLICATION
JOHN WILEY & SONS
New York • Chichester • Brisbane • Toronto • Singapore

Cover and interior design: Wanda Lubelska

Library of Congress Cataloging in Publication Data

Main entry under title:

Power and influence.

   (A Wiley medical publication)
   Bibliography: p.
   Includes index.
   1. Nursing—United States. 2. Nursing—Political aspects—United States. 3. Job satisfaction. I. Stevens, Kathleen R. II. Series.
RT4.P68   1983   362.1'73   82-13397
ISBN 0-471-08870-6

Printed in the United States of America

10 9 8 7 6 5 4 3 2 1

To Kelly

Foreword

Power and Influence: A Source Book for Nurses is an intriguing compilation of perspectives that addresses a number of deceptively basic, yet at the same time, quite far-reaching issues which confront the nursing profession today.

In fact, I have personally been pondering a number of these very issues for some time. In my efforts to ensure that your practitioners and clinical specialists will be accorded parity under our various federal health programs, and that you will receive appropriate representation on our national health policy advisory committees, I have become increasingly aware of the extent to which your profession has really not capitalized upon either its potential political clout, or its most laudatory public image. For example, although my colleagues in the United States Senate hold you in the highest regard, they unfortunately really do not understand the specifics of your clinical capabilities.

Similarly, after five years of intensive effort, I was finally successful in 1981 in amending the statute governing the Department of Defense CHAMPUS program in order to ensure that advanced practitioners would be allowed to bill independently for their services. This statute enabled the nurse to exercise power through billing directly for nursing services. Yet, few bills were submitted to CHAMPUS by the profession during our lengthy deliberations. This was in spite of the fact that this was a significant opportunity for you to demonstrate that practitioners could provide high quality and cost-effective care and, further, that your national association fully and enthusiastically supported my efforts.

Why, I asked myself, is the largest component of our health care profession—one which includes competent clinicians and researchers, as well as full professors at our most prestigious educational institutions—satisfied with paraprofessional status? Don't they appreciate the full extent of their potential contribution to our society? Are they really satisfied with serving as "handmaidens to physicians?" Why are they their own worst political enemies? Apparently, Dr. Kathleen Stevens heard my innermost thoughts, for the *Source Book* which she has compiled focuses upon these very questions.

In my judgment, if our nation is truly committed to fostering disease prevention and health promotion, which now appears to be the key to controlling our ever-escalating health care costs, then your profession must be in the forefront of our efforts. Our health payment mechanisms must provide "up front" coverage for your clinical services. We can no longer consider these important services to be "ancillary" or "supplemental."

We must begin to systematically address the all-important psychosocial aspects of health care, especially in delivering services to our nation's children and youth and the elderly. For example, we must insist that nursing homes are, in fact, *nursing* homes: institutions where your services are actively utilized.

I am personally convinced that your practitioners can provide from 80 to 90 percent of the health care for which we have traditionally relied upon physicians. Further, I have no doubt that your advanced practitioners are fully qualified to determine when a referral to a medical specialist would be appropriate; that is, that they can serve admirably as the entry point into our health care system, that there is no logical reason to continue to insist that they be supervised by another profession.

Perhaps, as is suggested (none too subtly) in a number of chapters in this *Source Book*, the prime reason for your political passivity is the fact that over 98 percent of your membership are female. Economists have pointed out that the average full-time employed woman earns just 50 cents for every dollar earned by men, and that women in technical and professional positions earn less than 71 percent of the men's median weekly salaries. Yet, as important as the implications of this data may be, in all candor, I feel that there is considerably more than "sex-bias" involved.

In my judgment, the most important factor has been the extent to which your profession has not really wanted to be accorded professional status—to be entitled to function autonomously and to be charged with the awesome responsibility for leading our nation's health care system. And this is the real focus of the *Source Book*, a glimpse of the "feeling of powerlessness" of our nation's professional nurses: educational and historical causes, as well as concrete suggestions for how nursing can modify the current situation.

As I reviewed the chapters in this *Source Book*, I was genuinely pleased with the depth of analysis, and the breadth of coverage, given to the many complex components of "Leadership" and "Power." As noted, there are many different types of power, each with its own unique assets and liabilities. Yet, from my personal experience, the common thread for long-term success has always been the development of trusting relationships. Accordingly, I was especially pleased with the extent to which this particular topic has been explored in considerable depth and the attention paid to the interpersonal ground rules and agency guidelines that have evolved in our society.

I was also intrigued by the authors' sensitivity to the extent to which professional nurses have not yet capitalized upon their natural alliances with nonnursing groups. For example, I have always been quite surprised by the extent of the lack of awareness to the many merits of your case exhibited by such politically powerful organizations as senior citizen spokespersons, the League of Women Voters, the National Organization of Women (NOW), the Children's Defense Fund, and the Junior League, to name but a few, who would instinctively share your views on a wide variety of issues. Further, although there is a tremendous commonality of professional interest between you and the other nonphysician health care providers—such as clinical psychologists and optometrists—rarely do I find your organizations working collaboratively on projects such as hospital admitting privileges, third-party reimbursement, etc.

Perhaps, however, in the long run, of even more importance to the readership will be the explanation of the different internal agendas within organized nursing as represented by the American Nurses' Association, the National League for Nursing, N-CAP, and the various specialty organizations. This clarification will be especially useful for those of us who do not belong to your profession, except perhaps in spirit.

For me personally, however, one of the most fascinating discussions in the *Source Book* dealt with the apparent discrepancy between the expectations developed in new graduates by our nation's schools of nursing and the "realities of practice." I found this discussion most timely both as to its impact on the individual nurse (resulting in periods of depression, acute stress, desire to leave the profession, etc.) and also for its clear implications regarding the very quality of care provided in our health care system today. No one can reasonably expect any professional school—whether we are thinking about nursing schools or law schools—to completely prepare their graduate for all of the strains of professional life ("reality shock"). However, by addressing this issue, constructive steps can be taken.

I was especially pleased to see the authors strongly urge their colleagues to become more actively involved in the political process. You should be proud of the fact that 91 percent of nurses are currently registered to vote. This is indeed significantly higher than the 70 percent national average for our general adult population. Nursing does indeed have "something unique and essential to offer patients and clients" and you should never forget this.

Our nation's health policy is shaped and created by politicians. It is your responsibility—both for your profession and for your patients—to become actively involved. We need you! The suggestions that the authors have made, such as meeting personally with your elected officials and writing articles for the public media, are excellent ones, and I sincerely hope that you will take them to heart.

To a very real extent, your destiny is in your own hands; those of us who are with you wish you the very best. However, you are the ones who collectively must take the next step.

Daniel K. Inouye
United States Senator
from Hawaii

Preface

For a number of reasons, nurses must use power. Situations calling for the use of power range from clearly stating what one wants, to dressing for an interview, to influencing legislation. To meet these situations, the nurse has at hand two broad categories of power: professional and personal. This book focuses on the professional and personal sources of power that will enable the nurse to have a positive impact on health care. The purpose of the book is to identify and describe ways the nurse can develop power sources to include in the repertoire of power strategy. The goal is to increase the personal self-determination of the nurse and to place professional self-determination where it belongs: in nursing.

Societal and evolutionary elements have limited, to a large degree, the development of power bases for nurses. In both the evolution of nursing and the socialization of nurses, business and political "savvy" has not been fostered. To the contrary, the nurse has been placed in a position of noninfluence. This is true with regard to the political process, independent decision making, key administrative positions, and budgetary matters. Even the expression of the individual nurse's thoughts is often disguised and indirect. Nursing, as an emerging profession, suffers double jeopardy in the effort to control its own development. As a result of these forces, many nursing students and practicing nurses lack professional, organizational, and political "know-how" as well as personal assertiveness and decision-making skills.

If nurses, physicians, administrators, legislators, and other health authorities are to create a responsive and responsible health care system, power must be developed and used. This book is designed to assist nurses—students and practitioners—in that development. It is intended to assist the nurse who wishes to make the ideal a reality. The book will prove helpful in basic courses, advanced seminars, continuing education programs, and self-development efforts.

Power and Influence: A Source Book for Nurses is a valuable resource because it presents the gamut of professional and personal power sources. In so doing, familiar topics are presented in a new light and related topics are presented for the first time in a comprehensive manner.

The organization of topics moves through the continuum of professional and personal sources of power. The first chapters provide broad introductions to (1) the concept of power and (2) change in nursing. The professional sources of power are presented in discussions of organizations, politics, bureaucracies, and publishing. The personal end of the continuum comes into focus as we discuss the topics of career development, personal effectiveness, decision making, and time management. The final chapter relates the nature of nursing to personal power.

Although the book concentrates on helping the reader to develop practical skills and strategies, the content is based on sound theory and available research. Each topic is described in a brief, easy-to-understand manner to provide the reader with a basis for action. The topic is then discussed in practical terms, with examples of how power is provided.

Most chapters contain exercises or thought questions that will assist the reader in applying the concept. As a special feature, the book identifies resources available for further self-development or for more elaborate theoretical explanation, as well as organizations, publications, and other sources that deal with a specific area.

Most books are the result of numerous interactions among people and their mutual supportive efforts. This book is no exception. I conceived the book as a result of interacting with the "ideal-holders" of the profession: senior nursing students who asked with sincerity, "How can I make a difference?" This book is my answer to them. It was made possible by the efforts and expertise of the contributors as well as friends and colleagues who encouraged me. My special thanks to Judy Williams for her vital role in typing the manuscript.

K.R.S.

Contributors

Janet M. Burge, R.N., Ph.D.
Professor and Chairperson
Graduate Program in Nursing
The University of Alabama in Huntsville
Huntsville, Alabama

Harriet S. Chaney, R.N., Ph.D.
Associate Professor
The University of Texas
    School of Nursing at Galveston
Galveston, Texas

Suzanne Hall Johnson, R.N., M.N.
Director of Health Update
Editor of *Dimensions of Critical Care Nursing*
Lakewood, Colorado

Clair Jordan, R.N., M.S.N.
Executive Director
Texas Nurses Association
Austin, Texas

Elizabeth A. Knebel, R.N., M.S.
Associate Dean for Administration and Coordination
    of Undergraduate Program
The University of Texas
    School of Nursing at Galveston
Galveston, Texas

Rae Wynelle Langford, R.N., Ed.D.
Associate Professor
Graduate Program
The University of Texas Health Science Center at Houston
School of Nursing
Houston, Texas

Harriet L. Sanders, R.N., M.S.N.
Assistant Professor of Nursing
Louisiana State University Medical Center
School of Nursing, Associate Degree Program
New Orleans, Louisiana

Kathleen R. Stevens, R.N., M.S., Ed.D.
Clinical Nurse Specialist
Nursing Research Section
The University of Texas System Cancer Center
M. D. Anderson Hospital and Tumor Institute
Formerly Assistant Professor
The University of Texas Health Science Center at Houston
School of Nursing
Houston, Texas

Katherine W. Vestal, R.N., M.S., Ph.D.
Assistant Professor of Pediatrics
The University of Texas Medical School at Houston
Assistant Professor
The University of Texas Health Science Center at Houston
School of Nursing
Associate Executive Director
Hermann Hospital
Houston, Texas

Marilyn D. Willman, R.N., Ph.D.
Professor and Director
School of Nursing
The University of British Columbia
Vancouver, British Columbia
Canada

Contents

POWER AND INFLUENCE

A Source Book for Nurses

1

POWER AS A POSITIVE FORCE

KATHLEEN R. STEVENS

Nurses must use power. It is imperative for nurses to exercise power in order to realize their full professional potential and maximize their contributions to health care and society at large. Clearly, nursing is at the center of health care, and from this vantage point nursing enjoys tremendous potential to change the health care system to the advantage of both health care providers and consumers.

Nurses must first understand the factors that have fostered their pervasive feelings of powerlessness, the nature of power, and the available sources of power. Once gained, this understanding can become a springboard to the nurse's development of power in the health care setting—a setting that has always been replete with power, influence, and politics.

The fact that nursing has not gained a strong power base in health care in the past is the result of two intertwined elements: (1) nursing is and has been a woman-dominated profession and considered to be the epitome of woman's traditional role; and (2) the health care system has evolved as a paternalistic one, suppressing the development of nursing and jeopardizing the quality of health care (Ashley, 1976). Still, these conditions are not a mandate for the future. Evidence shows that conditions are now changing. A new social consciousness has allowed us to recognize the abilities of women. With nurses leading the way, this consciousness will also increase consumer pressure to create an adequate and humane health care system.

However, nurses must develop and use power effectively in order to obtain results in both the nursing profession and the health care system. It is essential to understand the nature of power, for only this knowledge will enable the nurse to develop and use power and to resist the subversive power attempts of others.

At the same time, nurses must identify and develop the many personal and professional power bases available to them in order to be able to make a difference in health care as well as to survive as a profession. While they already possess some power, other sources of power, such as self-confidence, decision-making skills, political skills, and organizational skills, can be developed. Once developed, the nurse can use power as a positive force to obtain results beneficial to both patients and nurses. It is an undeniable fact that power is necessary to exercise any leadership role—from patient care to administration.

The following discussion

1. describes the factors resulting in the present state of relative powerlessness in nursing;

2. presents a useful conceptualization of power, using contemporary theories; and

3. identifies and justifies sources of power for nurses in both the personal and professional realms.

NURSES AND POWER

Nurses and power: in the past, these two terms have been likened to oil and water, not mixing well. With nurses playing the traditional woman's role in the past, little power was available to them. In addition, nurses have viewed themselves as powerless, the power game as useless, and the use of power "not commensurate with humanistic values inherent in the profession of nursing" (Claus & Bailey, 1977, p. vii).

Nursing as a Woman-Dominated Profession

Many of the reasons for nurses' lack of power are related to the fact that nursing is a woman-dominated profession. Traditionally, women do not possess power. Although there are several explanations of the differences between men and women's power, the conclusion generally drawn is that because of societal forces, men possess power and woman do not (Polk, 1974). One explanation that is particularly enlightening, when considering nursing, describes the division of labor between men and women. In the past, this division prescribed that men function in instrumental roles and women in expressive roles (Parsons & Bales, 1955). The instrumental role is oriented toward goal achievement and task accomplishment, while the expressive role is one of maintaining order and caring for others. "Traditional sex-role socialization assured that children, male and female, would grow up with the appropriate expectations" (Krueger, 1980, p. 374). Nursing embodies this traditionally female, expressive role. With women successfully socialized into this role and with 98% of those in nursing being women, it is not surprising that the nurse's role reflects to a large degree, woman's traditional expressive role.

Furthermore, even if a woman becomes educated and competent in a field, she still may not enjoy the success of her male counterpart. The reason is that she is not familiar with the game and rules of corporate politics (Harragan, 1978). Harragan contends that the socialization of men through the team model teaches them the rules of play where the goal is power and money. Women, on the other hand, learn noncontact sports and fail to learn team rules (Harragan, 1978). Health care is a system wherein a great deal of politics and power are used to control or create change. Women as nurses are at a disadvantage partly because their socialization has not taught them the corporate game. While nurses can and do creatively identify positive directions for health care, they lack the necessary sophistication in power and politics to produce the change.

Nurses are also handicapped in the power game for a second reason: the nurse *accepts* this traditional role. In some respects, it is comfortable to maintain this role because in holding to the status quo the nurse remains in a low-risk situation with little accountability. No power is gained by such a position; but this may be appealing to the traditionally socialized woman. May (1972) describes this condition as a psychological effort to protect self-esteem:

A great deal of human life can be seen as the conflict between power on one side (i.e., effective ways of influencing others, achieving the sense in interpersonal relations of significance of one's self) and powerlessness on the other. In this conflict, our efforts are made much more difficult by the fact that we block out both sides, the former because of the evil connotation of "power drives," and the latter because our powerlessness is too painful to confront. Indeed, the chief reason people refuse to confront the whole issue of power is that if they did, they would have to face their own powerlessness. (pp. 20–21)

Nurses, as professionals, must face their own powerlessness before they can move forward to develop power.

It is indeed painful to acknowledge our relative powerlessness, for nurses already have a diminished sense of self-esteem and self-confidence. The widely accepted image of the nurse as handmaiden to the physician assigns second-class status to the nurse's role. Women, in general, have largely been assigned "circumscribed, supportive, subservient, or other secondary roles" (McFarland & Shiflett, 1979, p. 5).

Fear of Power

The "evil connotation" of power to which May (1972) refers can create a fear of power, especially in those who have been the subject of unnecessary control by others. Often a fear of power results from having seen power abused. On the surface, the very topic of power in a humanistically oriented profession such as nursing may seem antithetic to its purpose. However, it is only through acquiring power that nurses will be able to improve the quality of care delivered to people. The fear of power also involves a reluctance to take risks and assume responsibility—for power implies action.

The Health Care System as an Inhibiting Factor

Another set of factors contributes to the present state of relative powerlessness in nursing. The system in which nursing has evolved is and has been a male-dominated one, which has essentially inhibited the growth of nursing as a profession. "The male physicians and hospital administrators were preoccupied . . . with control over others, profits, and male privileges" (Heide, 1976, p. v). Even in the face of these odds, the nursing profession managed to develop from a servant status to a collegiate-educated profession.

The Case for Power in Nursing

In order to realize the full potential of nurses to make valuable and unique contributions to effective and humane systems of health care, the nursing profession must acquire, develop, and exercise power and influence. Such power and influence must be used within the nursing profession, in the total health care field, and in society at large. Power and influence in nursing will result in the leadership needed to direct the profession of nursing and to revise the health care system to meet the needs of people. An awareness of power is also an awareness of its potential for making human endeavors more productive. As nurses and nursing develop and use power in a rational and organized fashion, nurses will emerge as leaders in health care reform. The results will be the improvement of both nursing and health care. Ashley points out that "Nursing is health care. If current and future crises in the health field are to be resolved effectively, society must face this fact" (1976, pp. 124–125). Nurses must also face this fact and set about to actively develop the power bases sorely needed to lead the way in health care.

As nurses acquire power, the profession will develop. And as the nurse's feeling of powerlessness is replaced by one of power, the reason for "nurses leaving nursing" may be dispelled (Kramer, 1974). The resulting greater commitment to the profession and the enhanced image of the nurse will strengthen the profession. With nursing at the center of health care and with nurses' commitment to quality and to the consumers of health care, such power would be well placed. Nurses must use power to develop the profession and to achieve its goals in health care.

THE NATURE OF POWER

Knowledge of the nature of power in and of itself affords a type of power. If one understands the sources of power, the methods of using power, and the array of possible responses to power, he or she has power. "Our success or failure in using and reacting to power is largely determined by realizing the bases of power available to us, knowing how to use them, and being able to anticipate their probable effects" (Jacobson, 1972, p. 19).

Definition of Power

It is important to understand power as a dynamic "property of the social relationship rather than an attribute of a person" (Jacobson, 1972, p. 166). Power can be defined simply as the ability to influence the behavior of another person (Gibson et al., 1979, p. 188); or as the "ability and willingness to affect the behavior of others" (Claus & Bailey, 1977, p. 17). Claus and Bailey fortify this definition by describing ability as being based on strength, and willingness being based on energy. Within this context, power is based on results. The pyramidal force of power is depicted as strength supporting energy which, in turn, supports the action (1977, p. 17).

An attempt to define power inevitably leads to a comparison of this concept to four others: influence, authority, leadership, and politics. Power and influence are compared by considering the following: "Power is a source of influence, whereas influence is the result of the proper use of power" (Claus & Bailey, 1977, p. 21). Influence is power applied; it is power in action.

Authority is a specific type of power that results from delegation within an organization. It is power legitimized (McFarland & Shiflett, 1979, p. 1). Authority tends to be the most reliable and stable type of power.

When compared to leadership, it is clear that power is a dimension of leadership behavior. However, power is not possessed only by leaders: individuals in an organization delegate power upward to the leader. (Stevens, 1978, p. 108). They allow the leader to influence them.

Another concept closely associated with power is politics. Politics can be described as the way in which vested interests or goals are promoted and protected by an individual or group (Leininger, 1977, p. 8).

Types of Power

The complexity of power has made its study difficult. Through all the attempts to study power, the categorization developed by French and Raven has received the widest application. French and Raven (1960) identify the following types of power.

Reward power rests on the belief that the influencing agent possesses a resource that can be obtained by conforming to the agent's request. The resource may be praise, recognition, income, or status promotion. If reward power is used, it is necessary for the influencing agent to maintain surveillance over the recipient. This type of power has a broad range since it can be used in any kind of behavior or attitudinal influence. When reward power is used and the reward is actually delivered, it increases power. Reward power is often exercised in the employer-employee relationship because of the employer's resources to provide such things as pay raises or promotions.

Coercive power is based on the influencing agent's ability to mediate negative sanctions or punish noncompliance. It is similar to reward power because it is based on the recipient's belief that the agent will deliver punishment for noncompliance. The actual punishment may be disapproval, withdrawal of love, or physical attack. As in the case of reward power, the agent must directly observe the noncompliance for coercive power to operate. The range of coercive power is limited to those situations where the agent can provide negative sanctions. In contrast to the exercise of reward power, use of coercive power may detract from the future power of the agent. The change in the recipient's behavior may only be outward in response to either reward or coercive power.

Referent power is based on identification with the agent. It is a feeling or a common bond shared with the agent by the recipient. As this commonality increases, the referent power held by the agent also increases. Referent power can be used when the patient emphasizes their commonality (i.e., "you and I are just plain folk"), and the agent needs no special resources. Unlike reward and coercive power, there is no need for the influencing agent to observe the recipient; however, it is vital that the relationship between the two be maintained for the power to continue. The identification of the recipient with the agent leads to additional attraction and increased referent power. This power type can be used when there is a desire to establish and maintain a positive interpersonal relationship. The range of referent power may be broad or limited (i.e., limited to members of the same organization). An outcome of the use of referent power is that it may preclude the agent's use of other types of power, particularly reward and coercive.

Legitimate power is based on the recipient's internalized values that specify the agent's right to influence the recipient, or the obligation to accept the influence. Acceptance of the social hierarchy or role perception are often the basis of legitimate power, such as in employer-employee or teacher-student relationships and, to some extent, in nurse-patient relationships. Legitimate power may also involve cultural values, such as the social obligation to return a favor. This type of power does not require surveillance by the agent to insure compliance, but it is dependent on the continuity of the hierarchal relationship. The range of legitimate power is limited to those situations in which the recipient believes the agent has the right to influence.

Expert power arises from the perception that the agent possesses superior knowledge or skills. It is also critical that the recipient perceive the agent as trustworthy and credible. Medical advice is often influential because of the physician's expert power base. The agent does not need to observe the recipient in order to exert expert power, but the relationship must continue. The effect of expert power is that, while it does not create a negative response, the recipient may move away from the agent to avoid further influence. The range of expert power is limited to the area of the agent's expertise. If used successfully, expert power will build because the agent will be established as well informed and trustworthy.

Informational power is based on information communicated by the influencing agent (Raven, 1965). It involves the ability of the agent to persuade the recipient to behave differently. The persuasion consists of good reasons for the recipient to behave as the agent prescribes. If the recipient sees these as valid, and if the information is consistent with the recipient's value system, then he or she complies. For example, an explanation of the relation between a high-cholesterol diet and heart disease may influence a person to change eating patterns. Surveillance is not necessary and the power base is independent of the agent because the reasons themselves become the source of influence. The range of informational power is limited to the situation in which the agent can give information to the recipient. The effect of this power base is that it has the potential to produce cognitive change since the influence is immediately internalized. Both private beliefs and public behavior are changed with this power base.

Other Categorizations of Power

Positional power that is combined with the authority existing in an organization inherently has legitimate and reward power. Legitimate power exists as authority; reward power may include the right to hire, fire, promote, recognize, and grant raises. This combination is referred to as *formal* or *positional power*.

Functional or *personal power* may be independent of formal power and may exist with or without it. Functional (referent) power may exist with or without formal power. Yet the impact of combined formal and functional power is obviously much greater than the impact of either alone. However, functional power may be used to convince others to grant more formal power to one's position (Stevens, 1980).

Power also exists in the following five forms, all of which are present in the same person at different times. These forms of power describe the relationship between the influencing agent and the recipient.

1. *Exploitative:* power identified with *force,* subjecting persons to the use of the powerholder; this is the most destructive type of power presupposing violence or threat of violence;

2. *Manipulative:* power *over* another person, although the recipient may have originally initiated the power out of desperation or anxiety; while necessary in some situations, this power should be used sparingly;

3. *Competitive:* power *against* another person, which may be destructive or constructive; in its destructive form, one gains ground because one's opponents lose

ground; in its constructive form, it adds zest to human relations and may bring out dormant capacities;

4. *Nutrient:* power *for* the other, which is illustrated by the parent's care for the child; it comes out of a concern for the welfare of another; and

5. *Integrative:* power *with* another person, which abets the other's power; it is growth-producing as it proposes antithesis against the other's thesis, at which point the other generates a synthesis. (May, 1972, pp. 105–113)

Since all five forms of power are present in all persons, the goal is to learn to use the different forms appropriately in given situations (May, 1972, p. 113).

Power and Corporate Politics

Developing power is just the first step in making changes. A critical step remains: to learn the rules by which the game of organizational politics is played. Any setting where people work together is steeped in corporate politics where the rules are rigid and applied to everyone—even to those who are unaware of the rules. Private business, large hospitals, and small clinics are all run according to these rules.

Knowledge of and orientation to these rules are acquired differentially among boys and girls in their formative years. According to Harragan (1978), during their formative years, women learn to perform skills but do not play competitive games. Men, however, through the military and sports models of cooperative competition, learn the parameters of the game in which the skill is applied. "The objectives of girls' games are never to beat anybody or perform under competitive stress, but merely to improve an agility in a vacuum." (Harragan, 1978, p. 72) This perspective is extended into women's job orientations. Harragan points out that women do not learn from their childhood games a fundamental rule of corporate politics: ".... it doesn't matter how good you are but how well you perform in the game, as part of the team, that counts" (Harragan, 1978, p. 73).

The rules of play become part of the secret of success and are part of the enjoyment of the game. Within the confines of the rules, a skilled player can try to outmaneuver an opponent. But the rules are applied equally to all—skilled and unskilled alike. Other perspectives of corporate politics are that losing—as well as winning—is part of competition; defeat should be taken as a signal to correct errors and go forward with a determination to win; and, nobody is good at everything (Harragan, 1978). Clearly, such perspectives lead to greater risk taking in competitive situations.

The application of these concepts to nursing exposes the fact that nurses (along with most women) have not learned corporate politics. Harragan observed in 1978 that nurses had a very narrow role in relation to the health care agency. Fortunately, this has changed. Nurses have made inroads into high-level health care administration and today there is more than one nurse administrator on the executive administrative boards of this nation's health care institutions! The nurse administrator who capitalizes on the rules of the game can move to win the two objectives of corporate politics: power and money. Then the nurse administrator is in a potentially powerful position because nurses represent the majority of workers in a health care agency. By identifying this power in numbers, the nurse executive can lay a course of action to acquire control of the budget (money) for her or his division. But the moves must be made within the rules—"The team and the players conform to the rules, never vice versa" (Harragan, 1978, p. 72). The rules for "rookies" that must be observed are:

1. Know your job duties and perform them well.

2. Don't let anger or fear drive you to impulsive actions that you may regret.

3. Never criticize or challenge your boss at meetings where others are present.

4. Don't try to do everything or be all things to all people.

5. Learn from mistakes and putdowns. Figure out better tactics for the next try.

6. Don't disparage any success you achieve. Publicize and promote yourself at every opportunity. (Harragan, 1978, pp. 91–92)

Nurses do not need to look far for a situation in which to heed this advice!

A thorough understanding of the corporate game will reveal that the rules are written to allow the proficient player to outmaneuver, deceive an opponent, and disguise an action without crossing the fair line. Not realizing this, the inexperienced nurse may interpret some actions as "unfair" when in fact they fall within the fair line. An example of action which falls close to the line is the situation in which the leader of one lobbying group withholds information vital to the successful performance of an opposing lobbying group.

Perhaps those who are averted from gaining power because of their fear that it will be "abused" are not correctly identifying abuse. In some instances, it is conceivable that an act of power may be identified as abusive when, in fact, it is the onlooker's ignorance of the rules that distorts the assessment.

As nurses move into power, two cardinal rules must be heeded:

1. Power is not a skill to be gained for itself but must be applied toward respectable ends, according to the rules.

2. The use of power should not be labeled "abuse" if it is within the rules of the corporate game and is intended to create a more humane system of care.

Power as a Positive Force

Power should be a means and not an end. As such, it can be used for rational or irrational ends, for benevolent or malicious intent, to be inspiring or stifling. It is the ends to which power is applied, rather than power itself, that determine its "good" or "evil" nature. "So long as interest in power can remain attached to universal ideals, the risks of abusing power diminish" (Zaleznik & Kets Devries, 1975, p. 8). With the profession's strong record of benevolence, surely power in nursing will be a positive force.

The desire to use power implies the desire to lead, to influence others (Claus & Bailey, 1977). Nurses should use power with other nurses to improve the nursing profession; nurses should use power with physicians and hospital administrators to revitalize the present health care system; nurses should use power with consumers to increase awareness of the possibilities and potentialities of health care. Through the positive use of power, the nurse will lead each of these groups to accomplish goals common to the good of all.

POWER SOURCES FOR NURSES

It has been said that ". . . power and politics exist, to be used or abused, in practically every situation" (Leininger, 1977, p. 6). The plentiful power sources available to nurses can lead to the profession's becoming a decisive force in the reform of today's health care system. In small beginnings, such as guiding a patient through the outpatient clinic, as in larger endeavors, such as influencing health care legislation, the nurse must use power.

The Power Nurses Hold

To begin, nurses must take note of the power they already hold. Ashley (1973) pointedly assessed this power when she said, "Nursing power, as a productive force, is the single most important factor maintaining our health care system today" (p. 632). Now that is a great deal of power! Nurses keep the health care system operative. We must now consider the choice of exerting this power to create the needed changes. The mounting influence of nurses is becoming evident. Social consciousness of the unique abilities of nurses is reflected in the sales of the book *Nurse* and the interest in its television dramatization under the same name. The nurse's actions have captured the public's attention, indicating an increased public awareness of the profession.

The Power Nurses Need

Although some power exists in nursing today, much more can and must be developed. The identification and development of multiple power sources for individuals and organizations will place a tremendously positive force in the hands of nurses. No longer will frustrated nurses leave nursing because they *could not make a difference.*

The sources of power fall broadly into two categories: professional bases and personal bases. The line between the two is not distinct, but the concept is more of a continuum. Professional power bases are largely anchored in groups of people. Examples include professional organizations, organizational gamesmanship, and publishing. Personal bases of power focus on the individual's ability to project a positive image of self-confidence, self-esteem, and competency. Some of these abilities are decision-making skills, value clarification, and assertiveness. The more power sources the nurse develops, the greater influence he or she can exercise.

PROFESSIONAL SOURCES OF POWER

Professional sources of power stem from groups of people, be they in a professional association, an organizational situation, or the readership of a journal. In order to tap these professional sources of power it is vital to understand how nursing functions within the broader context of health care delivery and the way in which it is evaluated. We would have no perspective for the goal of power in nursing without this understanding, plus a knowledge of the issues facing nursing. Close study of Chapter 2 will reveal this perspective, which is the "universal ideal" to which power must be attached in order to preclude its abuse. The role of the change agent is also discussed.

A most impressive source of power available to the profession lies in its relative numbers. Power in numbers is captured through professional nursing associations. The purpose of our long-standing nursing organizations, which represent nursing as a whole, has been the development of the profession. Membership is but a small beginning; active participation must ensue if this source of power is to be realized. We must also consider the possibility that power bases exist in associations outside of nursing: for example, in organizations of college educators, women executives, and consumer groups which may share goals with nursing. Chapter 3 examines the power bases of nursing and nonnursing organizations.

The societal need for professional nursing is reflected in public laws governing the profession. Nurses must guide the revision and updating of these laws to better meet public needs. This is accomplished through political activity and participation in the legislative process on local, state, and national levels. Numerous opportunities for nurses to become involved in the legislative process and create an impact on the political and legislative arenas are described in Chapter 4.

Organizational gamesmanship is requisite to the nurse's developing power. The overwhelming majority of nurses work in a health care agency, most in hospitals. These institutions strive to maintain organizational integrity and therefore display many bureaucratic characteristics. The nurse must know the "rules of the game" to effectively develop and use power in such a setting. Chapter 5 examines power in the health care agency.

Another source of power for nurses is that of publishing one's ideas. While publishing is not traditionally considered a source of power, one of the surest ways to add impact to a viewpoint is to widely disseminate supporting information. The outlets and channels for publishing for both nursing and lay audiences can and should be used to influence the nursing profession and the consumers of health care. Publishing as a power source is discussed in Chapter 6.

Career development involves some elements of personal sources of power. If thoroughly developed, career development dovetails the nurse's expert power within the evolving health care system. Nursing is one of the few careers in which there are a multitude of options and readily available jobs. Therefore, not only must the nurse give serious thought to opportunities afforded in a given job, but she or he must also consider the overall development of a career. As discussed in Chapter 7, career development and job planning involve setting goals and being cognizant of the expert power one possesses.

PERSONAL SOURCES OF POWER

When considering personal sources of power, one must focus clearly on individual abilities. One must first believe in her or his own power before becoming truly influential with others. At present, the nurse's self-image is wrought with feelings of powerlessness and decreased personal confidence, which precludes using the power that she or he may already possess. Increasing self-confidence, self-esteem, and assertiveness skills build personal effectiveness and make other sources of power accessible. Chapter 8 examines personal effectiveness as a power source.

Whether or not the nurse is an administrator, the personal use of specific management techniques can result in influence. Since two of the nurse's most crucial assets are his or her decisions and time, decision making and time management skills can increase personal effectiveness. The resulting strength, energy, and action are power. Chapter 9 discusses decision making and time management as they relate to power.

The very nature of nursing has an impact on personal power. Factors such as educational level contribute to the nurse's power base. Yet other factors like the tumultuous transition from school to work setting and the high stress present in nursing distract from power. These topics are considered in Chapter 10.

SUMMARY

Nursing has not enjoyed a power base broad enough to enable the nurse to make a significant difference in health care although she is in an excellent position to do so. The development of nursing power has been delayed by characteristics of the profession and of the setting in which nurses practice. Still, these factors are amenable to change. The nurse must not only prepare for these changes; she must create them.

Power as a positive force will be the nurse's instrument for change. It will serve as the means to the end of a reformed health care system and a strengthened nursing profession. The nurse must accept power as an essential part of her role in health care and cultivate multiple power sources from both the personal and professional categories.

For nursing, the question is not whether nurses *should* use power, but *how* they will use it.

BIBLIOGRAPHY

Ashley, J.A.: This I believe about power in nursing. *Nursing Outlook* 21:631–641, 1973.

Ashley, J.A.: *Hospitals, Paternalism, and the Role of the Nurse.* New York, Teachers College Press, 1976.

Brooten, D., Hayman, L., & Naylor, M.: *Leadership for Change: A Guide for the Frustrated Nurse.* Philadelphia, J. B. Lippincott, 1978.

Clark, C.C. & Shea, C.A.: *Management in Nursing: A Vital Link in the Health Care System.* New York, McGraw-Hill, 1979.

Claus, K.E. & Bailey, J.T.: *Power and Influence in Health Care: A New Approach to Leadership.* St. Louis, C. V. Mosby, 1977.

Donnelly, G. F., Mengal, A., & Sutterly, D.C.: *The Nursing System: Issues, Ethics, and Politics.* New York, John Wiley, 1980.

French, J.R.P., Jr. & Raven, B.: The bases of social power. In Cartwright, D. and A. F. Zander (eds.): *Group Dynamics,* 2nd ed. Evanston, Ill., Row, Peterson, 1960, pp. 607–623.

Gibson, J.L., Ivancevich, J.M., & Donnelly, J.H.: *Organizations: Behavior, Structure, and Processes.* Dallas, Business Publications, 1979.

Goldsmith, D.M.: Power and influence in the organizational setting. In *Power: Use It or Lose It*, National League for Nursing Publication No. 52–165, pp. 19–21, 1977.

Harragan, B.L.: *Games Mother Never Taught You: Corporate Gamesmanship for Women.* New York, Warner Books, 1978.

Heide, W.S.: Introduction, in J.A. Ashley: *Hospitals, Paternalism, and the Role of the Nurse.* New York, Teachers College Press, 1976, pp. v–viii.

Jacobson, W.D.: *Power and Interpersonal Relations.* Belmont, Ca., Wadsworth, 1972.

Kramer, M.: *Reality Shock: Why Nurses Leave Nursing.* Saint Louis, C. V. Mosby, 1974.

Leininger, M.: Territoriality, power, and creative leadership in administrative nursing contexts. In *Power: Use It or Lose It,* National League for Nursing Publication No. 52–165, pp. 6–18, 1977.

McFarland, D.E. & Shiflett, N.: The role of power in the nursing profession. *Nursing Dimensions* 7:1–131, 1979.

May, R.: *Power and Innocence.* New York, W.W. Norton, 1972.

Parsons, T. & Bales, R.F.: *Family, Socialization, and Interaction Process.* Glencoe Ill., Free Press, 1955.

Polk, B.B.: Male power and the women's movement. *Journal of Applied Behavioral Science* 10:415–431, 1974.

Raven, B.H.: Social influence and power. In Steiner I.D. & Fishbein M. (eds.): *Current Studies in Social Psychology.* New York, Holt, Rinehart and Winston, 1965.

Stevens, B.J.: *The Nurse as Executive,* 2nd ed. Wakefield, Mass., Nursing Resources, 1980.

Stevens, W.F.: *Management and Leadership in Nursing.* New York, McGraw-Hill, 1978.

Stogdill, R.M.: *Handbook of Leadership: A Survey of Theory and Research.* New York, The Free Press, 1974.

Yura, H. & Walsh, M.: Concepts and theories related to leadership. *Nursing Dimensions* 7:75–86, 1979.

Zaleznik, A. & Kets Devries, M.F.: *Power and the Corporate Mind.* Boston, Houghton Mifflin, 1975.

RECOMMENDED READINGS

Claus, Karen & Bailey, June T.: *Power and Influence in Health Care.* St. Louis, C. V. Mosby, 1977.

This book presents a model of power/authority/influence for leadership in health care. The model is especially useful in examining power from a theoretical framework.

Harragan, Betty Lehan: *Games Mother Never Taught You: Corporate Gamesmanship for Women.* Warner Books, 1978.

> Although this book is addressed to a business-woman audience, any nurse will find the corporate game rules she describes well worth knowing. However, be cautious of her advice on clothing since it is not research-based.

McFarland, Dalton E., & Shiflett, Nola (eds.): Power in Nursing. *Nursing Dimensions 7,* 1979.

> This topical volume is a collection of articles related to power. It examines politics, territoriality, organizational power, and leadership. The eleven articles represent an outstanding collection not often found in one resource.

Polk, Barbara Bovee: Male power and the women's movement. *Journal of Applied Behavioral Science 10:*415–431, 1974.

> Four different perspectives which explore the power relationship between females and males are concisely presented in this analysis. Activities and their potential impact are discussed.

Reiff, Robert: The control of knowledge: the power of helping professions. *Journal of Behavioral Science 10:*451–461, 1974.

> In this thought-provoking article, the author analyzes the control of knowledge as a power source in the helping professions. His philosophical perspective could serve as a basis of consumer rights.

CHANGE AND POWER

MARILYN D. WILLMAN

Change is an all-pervading influence on our lives today. This kind of statement is made so often that it loses its impact and is perceived as one of those things that goes without saying. The fact of change per se is essential and, indeed, is the basis for survival and progress. However, the rapidity with which change now occurs and the magnitude of its impact on our lives is potentially overwhelming. In part, this arises from failure to anticipate and prepare for change. It has become important to plan for change rather than just let it come in the natural course of events.

Successful use of the change process as a source of power requires not only a knowledge of change theory but also an appreciation and understanding of the evolution of nursing within the broader context of the health care system. The purpose of this chapter is to elaborate on the topic of change as a power source for nurses. Specifically discussed are change models, purposes for change, areas in nursing in which further change is desirable, and facilitators and deterrents to change. A brief review of the change process and its relevance to nursing will serve as a background for the discussion.

As professionals, nurses must not only cope with change as a factor in their personal lives, but must also be knowledgeable about its influence on the image and practice of nursing and, ultimately, on the health care system. Historically, professional nurses have most often reacted to, rather than initiated, change. Nurses became the recipients of duties cast off by physicians as the medical profession evolved. Skills such as intravenous and intramuscular injections, the taking of blood pressures, and the majority of physical assessment techniques were once carried out exclusively by the physician. As bureaucracy in health care increased, the nurses accepted the role of "paper coordinator." Nurses have permitted themselves to be moved farther and farther away from the patient as others made decisions about the delivery of nursing care. Furthermore, nurses have not been entirely unwilling or unwitting victims of the system. Despite our numbers and potential influence, nurses have diluted the power and potential of the nurse's role as change agent by internecine struggles and failure to seize opportunities for change as they arose. For example, nurses have only very recently begun to capitalize on the shortage of skilled nursing personnel as an argument for improved working conditions and as a means for garnering public support for the maintenance of high-quality nursing care.

Nurses are now coming to realize that initiation of change is a professional responsibility and one source of power where the potential has yet to be fully realized. Professional literature is replete with articles on change theory applied to nursing, the role of the nurse as change agent, leadership and the initiation of change, to cite only a few examples. Educational programs describe how they prepare graduates for the change agent role and continuing education programs provide information about change theory and its application in a variety of care settings. There is the temptation to suggest that the subject, like the "integrated curriculum," is but another of the bandwagons that nursing is so fond of jumping on without sufficient evidence of validity or effectiveness. While this may be true to some extent, the situations considered in this book clearly indicate that nurses must become more knowledgeable initiators of change and participants in the process. Planned change is a means of exercising control over one's personal and professional destiny. The development of such control represents one source of power for nurses.

As we consider the change agent role as a source of power for the nurse, we must bear in mind that it is only one such source and that its effectiveness may depend on the presence of certain precursors, some of which are dealt with in this volume. In other words, effective use of a means to increase one's power sources may depend on other power bases such as nursing expertise and competence, assertiveness, and affiliation with professional organizations. Thus, the process is a circular one, reminiscent of the old adage that "it takes money to make money." A certain amount of power is necessary to fully exploit the potentials of other sources of power.

THE CHANGE PROCESS

Planned change is defined as a "deliberative and collaborative process involving a change agent and a client system." (Brooten, Hayman, & Naylor, 1978, p. 81). The client system may be "an individual, a group of people, an agency, an organization or a social institution" (Brooten et al., 1978, p. 81).

Several models have been developed to explain the process of change. Study and comparison will reveal that these models have many elements in common. It will be most helpful for nurses seeking to understand and use planned change as a strategy to select the model that is clearest to them and has the most relevance for their practice and purposes. The following is a discussion of four change models: (1) the Lewin Model; (2) the Havelock Model; (3) the Lippitt Model; and (4) the Problem-Solving Model. Table 2.1 sets out in specific terms the elements of each of the change models presented so that the commonalities among them can be easily seen.

The Lewin Model

The work of Kurt Lewin serves as a basis for classical change theory. He described the process of change as having three phases: unfreezing, moving, and refreezing. Unfreezing is the stage in which the need for change is identified: a problem is identified which must be addressed in order to improve the functioning of the system, or it be-

Table 2.1
ELEMENTS OF FOUR CHANGE PROCESS MODELS

Levwin	Havelock	Lippitt	Problem Solving
1. Unfreezing	1. Building a relationship 2. Diagnosing the problem 3. Acquiring the relevant resources	1. Development of need for change 2. Establishment of change relationship 3. Diagnosis	1. Assessment
2. Moving	4. Choosing the solution 5. Gaining acceptance	4. Action planning 5. Action implementation	2. Planning 3. Implementation
3. Refreezing	6. Stabilization and self-renewal	6. Generalization and stabilization of change 7. Termination	4. Evaluation 5. Stabilization

comes apparent that there may be a better way to carry out a given activity. Moving is the stage of change per se during which the actions required to effect the change are identified and carried out. The refreezing stage is the period during which consolidation, integration, and stabilization occur. That is, the change has been initiated and now must be firmly incorporated or refrozen into the system. Lewin described two sets of forces: driving and restraining, which respectively either facilitate or deter the process of change. Both sets of forces must be properly identified so that facilitators may be maximized and deterrents minimized as much as possible (Welch, 1979, pp. 307–309).

With Lewin's framework as a basis, others have developed change models. Three models with particular relevance in nursing are presented below.

The Havelock Model

Havelock's modification of Lewin's work has six elements: "building a relationship, diagnosing the problem, acquiring the relevant resources, choosing the solution, gaining experience, and stabilization and self-renewal" (Welch, 1979, p. 313). This model emphasizes the planning stages of the change process and obviously supports the idea that planning for change may well be more time-consuming than the actual implementation of the change.

The Lippitt Model

Lippitt, in cooperation with others, expanded upon each of Lewin's three phases. The unfreezing phase is seen as having two phases: "development of a need for change and establishment of a change relationship" (Lippitt, Hooyman, Sashkin, & Kaplan, 1978, pp. 4–8). In other words, once the client system has recognized a need for change, the change agent is called upon to use the full repertoire of skills available in collaborating with the client to imple-

ment the change process. Within the "moving" aspect of
Lewin's model, Lippitt and his associates define three
phases: "diagnosis, action planning, and action implementation" (1978, pp. 9–15). In Lippitt's model, Lewin's refreezing phase is translated into two phases: "generaliza-
tion and stabilization of change and termination" (Lippitt,
et al., 1978, pp. 17–19.

The Problem-Solving Model

Brooten and associates describe a problem-solving approach to change which is derived from several sources.
This approach is particularly meaningful to nurses because
of its similarity to the nursing process. The use of terminology such as assessment, planning, implementation, and
evaluation removes any mystery which might surround
the change process. Brooten and her colleagues discuss the
problem-solving approach in some detail; the highlights of
that discussion follow.

The assessment phase is concerned with identifying the
interest in and motivation for change, and the environment in which the change will occur. Planning, the second
phase, requires the development of a support group which
formulates short-term and long-term goals and develops
strategies for action and methods of evaluation. Elements
to be considered in the planning phase are centers of
power and possible sources for conflict and resistance to
the proposed change. Once resistance is identified, the
support group is prepared to develop specific strategies.
The next step in the process is implementation. It seems
clear that, if the planning phase is properly carried out,
implementation is primarily a matter of translating the
plans into reality. Evaluation of progress against the established goals is built into the implementation phase in order
to measure progress to a given point, to identify activities
yet to be carried out, and to develop new strategies if required. The final phase of the process is stabilization when
no further change is needed or desired. It is appropriate in
this phase to emphasize consolidation of the gains while

leaving open the possibility of innovation (Brooten, Hayman, & Naylor, 1978, pp. 83–97).

RELEVANCE OF THE CHANGE PROCESS FOR NURSING

The use of planned change is one source of power for the nurse because it promotes the exercise of control over events rather than mere reactions to events initiated by others. It is important that nurses as potential change agents be knowledgeable about the change process and have an acquaintance with the more commonly used change process models. In addition, the change agent requires well-developed problem-solving and decision-making skills and the ability to work effectively with both individuals and groups (Welch, 1979, p. 307).

The importance of planned change in nursing has been stated as follows:

> Participation in planned change demands a heavy investment of individual and collective time and energy. But the rewards are commensurate. Planned change can have a unifying rather than a divisive effect on the client system. Applied within nursing, it can help the profession clarify its purposes and increase it effectiveness in seeking to improve its own status and to create a better health care system for people. (Brooten et al., 1978, p. 82)

As can be seen, change theory and the process of change have an almost endless variety of applications. The concern here is with change as it relates to the nursing profession. What is it that we hope to achieve for the professional through the change process? If a group of nurses were polled, the specifics would no doubt vary, but a general theme would prevail. It would be the wish to see nurses assume their rightful place among health professionals and have the opportunity to develop their potential for influencing and improving the quality of health care wherever it is provided. Change is not sought for its own sake nor for the aggrandizement of the profession or the individuals within it, but rather for improvement of health care and its delivery. In addition to promoting the improvement of health care per se, nursing has the potential, indeed the responsibility, for helping to improve the quality of life through emphasis on health maintenance, prevention of disease, and rehabilitation. Nurses wish to be recognized as colleagues, consultants, and collaborators rather than as handmaidens; as providers of care rather than as coordinators who delegate responsibilities for care to others; as initiators and principal investigators of nursing research projects rather than as research assistants on the research projects of others; as nursing educators/practitioners who participate actively in the functioning of health care agencies and in the provision of care rather than as visitors engaged for a few hours a week in the supervision of students; as members of a professional discipline that has established its legitimate place in the university community rather than as a group of nurse faculty who seek exemptions from expectations for research and scholarly work held by other disciplines and maintain a presence by virtue of the sufferance of the traditional academic disciplines. The reader will no doubt identify other "rather thans" from his or her own professional experiences. All are cogent examples of the need for change.

AREAS FOR CHANGE

What, then, are the areas within nursing that we seek to change? It seems clear that these are nursing practice, the practice setting, the educational preparation, and the image of the nurse. All are so intimately related that it is difficult to separate one from the other. Nevertheless, what follows is an attempt to address each area in turn.

Nursing Practice

In its early years, nursing was seen as a calling as defined by Florence Nightingale rather than a profession. Many of the functions carried out by nurses were dependent ones in the sense that they required action in response to the orders of another—namely a physician. The orders were quite specific in terms of both actions and the frequency with which they were to be carried out. Relatively little judgment on the nurse's part was required or wanted by either party—nurse or physician. Even so-called "p.r.n. orders" demanded only minimal judgment on the part of the nurse. Thus, the nurse was perceived and, indeed, perceived herself as the assistant to and supporter of the physician; she was the doer, the implementer of a plan of care, albeit a plan for medical rather than nursing care.

The change in this dependent role did not evolve primarily as a result of planned and organized transfer of responsibility, but in part because medical practice and technology changed. The changes were of such a degree that it was no longer possible for the physician to care for the same number of patients without turning over certain responsibilities for care to other members of the health care team, most often nurses. Thus, nurses came to include in their repertoire a wider variety and a larger number of independent functions. Still, it is incorrect to suggest that the only impetus for these developments was the change in the role of the physician. Nurses, by virtue of changes in educational programs and their developing sense of nursing as a profession in its own right, were better prepared to accept and develop the independent role and to become something more than adjuncts to physicians.

As the profession has continued to evolve, the development of the independent aspect of practice with its judgment and decision-making facets has become paramount.

The situations in which the autonomous nursing role is exercised continue to increase and to be documented in the literature. Extrahospital practice settings, most often thought of as those in which the independent functions come to the fore, are numerous. An obvious example is the location remote from other health personnel and facilities where the nurse makes critical judgments with access only to long-distance telephone consultation. Closer to the experience of most nurses are community health, nurse-operated clinics of various types, nurse-physician joint practices, and private practices and consulting firms established by nurses. Nevertheless, it remains true that large numbers of nurses work in hospitals. It is in these settings that the autonomous aspect of nursing practice must increasingly be emphasized as essential for the provision of quality care and as a power source for nurses as providers of that care.

In intensive and coronary care units, there is little question about the existence of the independent practice of nurses and their concomitant colleagueship with other health team members, physicians in particular. The unique and independent contributions of nursing seem to be recognized in such areas as neonatal intensive care units, burn units, psychiatric units and, interestingly enough, in a variety of long-term care units. In fact, nursing might well be a far different profession in terms of independence of function had its major development been in long-term care settings. The care of long-term patients has traditionally been of less interest to physicians and the needs are often for nursing rather than medical care. It is in the less specialized care areas, where the majority of nurses practice, that nursing has failed to strongly define and establish the role of the autonomous practitioner with all that the designation encompasses. Perhaps this lack of role definition and autonomy is the reason that nurses in such clinical settings seem to perceive themselves as relatively unimportant and powerless members of the patient care team, why many nurses leave the profession, why there seems to be so little commitment to the profession among those who stay, and why nurses find their work un-challenging and unsatisfying. This is a major area which nursing must address and where changes must be instituted which will promote autonomy, influence, and increased power for nurses and nursing.

Nursing Practice Settings

Let us assume for the moment that by waving a magic wand it were possible to provide a generation of nurses educated and socialized to function as autonomous practitioners in all clinical settings. What changes would be required in practice settings to accommodate this new wave of nursing practitioners? First and foremost, nurses would expect to have more to say about the conditions under which care is provided for patients or clients. For example, they would promote the development of a climate in which health professionals function as colleagues and in which each is respected for a unique contribution to care. More stringent stipulations would be set forth regarding levels of care required in a given setting and the categories of personnel who could best provide them; regarding numbers of personnel in the defined categories needed to maintain high-quality care; and regarding the development of patterns of use that would provide the most efficient and effective use of nursing personnel.

At the same time, satisfying work experiences must be available for individual practitioners. More flexible approaches to assignment of personnel would be emphasized to accommodate the personal life-styles of the care providers and to meet the needs of patients and clients. In some situations, primary nursing might be the choice, but flexibility of pattern would be the key rather than the exclusive use of whatever may be the current popular trend. As can be seen from these examples, change and innovation do not always demand totally new and revolutionary approaches. They are frequently the outgrowth of a reexamination of ideas and patterns that are not new in and of themselves, but whose time has come—or whose time has come again.

Innovation and change in delivery of nursing care in the wide variety of practice settings depends greatly upon the availability of leadership from nurse administrators prepared at the graduate level. It is still true in too many situations that nursing administrators have obtained their positions by virtue of seniority alone. Frequently, they are unable to communicate with administrative colleagues as equals and, as a result, their recommendations and rationales carry relatively little weight in the organization. It is unlikely that even the best prepared and most dedicated change agent can have much effect in a setting in which innovation and the innovator are viewed as a threat to the status quo and to the power of an administrator whose authority is challenged. Although the educational preparation of the leader may not be totally and directly related to establishing a climate conducive to change and growth, the potential for both is certainly greater when that preparation is present. Educational preparation provides a basis of expert power for the nurse administrator.

For years, nurses have talked about the recognition of clinical knowledge and skill as a basis for upward mobility in practice settings. Relatively little evidence exists in the majority of settings that this particular ideal has become a reality. Unless and until clinical competence in itself is seen as meritorious, the movement of nurses into administrative roles will continue to be the main method of achieving recognition in terms of promotion and salary increases. Extrinsic incentives for development and maintenance of excellence in clinical skills and the concomitant autonomy of practice will continue to be virtually nonexistent.

Nursing Education

If nursing practice is to change along with the settings in which it takes place, what are the ramifications for nursing education? Although change is a constant in nursing education, as elsewhere in nursing, controlled and planned change is vital. Certain desirable changes are presently occurring and should be encouraged. As never before, there is a need for professional nursing education to be based in institutions of higher education. Nurses who are to function as autonomous practitioners in a variety of clinical settings require at least baccalaureate level preparation and many would argue that even that level is inadequate.

The composition of undergraduate student bodies has changed markedly within the past ten to fifteen years. The present students are highly diverse in age, sex, ethnic background, life-style, academic background, intellectual ability, and motivation. Many are mature students, often pursuing preparation for a second career. In some cases, these students are women who have raised families and now have the time to pursue an education that may have been interrupted by marriage and childbearing. In other cases, they are individuals, both men and women, whose initial career choice has proven to be one in which they cannot earn a livelihood. In addition, registered nurses returning to school to obtain a baccalaureate degree represent a significant percentage of the enrollment in many programs. Within the latter group there is a diversity in basic preparation and in the years since the preparation was acquired as well as in the nursing practice roles from which they come. The learning needs of all of these groups vary and call for innovative approaches to program development. Among these students are the best qualified and most able we have ever had as well as some of the least prepared, by virtue of the educational disadvantages of which they have been the victims. The diversities noted should be respected, welcomed, and, in many cases, fostered, as they may reflect behaviors and characteristics that will be influential in changing the practice and the image of nursing.

Today's nursing students expect to have input into decisions that affect them. Their input is valuable and responsible and they are thoughtful participants in the educational experience. They are also more prone to challenge policies and procedures and to appeal decisions regarding their performance. These are desirable behaviors that must continue to be supported and encouraged because they, too, are bases for autonomous and creative nursing practice.

Along with changes in the composition and expectations of student bodies in nursing have been changes in the composition of nursing faculties and expectations of individual nursing faculty members, especially within the universities. Gone is the time when the master's degree was acceptable as terminal educational preparation for nursing faculty. Nursing education seems to have moved past a period in which the majority of nurses with doctoral preparation were recruited into administrative positions. Larger numbers of nurses with such preparation are now opting for faculty positions in which they expect that time will be available for both teaching and research, as is the case in other disciplines within the university.

Additionally, faculty are becoming more committed to clinical practice as an essential component of the teaching role. They seek positions in which joint appointments are possible and in which time is available to maintain and enhance clinical skills. Most nursing faculty members are women, but their new awareness, growing out of the women's movement and involvement in political action, influences their perceptions of the faculty member's role within the school of nursing and the university at large. They, like students, seek more involvement in decision making that affects ways in which programs develop and in which they function as faculty members. To be more influential, nursing faculty members are becoming active participants in university administrative committees, research review committees, governing bodies, and faculty bargaining units. These actions firmly establish the place of nursing in the academic community and identify nurse faculty members as valuable contributors to that community. Such activities, responsibly and creatively carried out, can serve as examples for students of the change process and of nurses as change agents.

One major area in which ongoing change is required is the relationship between nursing education and nursing service. Traditionally, the roles education and service administrators in nursing were joined. Over the years and with the movement of nursing education into universities, the duality of function has been de-emphasized. Increasing numbers of students and curricular changes have forced expansion from one or two hospitals, which provided all or a major portion of the clinical experience, into larger numbers of hospital and a wider range of health care settings. In addition, the belief that educational purposes were often subverted to meet service needs has promoted a separation between them. All of these factors have widened the gulf between service and education; however, health care agencies not only serve as laboratories for students but they are also the employers of the graduates. Collaboration, communication, and mutual support are essential to promote change and innovation in both areas. For example, nursing faculty members who hold clinical appointments in service agencies can provide consultation, assistance, and a different perspective for those coping with administrative and patient care problems. Conversely, nursing service personnel holding joint appointments with schools of nursing can provide valuable input to curriculum development and serve as preceptors and mentors for students in the clinical setting. In this way, nurses in both service and education become change agents, exercizing expert power.

Finally, increased emphasis upon nursing research is required in nursing education programs, particularly in universities. Traditionally, universities are centers of research activities that support and expand professional practice and education for such practice. However, there is also a need for research in clinical settings and for practitioners with well-developed research skills.

Although most of the ideas discussed above have implications for nursing research, some specific areas would be particularly valuable in promoting and evaluating change. These would include studies of the differentiation of function and utilization of nurses with varying levels of preparation, including specialized graduate preparation; the effects of nurses prepared at the various levels on the quality and level of care in various settings; the development of innovative nursing roles, explored in collaboration with medicine and other disciplines; and nursing interventions and measurement of their effects in terms of patient welfare, including development of objective criteria for quality patient care.

Image of the Nurse

The low esteem in which nursing is held is well documented. The problem is most serious among nurses and—to the degree that nursing's internal struggles and disunity are made public—among our fellow professionals. Yet the image held by consumers and potential consumers of nursing care is generally positive although the nurse's role is still seen as very traditional. This more positive public view of nursing has been studied by Wooley (1981) whose findings are of particular interest with regard to the image of nurses held by nonnurses in an academic setting typical of those in which many nursing programs are located. The self-image and public image of the nurse will be explored in greater detail in the following pages.

SELF-IMAGE

Because the nursing profession is so seriously divided with regard to its identity and self-image, it becomes difficult to project to the public and other professionals the image of a powerful and autonomous profession. What are some of the bases for our division? We must identify them if they are to be addressed as areas requiring change.

A major divisive point concerns the educational level for entry into practice. In no other profession are there so many routes to licensure. Basic programs may be two, three, four, or five years in length with graduates all taking the same examination for licensure as registered nurses. Despite years of discussion and repeated recommendations concerning basic preparation for professional practice, nurses have not yet resolved this problem. Nonbaccalaureate preparation—both diploma and associate degree—is perpetuated while nurses continue to seek ways to help registered nurses move through the baccalaureate program. These efforts no longer reflect efforts to overcome an educational lag; the pool of registered nurses from diploma and associate degree programs who seek baccalaureate preparation continues to be replenished. As long as this persists, the task will never be finished and the divisiveness sparked by differences in educational background continues.

Loyalty to a particular pattern of education is translated into hostility toward other kinds of nursing programs and their graduates. The perceived threat posed by baccalaureate graduates leads to attempts by graduates of other types of programs to denigrate such preparation, thus neutralizing the beneficial effects of baccalaureate preparation.

The issue of basic educational preparation and its potential for dividing the profession is further complicated by a wide variety of post-basic programs. These include academic programs leading to the master's or doctoral degree, certificate programs preparing for advanced or expanded practice but granting no academic degree, and short-term continuing educational programs. Furthermore, some practitioner programs lead to a graduate degree while others only to a certificate.

These many patterns of preparation weaken professional cohesion and create a confused image of nursing. Adding to this chaos is the lack of clearly defined practice levels. For example, how does the practice of the baccalaureate graduate differ from that of the diploma or associate degree graduate and what differences in patient outcomes might be identified depending upon the level of care provided? In certain settings, notably community health and some hospitals as well, the baccalaureate degree is recognized as a requirement for employment. However, in the majority of settings where nurses are employed there is no attempt on the part of the institution or, indeed, of the nurses themselves to delineate levels of practice in accord with basic educational preparation. The lowest level of practice becomes the common denominator. As already noted, the situation is further complicated by the introduction of nurses holding master's degrees who identify themselves as clinical specialists, by nurses holding certification as nurse practitioners or specialists in neonatal, critical care, or coronary care nursing, and by nurses holding the doctoral degree who identify themselves as nurse researchers.

The schism between nursing education and nursing service previously discussed bears reemphasis as we consider changing the image of nursing. Failure to communicate and, thus, to speak with one voice for the common concerns of education and service supports perceptions of a divided profession and, in fact, promotes a view of educators working in a vacuum to prepare a product that is seen by the employer as unusable.

Thus, nursing is a profession composed largely of women with a variety of patterns of basic and post-basic education, lack of clarity of levels of practice based on that education, and an ideological split between those who educate nurses and those who employ them. Nurses do not project one image, but many. Often the images are contradictory rather than complementary. We do not speak with one voice for nursing, but with a chorus of voices that do not always blend well. Despite large numbers, the image is not that of a powerful profession, secure in the knowledge that its role in the health care system is unique and irreplaceable. Instead, nurses reflect fragmentation, uncertainty, and powerlessness. We desperately need to "get our act together," agree upon what will constitute education for professional practice, define levels of practice and project numbers required at the several levels, and, above all, begin to speak and act in concert. The primary vehicle for this kind of change is the professional organization and individual participation in its many activities. Jordan reminds nurses that "ANA is not an inanimate object; it is a collectivity of nurses who jointly make the decisions necessary to govern and direct the profession." (1981, p. 483) Nevertheless, *The American Nurse* carries the information that ANA's present membership is 165,000, representing a loss of nearly 19% of its members over the past five years. Only 13% of all practicing nurses were represented by the professional association in 1980 (1981, p. 11). Clearly, the issue of change and the potential power of a professional group that speaks with one voice is a real one for nursing.

In order to fill the role envisioned for nurses in the health care system, a continuing supply of nursing graduates is required. Preferably, the majority of these will be at the baccalaureate level. At this time, nursing program enrollments are dropping in the United States while, concurrently, serious nursing shortages exist across the country. Kalisch and Kalisch discuss the shortage in 1979–1980 in relation to the issue of federal support. The shortage is documented in a review of newspaper articles with a figure of 100,000 vacant nursing positions nationwide (1980, p. 140). Since then, it is likely that the situation has worsened rather than improved. Some continue to hope that larger numbers of men will enter the profession, believing that their presence may help to improve the economic and general welfare situation of the profession and to resolve some of the problems that have resulted from the image of nursing as a woman's profession only. It seems unlikely, however, that in the near future at least, men will make up the bulk of admissions. Women will remain the main source of recruits for nursing while, at the same time, career opportunities for women in a variety of fields will continue to be more plentiful than ever before. The same women's movement that is helping nursing to grow is also creating obstacles to the recruitment of students. Where once nursing and teaching were obvious choices for women, both may now be relatively low on a list of possible careers. Given, in addition, a professional image that leaves something to be desired, the problem of recruitment becomes serious.

Nevertheless, students of varying backgrounds are

being recruited and their potential for changing the image of nursing is great. Still, their introduction to the profession and its current image is sometimes sufficiently negative to discourage completion of the educational program. These students are often mature persons, experienced in the world of work, who are intolerant of what they perceive as a stultifying bureaucratic hospital system in which nursing is practiced. With the additional negative factors of night and evening shifts, little autonomy, and the difficulties of providing quality care, they see little in nursing to encourage commitment and to provide the kind of work satisfaction they want.

Students who enter nursing programs immediately after high school—and there are still many who do so—too often come with an inaccurate image of nursing and, therefore, inappropriate expectations of the educational program. There is still a prevailing view of nursing as acute care oriented and many prospective students see only the white uniform and cap as symbols of their role. The nurse's role in health maintenance, disease prevention, and promotion of good health with all of the related knowledge and skills seems not to have been made explicit. Furthermore, there is insufficient information available to prospective students about the nature of different routes to a nursing career. Many choices must be made for practical reasons, such as geographic proximity or cost, but some potential students with no such restrictions find it difficult to determine the most appropriate route to take. Often program descriptions fail to indicate how one differs from another. Philosophies and objectives are very similar, with little variation in descriptions of the roles for which graduates are prepared. This blurred image of the profession confuses prospective students.

Finally, the motivation of those who enter nursing sometimes seems to be more vocational than professional. Nurses can always obtain employment and it is relatively easy to move in and out of the work force. For these reasons, nursing is seen as a good career for women whose interest is primarily in marriage and a family. This image of nursing as a vocation rather than as a profession persists because little has happened over the years to change it.

Students are recruited through mixed messages, followed by varying degrees of disillusionment with both educational programs and practice and very high attrition rates in both. The changes required are self-evident and reflect the interrelatedness of image, education, practice, and the characteristics of settings in which the practice occurs.

PUBLIC IMAGE

The recipient of nursing care, the patient or client, also holds an image of the nurse. In general, it is positive and frequently reflects more acceptance of change and expansion in nursing roles than the image held by other professionals or those who fund health care programs. For example, consumers have supported the development of the health maintenance role of the nurse even to the point of willingness to pay for the services provided. It would appear that nurse practitioners are well accepted by consumers and that their contribution to health care is valued. Woolley's study (1981) has been cited previously as support for the assertion that consumers hold nursing and nurses in high esteem. A brief report in *RN* indicated that 93% of a sample of Maryland residents, responding to a study by the Maryland Bar Association, held positive attitudes toward nurses. That proportion was higher than for either dentists (86%) or doctors (80%), and lawyers were much lower at 64%. (1979, p. 11). The questions of territoriality raised by professionals do not enter into the considerations of consumers; the contribution of each professional provider of care to the whole is assessed in terms of its quality and its influence on the consumer's life.

Consumers have also been supportive of the movement in nursing to assume the role of patient advocate. The changing composition of society to include a larger percentage of elderly persons, the increasing emphasis upon the special needs of infants and children, together with an increasingly complicated, expensive, and unresponsive health care system all indicate the need for patient or client advocacy. The nurse is admirably suited to act in this capacity by virtue of preparation and continuity of presence in a variety of care settings. In this kind of role, the nurse uses a full repertoire of skills and knowledge that adds an additional dimension to the nurse's unique role in health care. Most important, consumers have readily incorporated advocacy into their already positive image of nursing.

Consumers of nursing care may be among the strongest sources of support for change and the development of autonomy and power for professional nursing. *The American Nurse* reports that in a labor strike of nurses in the Berkshire, Massachusetts Medical Center "Community residents had joined nurses on the picket line as well as donating cash, food, and even umbrellas and raincoats to the nurses" (1981, p. 13). Woolley's findings in her study of the image of nursing on campus also support the concept of consumers as nurse advocates:

The fact that many respondents believed nurses know just as much as physicians and are simply inhibited by custom and by law from doing as much, and are also more pleasant to deal with, indicates the possibility of strong public support for the expanding role of the nurse and changes in nurse practice acts to accommodate it.

They (the respondents) tended to impute more power to nurses than nurses themselves often do. This suggests that the assumption of the client advocate role could be an important factor in support of a positive public image of nursing. (1981, p. 406)

Nurses have not really cultivated nor capitalized on consumer support. Having sought and quite effectively developed the role of patient advocate, nurses should now work equally hard to develop the potential power base of consumers as nurse advocates.

Clarification for ourselves of the image we wish to project and concerted action to promote it can only help to enhance the image of nursing in the view of the several publics with which nursing relates. The image of nursing as a profession is in disarray. As a result, nurses are unable to come to grips with a changing health care scene and nursing's place within it. We must establish very clearly for ourselves and for our public the unique and autonomous role of nursing in the system.

AND NOW WHERE?

Although a number of deterrents to change are implicit in the foregoing discussion, the following excerpts from the January 1978 issue of *Nursing Outlook* set forth four perceptions of nursing and its future and, in so doing, summarize eloquently the major reasons why power and change in nursing are so slow in coming. The section of the journal is entitled "Outlook on Nursing: State of the Profession" and consists of a series of articles by a group of distinguished nurses: Dr. Margretta Styles, Sister Dorothy Sheahan, Dr. Ada Jacox, and Dr. Beatrice Kalisch. While there is no reason to believe that the authors collaborated, the theme of all is disturbingly similar.

STYLES
It seems that, as a profession, we violate a physical principle; We are somehow *less* than the sum of our parts and much, much less than the sum of our potential. (Styles, 1978, p. 29)

SHEAHAN
What was needed was the isolation of and agreement upon, a set of basic integrating beliefs on the nature of nursing and the preparation of its practitioners . . . . Without making such a . . .decision . . .a disinterested observer in the year 2003 might find nursing to be a "profession of great promise" but too crippled by internecine issues to change the course of history. (Sheahan, 1978, p. 29)

JACOX
In short, we were collectively unable or unwilling to place a moratorium on our internal fighting so that we might redirect our energies

to deal positively and constructively with the promotion of health and prevention of disease and with nursing's role in these areas. By thus dissipating our energies we were not able to face up to the more important issues of the day. (Jacox, 1978, p. 41)

KALISCH
American nursing . . . is in such a period of flux and there are so many diverse forces at work that it is often difficult to tell if the profession is moving forward, backwards, or sideways. The critical challenge facing nursing over the next twenty-five years will be to acquire a solid resource and power base upon which to move the profession forward. (Kalisch, 1978, p. 43)

The overriding theme is one of disunity and fragmentation with the resulting inability to capitalize on opportunities to strengthen the profession and increase its power, autonomy, and potential for influencing the health care system. The resolution, to some extent, obviously lies with all of us and the degree to which we are able to project a clear image of what we believe nursing should and could be, to speak with a united voice, and to act in concert to present our case. Out of some of the changes already in progress a new generation of nurses seems to be emerging; nurses who are creative rather than conforming, initiating rather than reacting, assertive rather than passive. They are change agents rather than change retardants, political activists rather than political victims, independent rather than dependent. Our potential for power and influence is enormous.

SUMMARY

In this chapter, the use of the change process has been promoted as a power source for nurses. Nurses can actively apply the process of change to accomplish a variety of goals. Some purposes of change have been identified as have areas in nursing where change is highly desirable: nursing practice and the settings in which it occurs, nursing education, and the image of both the nurse and of nursing. As positive changes are produced in these areas, the net effect should be that nurses will exercise more control over their personal and professional destinies. Much of the desire for power in nursing arises from the need for nurses to positively influence the health care system for better patient care. To successfully accomplish such changes it is necessary that the change agent possess a knowledge of change theory, an understanding of the broader contexts of the health care system and the nursing profession, and have developed other personal and professional sources of power.

BIBLIOGRAPHY

Brooten, D., Hayman, L., & Naylor, M.: *Leadership for Change: A Guide for the Frustrated Nurse.* Philadelphia, J. B. Lippincott, 1978.

Jacox, A.: Address to the next generation. *Nursing Outlook 26* (1):38–41, 1978.

Jordan, H.: To advance, we must unite. *Nursing Outlook 29* (8):482–483, 1981.

Kalisch, B.: The promise of power. *Nursing Outlook 26* (1):42–46, 1978.

Kalisch, P. & Kalisch, B.: The nurse shortage, the President and the Congress. *Nursing Forum 19* (2):138–164, 1980.

Lippitt, R., Hooyman, G., Sashkin, M., & Kaplan, J.: *Resourcebook for Planned Change.* Ann Arbor, Human Resources Development Associates of Ann Arbor, 1978.

The public's love affair with nurses. *RN 42* (11):11,13, 1979.

Sheahan, D.: Scanning the seventies. *Nursing Outlook 26* (1):33–37, 1978.

Styles, M.M.: Dialogue across the decades. *Nursing Outlook 26* (1):28–32, 1978.

Welch, L. B.: Planned change in nursing: the theory. *Nursing Clinics of North America 14* (2):307–321, 1979.

Woolley, A. S.: Nursing's image on campus. *Nursing Outlook 29* (8):460–466, 1981.

RECOMMENDED READINGS

Brooten, Dorothy A., Hayman, Laura L., & Naylor, Mary D. *Leadership for Change: A Guide for the Frustrated Nurse.* Philadelphia, J. B. Lippincott, 1978.

An excellent and practical reference in which the authors first discuss changes that have been effected in nursing by both individuals and groups. It also serves as a background for the identification of areas in which change has yet to occur and reviews the nature of change with particular emphasis on the problem-solving model. Finally, a series of eight problem situations requiring change are presented. Two of these are unresolved and the reader is invited to apply his or her knowledge and skills as a change agent to their solution.

Freeman, Ruth. Practice as protest. *American Journal of Nursing 71* (5):918–921, 1971.

The author writes eloquently of the social action aspects of nursing and of the nurse's role as patient advocate. The content is as relevant today as at the time of publication.

Outlook on nursing: State of the profession. *Nursing Outlook 26* (1):28–46, 1978.

A series of articles by four nursing leaders from different areas within the profession. Each presents her view of nursing on the threshold of the 1980s. The resulting whole is an excellent summary of the status of nursing, setting forth both problems and potentials.

Symposium on the nurse as change agent. *Nursing Clinics of North America 14* (2):305–382, 1979.

This excellent series of articles presents an overview of change theory, a discussion of the nurse as change agent, and examples of planned change carried out by nurses in several different practice areas.

Whoolley, Alma S. Nursing's image on campus. *Nursing Outlook* 29 (8):460–466, 1981.

The author presents interesting findings concerning the image of nursing held by nonnurses in an academic setting. Perceptions of nurses as students, faculty members, and practitioners are discussed and the relevance of the findings for nurses and nursing is explored.

THE POWER OF ORGANIZATIONS

JANET M. BURGE

There may be a temptation to skip this chapter because of the controversy over the nursing organization that represents the real power base in this nation. Some of us are tired of the endless debate while others are not convinced that *any* of our current professional nursing organizations have any real power in today's society. Few nurses recognize the value of active memberships in professional organizations as a necessary step in developing their personal power base. Even the words "organization power" have a negative connotation because they are often associated with the dominance of one group over another. Organization power can also be interpreted as being too closely linked with the feminist movement and therefore may be viewed negatively.

The intent of this chapter is four-fold: (1) to identify basic concepts of organization power in an attempt to explore the power now held by our professional nursing organizations; (2) to assess the impact that our nursing organizations can make toward changing the health care system; (3) to examine how nonnursing organizations can be used by nurses to strengthen the power base of nursing; and (4) to provide suggestions on how to assess current and potential memberships in nonnursing organizations.

WHY THE NEED FOR NURSES TO EXPLORE ORGANIZATION POWER?

There is a critical need for nurses to recognize that the most impressive source of power available to them is through the various professional nursing organizations. Nurses constitute the largest group of health care givers in the nation. Today there are approximately 1.4 million nurses functioning in a wide variety of roles. This fact alone is indicative of an enormous amount of potential power. In recent years it has become obvious to nurses that the larger the membership of the professional organizations, the greater the power and influence they will have in effecting needed health care changes. Although numbers are not the only criterion for evaluating the effectiveness and power of our nursing organizations, there is evidence that numbers have impact, particularly in the political arena at the local, state, and federal levels.

Nurses are not generally risk takers. This can be partially attributed to the fact that most are females who have accepted the traditional roles that women have assumed in our society. In the past nurses did not concern themselves with power and its use, either individually or collectively through professional nursing organizations. It is becoming more obvious to nurses that it will take more than the efforts of a few nursing leaders in our organizations to bring about needed autonomy, prestige, and power in the profession. Nurses are beginning to recognize that competition for power exists among all the major organizations involved in health care. Health related organizations are being asked to contribute to all levels of decision making related to health care. It is therefore imperative for nurses to unite in these efforts; otherwise, other organizations will assume the responsibility for us. Nurses cannot influence these decisions from the sidelines. It will take our active involvement to strengthen the power of the profession.

CONCEPTS OF ORGANIZATION POWER

Organization power has been studied from many different points of view. For the purpose of this discussion, power will be explored as a form of influence in effecting change.

The three basic concepts discussed here are generally accepted as being typical of most organizations, regardless of their type. If nurses are knowledgeable about organizational behaviors, they can then actively plan to deal with these behaviors and, if necessary, counteract them.

The first concept related to organization power is "the level of credibility of the organization." Much of what occurs in the political arena today is based on misrepresentation of facts and half-truths. Professional organizations have an obligation to counter half-truths with facts. By doing so they will increase their credibility as well as increase their power base. The credibility of an organization is largely determined by the way the organization screens and uses the information that filters in and out of it. This information flow involves two basic components: (1) that which members feed into the organization, and (2) that which the leadership of the organization disseminates to the members. Both components lay the groundwork for credibility and power.

It is not uncommon for opponents of an organization to deliberately feed inaccurate information to another organization with the intent of sabotage. In this situation, the members of the organization who receive such information are the real pivotal points. They can easily weaken the power of the organization by failing to verify the information before it is passed on to the leadership, or they can strengthen it by conducting rigorous research of the facts. The errors commonly associated with passing inaccurate information into an organization are that (1) the members of the organization are naive in not recognizing that all opponents do not fight a clean fight, and (2) the members assume that the prestige of the source of information automatically guarantees its truthfulness. For example, an officer of one organization may tell a member of another organization that they will be lobbying against legislation that is supported by the member's organization. The real fact of this communication is that the officer's organization has no real interest in the piece of legislation and does not intend to put any effort into it in any case. However, the tactic used by the officer in this situation diverts the attention of the second organization so that more important legislation may slip by unnoticed. In this example, the first error made by the member receiving the inaccurate information was failure to recognize the intent of sabotage by the officer. The second error was to assume that the information was correct because it came from an officer of the organization.

The second concept of organization power is that "power is not always explicitly evident." This concept assumes that there are always some strategies used by the leadership of an organization that are not obvious to the membership. The behaviors associated with these strategies are: (1) being seen in the right place at the right time, and (2) interacting with individuals and subgroups in other organizations who are known "power people." It has long been known that many important decisions are made and strategies planned over a lunch or dinner session. Two basic questions are inherent to this behavior: (1) who talks to whom outside the organization, and (2) who joins whom at certain meetings and for what purpose? Basic to these questions is the assumption that leaders of an organization will do their part to maintain open and official communication with leaders of other organizations.

When organizations fail to encourage their members and leaders to become actively associated with their counterparts in other organizations, this tends to create closed systems and usually does not promote strong power bases. One of the purposes of encouraging members and officers of an organization to maintain active relationships with another organization is to preserve a flow of information that may have directl or indirect impact on either one. Information is a source of power and organizations preserve their power by receiving and giving accurate information. If the president of a local nursing association does not talk to the president of the local medical association, there is reason to doubt that common interests relating to health care in the community can be accomplished effectively and collectively. Leaders of both organizations must use their time and opportunities at general meetings to plan and initiate strategies that will benefit the organizations and the community. Organizations with leaders who utilize these strategies are those that seek and usually have fairly strong power bases.

A third concept related to organization and power is that "one organization's power is enhanced by its relationship with other organizations that possess power." This concept is based on coalition building or the joining of two organizations for the purpose of accomplishing a shared goal. Coalition building is usually positive in nature because it is an attempt on the part of two or more organizations to strengthen their own competence and power in areas of importance to all concerned. For example, if a nursing organization is concerned about the establishment of a new hospital in the community and believes there are too few nurses to adequately staff the new hospital, then a coalition might be formed with another organization to support this position.

An important process to be used in strengthening the development of formal coalitions is networking. Nurses who hold membership in one nurses' association can disseminate information on the issue at hand to nurses in other organizations. As a result, the efforts are united and a stronger power base is established. Much of the real power of organizations depends on the joining or linking activities with other organizations. While some believe that the development of coalition with other groups weakens the power within the organization, this is usually not true if both organizations in the coalition know where they agree and disagree on the issues, plans, and strategies being considered. Efforts need to be made by all groups entering into a coalition to focus on strengthening their collective power on issues of agreement rather than on issues of disagreement. When coalitions among organizations disintegrate, it is usually because the parties allow the focus to be placed on the disagreeing aspects of the issue and the relationship becomes one of rivalry.

PROFESSIONAL NURSING ORGANIZATIONS

Two major professional nursing organizations are considered here: The American Nurses' Association (ANA) and the National League for Nursing (NLN). Our intention is not to establish which of the two organizations is *the* professional organization for nursing (an age-old debate) but to look at what both organizations are, what they do, and what they might do to strengthen the power base of nursing in our society. Each of the organizations has different purposes and objectives and each has made significantly different contributions toward the advancement of nursing over the years. It would be nearly impossible to discuss all the accomplishments of each organization; therefore, we will focus on what they have done and are doing to establish a strong power base for the profession and how the nurse can use them to strengthen his or her own personal power base. Since much of what both organizations do toward establishing the profession as a power base is in the form of published materials, we shall discuss selected documents with which nurses should be familiar. In addition, we analyze the issues confronting the organizations and their current activities.

American Nurses' Association

The American Nurses' Association (ANA), established in 1911, has long been recognized as the largest professional women's organization in the world. The ANA functions as the official professional organization for nurses in the United States. Its functions are: (1) to define the scope of nursing practice for licensed professional nurses, (2) to establish and maintain standards of nursing care that will assure consumer protection, (3) to provide information related to nursing and nursing practice to institutions, agencies, and groups associated with health care, (4) to promote nursing research, and (5) to promote the economic and general welfare of nurses. Three major documents from ANA are relevant to building a personal power base for nurses: "Standards of Practice, 1975"; "Policy Guide for State Nursing Practice Acts, 1980"; and "ANA Statement on The Nature and Scope of Nursing Practice: A Social Policy Statement, 1980."

"STANDARDS OF PRACTICE"

Standards of practice have been written for all specialty areas that are listed below:

1. Cancer nursing practice
2. Cardiovascular nursing practice
3. Community health nursing practice
4. Emergency nursing practice
5. Gerontological nursing practice
6. Maternal and child nursing practice
7. Medical-surgical nursing practice
8. Neurological and neurosurgical nursing practice
9. Nursing education
10. Nursing practice (general)
11. Nursing services (general)
12. Nursing services in camp settings
13. Operating room nursing practice
14. Orthopedic nursing practice
15. Pediatric oncology nursing practice
16. Perioperative nursing practice

17. Rehabilitation nursing practice

18. Psychiatric and mental health nursing practice

19. Urologic nursing practice

The standards identify assumptions and beliefs basic to the area of practice, definitions pertinent to the practice, descriptions of types of practitioners, qualifications related to educational preparation, and scope of practice. ANA standards may be used by nurses as a form of power to (1) maintain professional influence with employers for hiring appropriately prepared nurses for specific types of nursing care, and (2) define the scope of practice to the various public, private, and governmental agencies and institutions using the services of nurses.

"POLICY GUIDE FOR STATE NURSING PRACTICE ACTS"

The ANA "Policy Guide" reinforces the premise that the public's health and welfare should be protected with a minimum of governmental regulation and that there are checks and balances between governmental and professional regulation of the practice of nursing. This safeguard is needed to assure the public of protection from unqualified practitioners without unduly limiting innovation in nursing services. As a power base for nurses this document may be used when needed to: (1) lobby legislative committees for changes in the State Nurse Practice Act in order to define additional activities or acts of nurses functioning in expanded roles, (2) influence the state legislative body when changes in the licensure requirements of nurses are threatened by institutions that promote the administration of medications by nonprofessional personnel, such as aides, and (3) testify before state legislative committees when a threat exists of changing the disciplinary or investigative powers of boards of nursing.

"ANA STATEMENT ON THE NATURE AND SCOPE OF NURSING PRACTICE"

Through the years, nurses have had varying opinions about what nursing is, how it is done, and who should do it. The "ANA Statement on The Nature and Scope of Nursing Practice," a hallmark for the profession, is a definitive statement relating to the scope and practice of nursing, including expanded roles in nursing and specialists in nursing practice. The social policy statement gives very specific and clear interpretations of the practice of nursing while it also identifies nursing's responsibility to the public and other health professionals. As a power base the document may be used to (1) interpret nursing to individuals, institutions and agencies, legislative bodies, and other groups that interface with nurses, and (2) assist nurses to conceptualize their own practice.

In addition to the three documents discussed above, the ANA's real source of power for the profession may lie in its lobbying efforts. The organization maintains an office in Washington for the express purpose of lobbying for and monitoring federal legislation that will influence the profession and health care. Recently, the major efforts of the Washington staff have focused on health manpower and funding for nursing education.

Several issues currently confront the ANA. The way in which these issues will be resolved over the next decade will either give the organization the professional power it seeks or will cause additional fragmentation among various nursing groups, thus decreasing the overall power of the profession. The two major issues concern entry into practice and credentialing. Entry into practice involves a stipulated educational level of preparation required to practice nursing. Currently, an individual may enter nursing practice through one of three educational routes: (1) a hospital school of nursing granting a diploma, (2) a junior college granting an associate degree, and (3) a college or university granting a baccalaureate degree. Each of these three routes demands varying competencies of the graduate and varies in the amount of time taken to complete the program. Crucial to the regulation of entry into practice is ANA's attempt to establish the baccalaureate degree as the basic educational requirement for professional nursing practice. ANA takes the position that nursing will be recognized as a profession when only one educational level is required for entry into practice. Unfortunately, this position does not enhance the organization's reputation with other nursing groups, particularly those supporting diploma and associate degree nursing programs.

Credentialing is a process designed to assure quality care for the public, identify the members of particular professions, protect the public from substandard practices, and control the growth and development of professions. Currently, there are four major credentialing forms in nursing: (1) licensure, (2) certification, (3) accreditation, and (4) academic degrees. ANA has taken a stand on this issue by attempting to consolidate all aspects of credentialing under a free-standing credentialing center. Today, many nursing specialty groups offer their own form of credentialing and certification, which many view as more fragmentation within the profession. ANA believes that a free-standing credentialing center would achieve a unified, coordinated, and comprehensive credentialing system for nursing. Its purpose would be to study, develop, coordinate, provide services for, and conduct credentialing in nursing. ANA's intent is an honorable one. Whether or not there can and will be a consolidation of efforts on the part of the various nursing groups is to be seen.

National League for Nursing

The National League for Nursing (NLN) was organized, as now constituted, in 1952. The NLN's functions are identified in each issue of *Nursing and Health Care*, its official publication. Its functions are to: (1) identify and foster programs related to the nursing needs of society, (2) work with voluntary, governmental, and other agencies toward the achievement of comprehensive health care, (3) develop and support services for the improvement of nursing service and nursing education, and (4) respond to universal nursing needs. Most nurses have a rather limited understanding of the NLN's accrediting process of all types of nursing education programs. This is one of its major functions but there are many more.

The NLN provides numerous documents containing career guidance information on all types of nursing education programs, including master's and doctoral preparation. It also conducts research related to nursing, which is published annually in the *NLN Nursing Data Book,* including data on basic RN education, students in all types of nursing programs, faculty characteristics, and student follow-up.

The NLN's efforts to promote power in the profession are best reflected in the position statements on issues affecting practice, education, and research, as well as consumerism. All of the following position statements are used as power sources in the form of information for nurses at the local, state, and federal levels:

1. Position Statement on Education of Nurse Practitioners

2. Position Statement on Nursing Licensure

3. Position Statement on Quality Review of Health and Professional Standards Review Organizations

4. Position Statement on National Health Insurance

In addition to the resources identified above, the NLN has developed structured councils for special interest groups. There are councils related to vocational, diploma, associate degree and baccalaureate educators and councils related to nursing service and nursing administration. These, too, are sources of power because they provide the opportunity for nurses with similar backgrounds and interests to consolidate their efforts toward setting goals and implementing policies that have an impact on the public image of nursing.

The NLN, like the ANA, has two major issues (1) support or nonsupport of ANA's entry into practice resolution, and (2) exclusion of nonnurse members from the organization. The three different educational routes by which individuals may now enter professional nursing is the basis for the entry into practice issue. Since nursing is the only profession that promotes three distinctive routes for entry, the real question seems to be: if nursing seeks true status and recognition as a profession that is distinctive, yet comparable with other professions, then why would nursing promote educational entry levels that are significantly different from those held by other professions? Two professions come to mind in relation to this question: law and medicine. Neither of these professions have multiple routes for entry into practice; both require a basic educational degree from a college or university in order to practice in the profession.

Whether or not the NLN should maintain nonnurse memberships in its organization raises two questions. The first is: does the NLN have power as a professional organization as long as decision making and policy determinations about nursing are being influenced by nonnurse members? The second is: would not the power of the NLN be better professionally preserved if membership consisted only of nurses speaking and acting for nursing? The strategies now used by the NLN would, of necessity, have to be changed, but this could be effectively accomplished through coalitions and by maintaining liaison relationships with the organizations currently represented by nonnurse members.

What Should the Nursing Organizations Be Doing?

Nurses have long been advocating the need for power in the profession. When one looks at the role and functions of both nursing organizations, it becomes obvious that there is duplication of efforts and fragmentation of responsibility. As a result, the needed power base in nursing is critically eroded and weakened. At this point, several considerations should be given to increasing the power of nursing. The first is to explore the consolidation of all federal lobbying efforts of the profession into one organization. Currently, both organizations maintain legislative activities within their separate structures. The organizations should meet and establish which of the two is in a better position to assume this responsibility and move to that end. The writer believes that the ANA is now the stronger of the two organizations because its office is located in Washington, D.C. It is vital that the image of nursing presented in Washington be one of unity and power.

A second consideration is that of consolidating the practice-related groups, councils, and commissions of both organizations. A nurse who joins any nursing organization is looking for an avenue by which he or she can meet with other nurses with common interests to discuss issues and needs that have a direct impact on their practice areas. It is therefore vital that the profession retain this structure for its members. In the opinion of this writer, currently the NLN may be in a better position to assume this responsibility, assuming that the NLN would work closely with state nursing associations to develop stronger practice-related groups to meet the needs of nurses in each state.

The third consideration of what nursing organizations should be doing relates to the issues of entry into practice and credentialing. Both the ANA and the NLN have a responsibility to continue exploring these issues and to determine how the conflict will be resolved. Various types of compromise must be reached, perhaps in terms of the historical development of each organization. On the issue of credentialing, the NLN probably has greater strength for assuming the responsibility because of its past and current record in the educational accreditation of schools of nursing. Could not the NLN then assume the responsibility for directing and monitoring all forms of credentialing within the profession? This would necessitate some restructuring

of the NLN in order to accomplish more uniform credentialing. On the issue of entry into practice, the ANA position represents the direction of the profession. Is it not past
time for the NLN to recognize the strength inherent in this
position and begin to assist in the transition?

The profession needs both the ANA and the NLN since
the two organizations perform specific roles and functions
that can only be adequately implemented by each of them.
Our basic concern is rather the duplication of many functions which, if not changed, will contribute to continued
fragmentation within the profession, thereby, decreasing
our potential power. When both organizations lay aside
their vested interests and begin to work together to resolve
the areas of conflict, the nursing profession will gain the
power necessary for its development.

NONNURSING ORGANIZATIONS

The inclusion of two nonnursing organizations in this
chapter on organizational power reflects the fact that some
of the power nursing possesses comes from its associative
relationships and proximity to other organizations that
hold power. Nurses not only have to be affiliated with and
knowledgeable about other professional organizations, but
must also learn how to use their memberships in these
organizations to enhance their own personal and professional power bases. Nurses and nursing cannot operate
effectively in isolation from other groups and organizations.

The National Organization for Women (NOW) and The
League of Women Voters of the United States (LWVUS)
are two nonnursing organizations that have had significant
impact on nursing in today's society. Both organizations
are essentially female directed and focus on issues that

often are shared or overlap with nursing. Membership of nurses in either organization should be viewed in light of the power that can be derived from it.

The League of Women Voters in the United States

The League of Women Voters (LWVUS) was founded in 1920 and has almost 120,000 members. Approximately 3,000 of the organization's members are men. The primary objectives of the organization are to: (1) encourage and increase the number of people registering and voting at all levels of government, (2) provide nonpartisan information on candidates and ballot issues at election time, including all major issues of public concern, and (3) shape legislation at every governmental level to meet the public's need and strengthen citizen participation in the political process in order to have accountable and responsive government.

Two major aspects of the LWVUS make it a source of power for nurses. The first aspect lies in the fact that the organization is nonpartisan in nature, which means that it does not take a position of support or nonsupport for any candidate running for public office. It presents information and facts to the public, believing that an informed public will make the best choice when they go to the polls. This policy is an asset for nurses considering membership because health care policy and related issues always reach into the political arenas at election time. Indeed, health care issues are often major components of a political candidate's platform. It is therefore important that nurses be actively involved in preventing these issues from becoming partisan issues. Promises in the name of health made by would-be politicians do not often reflect the real needs of the general public. For example, in a recent situation during an election year, several senators in a state objected to the closing of a school of nursing in their district by the State Board of Nursing. The school was closed because standards for state accreditation were not being met. The senators advocated the dissolution of the Board of Nursing and actively campaigned toward this end. They were willing to use their political power and campaign platforms to persuade the community to disregard the professional standards set by the Board of Nursing.

The second aspect of LWVUS that makes it a source of power for nurses relates to the everyday workings of the organization. Judgments on issues are based on direct observation and consensus of its membership who have had the opportunity to weigh the pros and cons. These judgments are the results of the observer corps, which are composed of members who get firsthand information by attending special meetings, then reporting the results to the membership at a regular meeting.

National Organization for Women

The National Organization for Women (NOW) was established in the early 1960s to promote and insure the civil rights of women in the United States. Specifically, the organization continues to focus on: (1) actively engaging women in politics at the local, state, and national levels of government, (2) increasing the availability of education and economic stability for minority women, (3) decreasing sex discrimination against women in male-dominated professions such as law and medicine, (4) promoting federal and state legislation that insures free choice for women in childbearing and birth control policies, and (5) monitoring state and federal legislation on all issues related to the civil rights of women.

NOW is organized at local, state, and national levels. The national headquarters is housed in Washington and there are state headquarters located in every state. Most communities have local chapters and, if not, there are members who function as contact persons for the organization. Of interest to nurses is a subgroup of the organization called NURSES NOW. This subgroup reflects the efforts of some nurses who use their affiliation with a feminist group in order to gain support for issues confronting nurses—as women—throughout the nation. It also shows that nurses are becoming more politically active through an organization which may have more power in some areas than do nurses.

NOW is one of the more assertive—some would say aggressive—organizations in the United States today. Its voice continues to be heard in Washington and around the nation. It has been a major force in seeking ratification of the Equal Rights Amendment (ERA), and continues to hold impressive get-out-and-vote campaigns, public marches, demonstrations, and door-to-door canvassing in an effort to inform the public of the need to pass the amendment.

In addition to supporting ERA, the organization seeks defeat in Congress of the Human Life Amendment (HLA). NOW believes the amendment to be a basic violation of the free choice of women. NOW has interpreted that passage of the HLA will have the following detrimental effects on women: (1) threaten the lives of pregnant women, (2) promote unwanted pregnancies by outlawing the use of the IUD and some forms of the Pill, (3) classify abortions as a crime (premediatated murder and/or felony) in all states, and (4) promote prosecution by state governments of physicians, family, and friends who assist a woman with an abortion. For these reasons, NOW employs the strategy of developing coalitions with other major organizations with reputable power. For example, in seeking the defeat of the HLA, NOW has sought and obtained support from the National Planned Parenthood Association and selected physician groups across the nation.

How Can Nonnursing Organizations Be Useful to Nursing?

Five strategies can be used by nursing groups to increase their power base through nonnursing organizations. Since the strategies discussed here will not work in *all* cases, the nursing organization must assess its own situation in light of what it needs and the nonnursing organizations available to assist it in meeting those needs. It is important to note that the strategies discussed will also apply to organizations not mentioned in this chapter.

The first strategy is for local nursing districts and state nursing associations to hold regular annual meetings with nonnursing organizations for the purpose of identifying the health-related issues that both groups can and will support throughout the year. Groups taking this approach must realize that there will be issues on which the groups will be unable to agree because of their official organizational positions, which are likely to differ. This is all right. It is just as important for organizations to recognize that they "agree to disagree" on some issues. The point is that there is power in recognizing disagreement.

The second strategy is to invite local chapters or units of the nonnurse organizations to become involved—even to cosponsors—some of the health and nursing-related activities undertaken by the local nursing districts. The stereotyped role of nurses, as perceived by nonnursing organizations, is often limited to what nurses do in a physician's office, a nursing home, or a local hospital. Nursing groups have depended, far too long, only on other health-related groups for commitment to and support of nursing activities in the local community. Groups such as business and professional women's clubs and city or county commissioners could join nurses in conducting health screening projects in specified areas of a community. These nonnurse participants could help to keep the records of the screening projects and distribute health education materials. Other power groups must be made to see the full complement of nursing. And this strategy will serve to inform them of the contributions being made by nursing at the local community level, as well as to broaden those contributions.

A third strategy is to encourage individuals outside of nursing to see what activities are being accomplished by nurses. If cosponsorship of health-related activities and direct involvement of nonnursing organizations in these activities (the second strategy) are not possible, then invite the organizations to send observers to these activities and projects. This will give the observers information about nursing as well as firsthand opportunities to see nurses in light of their varied responsibilities.

The fourth strategy is to seek out public support of nonnursing organizations in campaigns where nurses are running for office at all levels of government. This support may be in the form of the leadership's signature on campaign materials or by speaking on behalf of the candidate at meetings of groups where nonnurses hold power.

The fifth, and possibly the most important, strategy is to seek the support of nonnursing organizations in sending members to testify before legislative bodies on issues that have a direct or indirect impact on nursing and health issues. There may be no greater impact on legislative bodies than to hear a nonnursing organization or individual speak in support of the same issues that are advocated by nursing.

Evaluating Memberships in Nonnursing Organizations

Joining an organization or maintaining a membership in one are actions not to be taken lightly by a nurse. The organization should contribute to the personal or professional power base of the nurse; if it does not, he or she should consider making a change. The nurse's decision to join an organization should be based on a very distinctive preliminary process which will be discussed here, along with three strategies that may be used to evaluate current membership in a nonnursing organization.

Every nurse must have a clear and unwavering philosophy about nursing and how they propose to practice nursing. This philosophy is developed, over time, by individuals who: (1) develop competence and proficiency as practitioners, (2) view nurses and nursing as a profession which makes significant contributions to the health of individuals, (3) periodically evaluate their personal involvement in the development of the profession, and (4) become politically active in the politics of health care at all levels of government. Generally, people do not know what nursing is and what is needed in nursing to assist in better meeting the health needs of our society. Many still believe that medicine and physicians are the primary sources for identifying and meeting the health needs of society, while they also believe that physicians control nurses and the practice of nursing.

Each nurse should be equipped to express the concerns and needs of nursing. This includes the ability to identify those needs and to have a plan for implementing changes so that the care given by and through nursing will benefit the general public. Nothing will take the place of a nurse who can articulate his or her knowledge about the profession. And it is through this knowledge that nurses will contribute to the organizations they join.

A nurse first has to assess the credibility of the organizations he or she plans to join by personally conducting a search for information. The record of an organization and whether or not, over time, it is perceived by other organizations as having power is important to know. It is an error to ignore these points before aligning oneself with an organization. Nurses need to complement their resources with organizations that can help them do their jobs better.

Two important questions can be asked by the nurse to help in his or her information search before joining an organization: (1) what official or unofficial liaison relationships does the organization have with other organizations in the local community, and (2) what meetings, programs, or projects has the organization cosponsored with other organizations in the last year? The answers to the first question may tell you who talks with whom and for what purpose. The answers to the second question may tell you whether the relationship of one organization with another is official, and publicly demonstrated or whether it is the type that takes place behind closed doors or over informal lunch or dinner sessions. In addition to talking directly to members of the organization, the nurse may: (1) ask to read the annual committee reports of the organization, specifically noting the plans and accomplishments of the program or projects committee, (2) ask to view the organizational chart noting formal and informal relationships with other organizations or groups, and (3) monitor the media for firsthand knowledge of public announcements of programs, projects, and meetings held with other groups or organizations.

Nurses also need to periodically assess their current memberships in nonnursing organizations. The following strategies—all in the form of questions—are identified to facilitate this personal assessment. By asking yourself how many times you have been appointed as a member or chairperson to a committee or subgroup of the organization in the last two years you can look at your leadership or ability as perceived by the organization. It is not enough to vote on the issues as presented by others in the organization, but more important to be involved in determining the issues to be voted.

The second question to ask yourself is how many times you have been asked by the leadership in the organization to compromise or modify a basic belief that is critical to maintain the autonomy of nurses or nursing. With this question you are assessing your strength in relation to knowledge and decision making. You may also be assessing the frequency with which the leadership has used your compromises to sway other uncommitted members in the organization. An example of a strategy often used by male leaders in organizations to gain compromise from female nurses is to approach the nurse privately, acknowledge that the nurse may not be supportive of the leader's position on an issue, and ask that she not be disruptive in the meeting by raising questions or by taking an opposing stand on the issue. Female nurses should recognize this strategy for what it is: an attempt to promote the attitude that a "respected" female nurse does not speak or fight openly with males.

The final question to ask in your personal assessment is what, in the last year, have been the areas of commitment by the organization to nurses in the community and to the issues that nurses have supported. This means that you should be able to see some tangible evidence, over time, of the organization's interest in and support of health care issues that have been determined by nurses. You can also keep your own written record of issues that have been supported or not supported by the organization. This type of record will serve to document: (1) the degree of influence and personal power you have had in the organization, and (2) whether or not continued membership seems advantageous.

SUMMARY

This chapter has focused on the power nurses hold and acquire through various professional organizations. There remains much to be done by our professional organizations to strengthen the power bases of the nursing profession. We have also outlined various strategies for nurses to use in strengthening their personal power bases through memberships in nonnursing organizations that have shared goals with nursing.

The author recognizes that some of the strategies proposed in this chapter may be unacceptable to nurses. Yet most of what has been proposed has been attempted by various nurses and nursing groups although not in any consistent, organized, or planned manner. The ideas contained in this chapter must be integrated into the way nurses think and act. Only when this occurs will nursing have the power it needs to truly influence the current health care system in the United States.

BIBLIOGRAPHY

Ashley, J.A.: This I believe about power in nursing. *Nursing Outlook* 21(10): 631–641, 1973.

Bagwell, M.A.: The nursing network. . . a united front. *Nursing Leadership* 3(2):5–8, 1980.

Claus, K.E. & Bailey, J.T.: *Power and Influence in Health Care: A New Approach to Leadership.* St. Louis, C. V. Mosby, 1977.

Grissum, M. & Spengler, C.: *Womanpower and Health Care.* Boston, Little Brown, 1976.

McFarland, D.E. & Shiflett, N.: The role of power in the nursing profession. *Nursing Dimensions* 7(2):1–13, 1979.

Peterson, G.: Power: a perspective for the nurse administrator. *Journal of Nursing Administration* 9(7):7–10, 1979.

Ver Steeg, D.: The political process, or the power and the glory. *Nursing Dimensions* 3(2):20–27, 1979.

RECOMMENDED READINGS

American Nurses' Association: *A Plan for Implementation of the Standards of Nursing Practice,* Kansas City, American Nurses' Association, 1975.

This plan contains the historical perspective of ANA's development of standards of nursing care with supportive rationale for implementing the standards. Use of standards with other disciplinary bodies is discussed. Quality assurance models are explained in relation to institutions, clients, private practice, and schools of nursing. An extensive glossary of terms and bibliography are included.

American Nurses' Association: *The Study of Credentialing in Nursing: A New Approach,* Kansas City, American Nurses' Association, 1979.

This report includes general observations on and basic principles of credentialing as they affect nursing; position statements on credentialing; credentialing definitions and their application in nursing; and a model for credentialing in nursing. Committee conclusions and recommendations are included in the report.

ADDITIONAL RESOURCES

Additional resources are provided for readers who wish to go beyond the contents of the chapter. These resources are in the form of addresses of the organizations discussed in the body of the chapter and additional reading materials. Documents discussed in the body of the chapter are not placed in the bibliography but may be obtained by writing directly to the organization under which they are discussed.

American Nurses' Association (ANA)
2420 Pershing Road
Kansas City, Missouri 64108

National League for Nursing (NLN)
10 Columbus Circle
New York, N.Y. 10019

League of Women Voters in the United States (LWVUS)
1730 M Street, N.W.
Washington, D.C. 20036

National Organization for Women (NOW)
425 13th Street, N.W.
Suite 1048
Washington, D.C. 20004

THE POWER OF
POLITICAL ACTIVITY

CLAIR JORDAN

Amid the outcry today about nurses feeling powerless, burned out, and abused there exists a power source that nursing has hardly tapped in its quest for self-determination. This is the power of politics. Webster's dictionary defines politics as the science of government (1977). This definition does little, however, to illustrate politics as the art of influencing the constantly changing community through human relationships (Abalos, 1978). The latter definition may relate more to nursing because nurses provide a humanistic service that is part of a community regulated by laws. Nurses hope to be able to influence the amount and kinds of these services as well as the standards by which they are delivered. But they must be aware that there is an art to being able to influence people through the human interactions of politics.

There are two reasons that nurses should elect to move into the political arena in greater than ever numbers: (1) The nurse today frequently expresses a desire to participate in decisions relating to his or her professional destiny. The political framework of the government, in fact, provides nurses with the opportunity to participate at one of the highest levels of policy making, that is, law making. Since the impact of decisions and policies made at this level often goes far beyond the local health delivery site, where the nurse practices, actively involved nurses can sometimes shape the future of health care. For example, nurses may lobby for a national health insurance law that will decide who will receive health care and whether it is a right or a privilege. Or nurses may speak to the need for additional funds for a clinic, or the right to provide services under a state license. (2) The health care delivery system of today *needs* nurses' input and influence at the policy-making and health-planning level. Nurses' beliefs and standards for health care will not survive in the future if exercised only at the bedside of patients and clients. Nurses' beliefs about health care must be transferred, via politics, into the actual health care system if nursing is to exist in the twenty-first century as a necessary component of health care.

NURSES MOVE INTO POLITICS

Historically, nurses have not attempted to use the political system on a conscious and continuous basis. Before the 1970s, professional nurses usually practiced a type of "reactionary politics;" they entered the political system only to try to stop certain legislation that threatened the profession's existence. The late 1960s saw nurses reacting in this way against federal and state legislative bills that called for institutional licensure as a replacement for professional licensure. In addition, they spoke out in support of "the great society" bills, such as Medicare, that mirrored part of the profession's beliefs about health care. In the 1970s, several factors led some members of the nursing profession to systematically plan and attempt to build political power for nursing. The factors leading to this concentrated political awareness were allied to important societal and professional movements, which we shall briefly review.

The 1970s saw the peak of government involvement in the health care industry. Nurses realized that government policies would increasingly regulate the health care industry in the form of legislation on Medicaid, health system agencies, and professional standards review organizations. In the 1970s, the activities of the women's movement also reached an all-time high, especially in attempts to educate women about their need for involvement in the political process. Many women involved in the movement put together thorough and well-defined plans for entering the political process. It was therefore natural that nursing, a 98%-female profession, should be strongly influenced by these endeavors and adopt some of the same directions.

The third reason for nurses' interest in political power in the 1970s stemmed from their realization that they desperately *needed* to influence the law-making process. This sense of urgency served to motivate professional organizations and groups to become more politically active. As a result, the nursing profession and its practices began to change during this period. Nurses began to take on new and more complex roles. As they began to foster preventative health care, the nurse practitioner movement came into being. All these changes necessitated revisions in state nurse practice acts. Then, in 1974, when the profession experienced a presidential veto against the nurse training act, which threatened funds that nursing had enjoyed for years, many nurses were strongly motivated to become more politically effective in order to maintain the profession's well-being (Kalisch & Kalisch, 1978).

The nurse today who wishes to become involved in political advocacy for nursing will need to adapt the model of those politically involved nurses of the 1970s to the issues of the 1980s. To accomplish this, the nurse will need to become skilled in the rudiments of the political process. In the past, and even today, nurses have deemed politics a slightly "shady" subject. This view is not entirely invalid since the rules of politics are not routinely open. Often, the key influencing factors in a political issue occur outside the law-making process.

The components of politics are power, competition, and conflict. However, not all who enter the *competition* have enough *power* to solve their *conflict*. Historically, the rules governing politics have been derived by men who are comfortable with the "old boy" rules that you never stop negotiating, that no one ever totally becomes your enemy, and that you never appear "uncontrolled" in public. Although nurses are secure about speaking to the needs of patients, they may not be as confident when speaking about the needs of a special interest group such as nursing. They need only to remember, however, that they are promoting the profession because they believe that nursing has something unique and essential to offer patients and clients. Nurses who shy away from certain elements of politics, such as collusion, threat, and financial investment, must remember that all other health professions use them. If nurses elect not to participate in the political process, the balance will tip in favor of other health professions.

To be successful in politics, the nurse must learn that the process for influencing legislation or governmental action is a continuous process which starts long before a vote is taken in the legislative body. Those who are just beginning to try to sway a legislator's or councilman's thinking at the point of bill development will find that the opposition has a greater hold because of previous groundwork. It is often at this point that nurses begin to understand the many powers are brought to bear on the legislator's ultimate decision to vote for or against certain issues. It is wise to learn and understand the different types and categories of power that play a part in each legislator's final decision.

POWER TYPES AND POLITICS

The following discussion relates "accepted categories of power" French & Raven, 1959) to the tools of the political process that culminate in laws.

Reward Power

Reward power involves the use of positive sanctions by the person wielding the power. These sanctions may range from verbal praise to economic compensation. In politics, an individual or group often holds power over a legislator because they have rewarded him or her in one or several of these ways. Thought by some to be the strongest categorical power, it is definitely the fastest growing power in the political process today. Examples of reward power have always been evident in politics. However, in the late 1960s and early 1970s, the advent of certain laws allowed incorporated groups to form political action committees, or PACs, which supplied campaign finances and other support such as manpower to certain candidates whose views coincided with those of the special interest group. With the rising cost of political campaigning, many candidates have become more dependent on this campaign help and, in turn, have become indebted to certain special interest groups. Nurses trying to influence the political process will need to use this type of political influence to fully be a part of the political game. They may exercise this type of political power through direct campaigning for an individual legislator or by actively participating in one of nursing's political action committees.

Nurses' Coalition for Action in Politics (*N-CAP*) the political action committee for the American Nurses' Association, was founded in 1973 to give nurses an equal chance to participate in the election of candidates with views similar to theirs. N-CAP endorses candidates, organizes work banks, and contributes monies to individuals who are running for federal office. Because a national political action committee can only participate in national elections, approximately 33 state nurses' associations have also formed political action committees to carry out similar functions in state elections. Likewise, nurses who are committed to local, city, county, or municipal races have formed local political action committees. Nurses interested in working with political action committees should write to:

N-CAP
1101 14th St. N.W., Suite 200
Washington, D.C. 20005

or, their state nurses' association, for further information.

At the current time, all major health professions have political action groups functioning in state and national elections. Nurses who participate in political action committees will find they will achieve better communications with the legislators they helped elect, and the legislator will find it harder to go against nursing's issues if he or she has had the profession's support during election.

Coercive Power

Coercive power is the opposite of reward power because it involves negative sanctions such as threats or punishment. In politics, this power type is most often used by special interest groups that approach a legislator to support a certain measure. The very subtle message given to the legislator is that if he or she is not cooperative, the special interest group will seek and support another candidate for that legislative position. Often the major issue at stake is whether the special interest group has the backing needed to carry out such a threat. To be able to utilize such political power, nurses would have to establish a clear identity as a group that could assist a candidate to win election. In some parts of the country, nurses have been able to organize their own resources and form coalitions to have new candidates elected. In some instances, however, nurses have threatened a legislator without having the resources to carry out the threat. This can leave nurses in the uncomfortable situation of having virtually severed their relationship with a legislator who will continue to make decisions about nursing issues.

Sometimes, the mere fact that an individual or group is keeping the record of a legislator's voting pattern in such areas as health care is enough to threaten the legislator. This strategy can be very effective if nurses request from their state or federal government the record of their legislator's votes, both in committee and on the Senate or House floor. Nurses may also contact nursing associations who usually maintain voting records on legislators.

Another technique nurses can use to subtly pressure legislators is to expose the legislator's position on particular issues through public media. A legislator from a rural area of the country may not want his constituents to learn through the media that he voted against a bill allowing nurse practitioners to provide care in rural areas. This exposure would therefore threaten the legislator's relationship with his constituents.

Legitimate Power

Legitimate power is the authority vested in a role, position, or office. In politics, the legislator will often look to individuals who hold positions of esteem in his or her home district for direction on particular issues. If the issue under discussion is education, the legislator might consult with all the presidents of the school boards in the district. If the issue is health care, the legislator might turn to the hospital board, the board of the health system agencies, or the local president of the nursing and medical associations. If nurses wish to have influence through this type of power they must actively seek appointment to those offices that confer legitimate power. Once nurses become key leaders in their communities, they will be sought out much more frequently for their advice on health care.

Referent Power or Mentor Power

Referent, or mentor, power is a subtle form of power that is based on the ability of one or more individuals or groups to share some of the power or esteem held by a more powerful individual or group. In politics, this power type frequently operates through the coalition of special interest groups. For example, the combining of a major political organization with two minor political groups through coalition would definitely produce more power for the minor groups. Another example of referent or mentor power would result from persuading a powerful group such as oil and gas lobbyists to speak out on behalf of employee health care issues that also interest nurses. In this case, nurses could borrow some of the power of the stronger oil group and thus use their referent power.

Expert Power

Expert power, which is most often based on the knowledge of the powerholder, is probably the most used power type in the political arena and, in some cases, the least effective. It is usually exercised by individuals or groups communicating with their legislator and pressuring the legislator to carry out a particular action on the basis of the former's expert knowledge and opinions. Special interest groups may either testify as experts at hearings or write or telegraph their legislators their opinions. If no one opposes the viewpoint, the legislator will probably listen to the expert. However, if nurses and physicians are both the experts on a health care issue and their views are opposing, the legislator may have to choose whom he or she thinks has the greatest degree of expertise.

Informational Power

Informational power is one of the most important requisites for the nurse who wishes to participate in political advocacy on state and federal actions that affect nursing. In order to communicate with legislators the first step the nurse must take is to establish an information network that will provide the necessary information. Few nurses, independent of a professional association or large corporate organization, will find the ready and available data needed to act at the strategic time. Moreover, without an information network, individual nurses will be unable to orchestrate collective nursing action from far-flung geographical areas or to bring about major pieces of legislation. Several strategies can be planned that will result in an information network.

Most national nursing associations, such as the American Nurses' Association and the National League for Nursing, have elaborate monitoring systems that track all health bills introduced at the national level. Most state nurses' associations do likewise and subscribe to services that give them ready access to proposed health bills, times and places for committee meetings, and actual agendas of Senate and House assemblies. Constituent members of national and state associations will usually be provided a concentrated synopsis of this information in a format appropriate to the need for action. Three common avenues of communication are the American Nurses' Association, communication networks, and direct personal contacts.

The American Nurses' Association communicates special legislative information in its regular publication, *The American Nurse*, under a special column "Capital Commentary." Several organizations use this format and, in addition, publish such information in smaller periodic newsletters that are mailed directly to key nurse leaders who might be instigators of action in their own areas.

Communication networks, another avenue of communication, are usually formed by professional associations in order to bring about quick and concentrated lobbying efforts from nursing. Using telephone trees, the network can provide information to 300 people in a two-hour period when the on-site lobbyist activates ten nurses by phone and reports that some specific activity on a bill is imminent and that help is needed to convince the legislator to take a certain path. Each nurse then calls ten more nurses until a mass of nurses is contacted. They can then bring about grassroots pressure by individually contacting their respective legislators. Through this system, the legislator experiences multiple contacts from the constituency and thus feels pressure to represent those verbal nurses in the ensuing action. This method may also be used to contact coalition groups or consumer groups that are especially interested in supporting certain nursing issues.

Still another avenue of communication is direct contact from the association to the legislator. Some associations ttempt to identify one nurse to work with each legislator or council member. This nurse maintains a close working relationship with the elected official and the staff of the association and will often have worked directly in the elected official's campaign. The contact nurse will stay in daily contact with the association during periods of debate because he or she has usually received the most up-to-date information from the legislator. Such a network will result in firsthand information on the total picture of the legislative issues affecting nursing.

In addition to the formal avenues of information, nurses will find that as their involvement in politics increases more information will come to them through the informal grapevine, that is, either though legislators' aides or other groups. However, nurses should evaluate rumors carefully since spreading incorrect rumors is often a strategy used by opponents to stop a bill's movement.

In summary, nurses will have to use all available sources of information as well as individual legislators to stay in control of information on legislators' endeavors. Association membership, or subscriptions to special publications will further assist nurses who do not have unlimited time.

LOBBYING

The word "lobbyist" often conjures up a mental image of an elderly man, with cigar, handing out dollar bills to legislators. In truth, the individual who lobbys today may do so through other means. The definition of the word lobby is to attempt to influence or sway a public official toward a desired action. (Merriam-Webster, 1977). The people who carry out this activity must therefore have an abundant source of background information upon which to draw. Lobbyists often act more as "educators" to the legislator on issues than anything else. Nurses need to remember that if they do not assume the role of educator to the public official on nursing, other health professions or interested parties stand ready to do so. But obviously these other groups will not express a true nursing viewpoint. With a knowledge of their profession, technical resources, and insights into speciality areas, nurses have a unique body of knowledge to share with legislators.

The first step to being a good lobbyist is to be a good citizen. Voting in elections is the most important contribution a nurse can make as a citizen. Nurses who are not registered to vote and have not assisted in the selection of their decision makers must go back to step one. The voter registration process varies from state to state, but information can be obtained by contacting the county courthouse or state election office where you can find out how to register to vote.

Some research has been done on nurses' political activities. A survey conducted by N-CAP, the political action arm of the American Nurses' Association found that 91% of nurses were registered to vote. This indicates that nurses may already be functioning in political activity at a higher rate than the general population where only about 70% of the adult population is registered. (Shorr, 1979)

The second step to being an involved citizen is to know your elected officials. To find the names and addresses of your state officials and congressmen, contact your local library or county courthouse. As a general rule, nurses will want to confine their contact to legislators and congressmen who represent them. Indeed, public officials are more accessible and more amenable to the constituents who have elected them. However, nurses may also wish to contact a legislator outside their district if he or she serves on a committee studying a health bill. In this instance, the legislator would be more open to influence by the general background and knowledge of the nurse, while the nurse's information can be valuable to the legislator.

Nurses who have decided to influence the political arena will do well to develop skills and gather tips on the lobby-

ing process. They should remember that the most successful lobbying or advocacy campaigns are multifaceted, coordinated efforts of many nurses. State and national nursing
organizations, consumer groups, and health coalitions will
all give the nurse a chance to work as part of an organized
lobbying network.

There are four general categories of activity through
which a nurse can lobby or advocate nursing's position:
telephone, mail, and telegraph communication; direct personal contact; testimony; and mobilization of support
through news media.

Telephone, Mail, and Telegraph Communication

Nurses who have information on a bill or who have been
contacted through a telephone network may write, telephone or telegraph their representative to express their
opinion. Through this method of lobbying, nurses may
notify the legislator or congressman that his constituents
are aware of an issue. In this instance, nurses are offering
their "expert" opinion on a health care subject. The purpose of this kind of lobbying is usually not to change the
public official's mind but to put him or her on notice as to
how local constituents view the issue and to offer background data. For each mode of contact there are several
points to consider in order to make the contact maximally
effective (Texas Nurses Association, 1980).

EFFECTIVE LETTERS

There are congressmen who agree that a letter is the most
effective means of communication since it shows that the
constituent has expended considerable effort and forethought on the issue, and hence is committed to it. In a
survey addressing nurse administrators, 83% said that
they thought writing the legislator was the most successful
political strategy. (Archer & Goehner, 1981) Letters also

provide a permanent mailing list for the legislator. However, they are often slow to be processed and should only be used when time is not of the essence.

During peak legislative activities, legislators' and congressmens' offices may receive hundreds, sometimes thousands, of letters a day on a variety of bills so that the impact of any single letter is diminished by the volume. Still, legislators from less populous rural areas may actually read all the mail, while legislators from densely populated areas may have their staff compile lists of subjects from the mail and do straw counts on the subjects. Rarely is the content of the mail not brought to a legislator's attention in some way. To insure that the letter's message gets through to the elected official, several points should be followed:

• Begin by using the correct salutation for the letter. A quick reference for most elected officials is included in Figure 4.1. Local libraries can supply more detailed addresses.

Figure 4.1
Salutations to Elected Officials

The appropriate salutation for letters to officials is:

President of the United States
    The President
    The White House
    Washington, D.C. 20500

    Dear Mr. President:

Vice President
    The Vice President
    United States Senate
    Washington, D.C. 20510

    Dear Mr. Vice President:

Figure 4.1
Continued

Senator
> The Honorable (full name)
> United States Senate
> Washington, D.C. 20510
>
> Dear Senator (last name):

Representative
> The Honorable (full name)
> House of Representatives
> Washington, D.C. 20515
>
> Dear Mr., Mrs., Ms. (last name)

Member of the Cabinet
> The Honorable (full name)
> The Secretary of (cabinet position)
> Washington, D.C.
>
> Dear Mr., Mrs., Ms. Secretary:

Governor
> The Honorable (full name)
> State Capitol
> City, State, Zip Code
>
> Dear Governor (last name):

State senator
> The Honorable (full name)
> The Senate
> City, State, Zip Code
>
> Dear Senator (last name):

State representative
> The Honorable (full name)
> House of Representatives
> City, State, Zip Code
>
> Dear Mr., Mrs., Ms. (last name):

Figure 4.1
Continued

Mayor
 The Honorable (full name)
 City Hall
 City, State, Zip Code

 Dear Mayor (last name):

Councilperson
 Council Member (full name)
 City Hall
 City, State, Zip Code

 Dear Mr., Mrs., Ms. (last name):

County commissioner
 Mr., Mrs., Ms. (full name)
 County Commissioner
 Precinct No.
 County Courthouse
 City, State, Zip Code

 Dear Mr., Mrs., Ms. (last name):

- The most widely used complimentary closing for letters to elected officials is "Sincerely yours." Most etiquette books recommend "Very respectfully yours" when closing a letter to the president.

- The letter should be no more than one page, straightforward, and to the point. If more information must be included, it should be condensed to a one-page fact sheet. It is preferable that the letter be typed.

- The letter should address only one bill or pending issue. Always refer to the bill by name, number, and bill purpose.

- The letter should include a direct inquiry to the elected official on his or her position on the bill in question. This will decrease the chances of a form-letter reply.

- The letter should include the nurse's own personal stand on the bill, the reason for the interest in the bill, and how the outcome will affect the nurse. Any personal experience and observation the nurse may have had in regard to the issue should be highlighted.

- The letter should point out the local impact of a bill so that the elected official can relate it to his or her local elected area.

- The timing of a letter often dictates some of its content. A letter written to a legislator before a bill is introduced might include language a nurse believes should be in the bill. A letter written the day before a committee hearing might include questions for the legislator to ask of individuals testifying.

- The letter should always include the nurse's name and address on the letter because envelopes often get thrown away. Include titles such as R.N. or L.P.N. so thet the legislator is aware of the nurse's credentials and interest.

- Remember, some of the most important letters to legislators are those that say "thank you for your vote and support of nursing's issues."

TELEGRAMS

When speed is a consideration in communicating a viewpoint, a telegram is the answer. Telegrams are usually reserved for upcoming votes in committee or on the floor of the chamber, while their purpose is usually not to educate the legislator, but to indicate the numbers of individuals from the constituency interested in the issue. Many of the points to remember in sending effective telegrams are the same as for letter writing. In addition, the following points relate specifically to telegrams:

- Most telegrams can be sent by telephone and charged to a business or home phone number. Western Union offers a "Public Opinion Telegram" especially designed for individuals to notify their legislators of their opinions. The rate is usually under $5.00 for a message of 15 words (not counting names and addresses).

- Overnight mailgrams are usually under $5.00 for 50 words or less and can be sent by calling Western Union.

- Telegrams should include the bill number and purpose with the individual's stand for or against the bill.

- Telegrams should include the name and address in the message so the legislator may identify the individual as a constituent.

TELEPHONE CALLS

Telephoning an elected official is a legitimate method for a constituent to express an opinion. Again, as with the use of letters, this method of lobbying is best used to alert legislators to views of the constituency. Since the legislator is seldom reached, the telephone call's success depends on the staff's ability to adequately summarize the call and pass on the message. Often, the staff does not have the materials on the issue at hand and will have difficulty relating to the concern. Before making a call, it is helpful to outline the points to be made and the arguments to support these points. The following guides are useful when telephoning an elected official:

- When initiating the call, ask if the senator or representative is available to speak to a constituent. If the person is unavailable, request to speak to the staff person assigned to the bill, giving its purpose and number.

- Early morning is usually a good time to make telephone calls to offices before the staffs are into their busy day of appointments.

- Telephone calls should be kept brief. If complicated information is involved, it is best to follow up with a letter or fact sheet.

Direct Personal Contact

Direct personal contact with a legislator is the most powerful form of influence available to a nurse when lobbying. It
gives the legislator a chance to view the nurse's legitimacy,
rational behavior, and dedication to the cause. In addition,
the legislator is able to receive positive feedback from the
nurse throughout the exchange. The only drawback is the
difficulty of securing a personal contact with the official;
because of their work load, many legislators limit their
contacts. When possible, two methods of personal contact
can be used: nurses may personally visit legislators in their
homes, local or capitol offices and may provide testimony
at hearings or meet with legislators at public gatherings.

MAKING A PERSONAL VISIT

Nothing is more effective in communicating nursing's
position on a given issue than face-to-face contact with a
representative. However, nothing is more detrimental to
nursing's cause than a meeting between an elected official
and a nurse where the official comes away feeling that the
time was wasted and the issues poorly verbalized. Representatives have an incredible number of bills to follow
whose topics are varied and often highly specialized. As a
result, a large part of lobbying is concerned with educating
the legislators. If a group of nurses can focus their representative's attention on a particular bill and present a few
basic arguments for the position, the nurses may well win
the legislator's support. Following are points to remember
when planning for a personal visit with an elected official.

PREPARING FOR THE MEETING

A visit to an elected official may be made to a home district's office or capitol office. Often, the legislator will have
more time in the home office but will not have as many
resources at his or her fingertips. The nurse should contact
the appropriate office to make the appointment and to ex-

plain to the staff its specific purpose. In preparation for the meeting, the nurse should become familiar with as much background on the representative as possible. Information on the representative's voting record, contribution list, and personal occupation will give the nurse an estimate of the legislator's thinking. Public libraries and associations are good resources for this kind of background information.

The nurse should thoroughly research the issue to be discussed with the legislator. To gain credibility as a lobbyist, a nurse must be able to do a thorough presentation of the facts and well-reasoned arguments and at the same time be prepared to respond to opposing views.

CONDUCTING THE MEETING

The nurse will probably wish to arrive at the legislator's office with a packet of information, which might include your address for further contacts as well as a summary of your concerns regarding the specific language of the bill. In addition, a brief fact sheet or summaries of larger studies that back up the nurse's position might also be included. This information will help to introduce the nurse, to provide an outline for the conversation, and to provide the office with a written summary of what you have said. A good impression is imperative. Dress should be neat and businesslike.

The nurse should introduce herself upon arriving in the office, giving information about her background and organization affiliation. While waiting for the elected official, the nurse can use the time to get to know the legislator's staff who are valuable resources.

Upon meeting the legislator, the nurse should start the conversation with a nondirective approach: "Senator, since you know that Mrs. Allison and I are nurses, I'm sure you understand our interest in the new public health bill." An opportunity should then be given to the legislator to verbalize his or her level of knowledge and concern on the issue. In discussion, the nurse will need to refer to the bill by content, not by number or sponsor. Legislators deal with thousands of bills and tend to remember them by subject.

The nurse keeps the conversation in the realm of the positive; if the nurse express the position firmly but not in a threatening manner, the discussion will be more profitable. Arguing with a legislator will simply place one in an adversary role. If a point of disagreement comes up, the nurse should offer to provide more data and offer a future discussion. If the nurse finds that she does not know the answers to some of the legislator's questions, she should say so and volunteer to find the answers.

FOLLOW-UP OF THE MEETING

The nurse should follow up the visit with a short note thanking the legislator for the meeting, restating your position and understanding of the legislator's views and including the answers to any questions that you may had been unable to supply during the meeting. The nurse should always volunteer further assistance.

Testifying

As bills work through the legislative process, they will be first referred to a legislative subcommittee. The committee is the body that most often "perfects" a bill. The committee chairperson will usually call a public hearing to allow the public to present testimony or input. It is important that nurses present testimony at these hearings to offer nursing's viewpoint. Nurses planning to testify will do well to prepare themselves as thoroughly as possible. Reading a prepared statement before a mirror or asking a peer to cross-examine you beforehand will help you to be more relaxed during the actual testimony. The testifying nurse should dress conservatively because appearance may be as important to legislators as what is said. Plan to augment the oral testimony with copies of a written statement presented at the time of testimony. The written statement may include support materials in the form of data, reports, or fact sheets to which the nurse simply refers during her oral testimony. Enough copies of the written statement should be available to give copies to each member of the committee, staff, and media. Upon arrival at the committee hearing room, ascertain if signed witness forms are necessary to testify. Check at the main entrance of the hearing room for directions on witness forms or check with the staff of the committee.

When the nurse is called to the podium or table to testify, you should begin with identifying remarks such as name, occupation and any groups represented. If the nurse represents an organization, she should be prepared to state the organization's purpose and the number of its members. The nurse may be sworn to tell the truth by the committee chair much as in a witness at a court trial.

The nurse should present testimony that is concise and brief—no more than five minutes. She or he should also be prepared to answer questions at the end of the testimony. Most questions will be "friendly," simply an attempt to gather more information. However, some officials, especially those with opposing views, may attempt to confuse you or discredit the nurse's testimony. The nurse should stand firm in her or his position but do not attempt to ridicule or strike back at the legislator. When presenting testimony or answering questions, the nurse should not use "nursing" or health care vocabulary. Most of the individuals hearing the testimony will be lay individuals.

Remember that testimony at a hearing rarely educates a legislator's mind. It takes legwork and individual meetings before the hearings to accomplish this.

Arguing Nursing's Viewpoint

Nurses have often entered the political process believing that they would be successful because they were right and because what they wanted was best for the public. Nurses should be aware, however, that part of their success depends on how well they are able to plan and prepare their arguments. In writing letters, testifying, or in direct visits with legislators, nurses should adopt techniques for arguing their position. (Johnson, 1979)

Some of the techniques are obvious while others speak to hidden ways to convince legislators. An argument, of course, must be logical, but it should also have an element that appeals to the emotion. Nurses can use patients' human-interest stories to support logical argument; pure factual information alone is not enough. However, they must also learn to support their conclusions with relevant statistics.

Arguments usually fall into four categories. Strong arguments will focus one one of the following:

- society how the nursing position will enhance people's lives

- economics how the nurse's position will save money or stimulate business

- ethics why the nurses' position is morally right

- scientific a conglomerate of facts that justify the nurse's position

Nurses should be concerned not only with their own argument, but the arguments of opponents as well. It may be strategically important *not* to continue to press points but to attack your opponent's arguments. Some ways to counter opponents are to:

- challenge the opponent's "facts." Look for every flaw and exaggeration. Turn to governmental agencies or local universities for factual help.

- look for weak assumptions. All arguments are based on certain assumptions and weak ones, that lacking sufficient documentation should be attacked first.

- challenge the "rightness" of the opponent's arguments, especially if the opponent has based the argument on a moral or ethical issue.

- point out inconsistencies. Research arguments the opposition has used in past causes and look for "changes" in attitudes.

- point out conflicts of interest.

In preparing her or his viewpoint, the nurse will need to remember that many legislators and lobbyists are attorneys and highly skilled in argumentation. The nurse will be more successful if he or she uses some of the attorney's techniques.

Mobilizing Public Support

Most of nursing's issues in the political arena have a direct impact on the quality of health care the public receives. For this reason, some nurse lobbying campaigns will reach out to mobilize support from the public, the consumer of health care. This is most often carried out through the media and through contact with local organizations and influential persons in the community.

MEDIA RELATIONS

Nurses can use any channel of the media—television news, radio, talk shows, newspapers—to distribute the concerns of the profession to the public. The purpose of presenting the nurse's case is to educate the public and offer health care consumers political ways to fight for an issue. Nurses should remember, however, that it is extremely difficult to motivate the general public to take up a cause to the extent of persuading people to become politically involved. Nevertheless, nurses can use the media to motivate the public to call legislators on the day a hearing takes place on the funding of health care clinics. Nurses need to work together to create a media impact that coincides with an important event concerning a bill, and this often means bringing public attention to a peak at the right time.

The "press release" and the "press conference" are two tools used in dealing with the press that nurses should be aware of. The press release is simply a written story about the *action* of the nursing group's project, which may be mailed or hand delivered to the news media or used in conjunction with a press conference. Its content should be "new" news or should at least offer a new focus on the issue. The release should contain a release time and date indicating when the media can use the material in the release, and the name and telephone number of a person to contact if a reporter has a question about the material or wishes further information. The release should never be more than 1½ to 2 pages long. It is best to use press releases when there is a need to get educational information blanketed throughout an area and when the timeliness of the message is not crucial.

A press conference is simply a conference of the press called by an individual or group when they believe they have important information and where timeliness *is* a crucial consideration. The press conference should be used very sparingly and only when critical points concerning an issue or project need to be made. It should be held in a central, accessible location, and announced by a short press release and follow-up phone calls to alert wire services and reporters to the event. The timing of press conferences vary according to different medias. To get TV coverage the same day, the press conference should be held about midmorning. To make newspaper coverage the next day, it should be held no later than noon. It should begin by distributing copies of the statement to the press, while the person who reads the statement should be the most articulate in the group. The statement itself should take no more than seven minutes to read, with concluding time for questions. The speaker must always be prepared to provide factual, background information on statements made to reporters. Sometimes the use of "horror stories" may be used to secure press coverage, but these must be used with caution.

Several other kinds of media coverage that can be used throughout the legislative process to build public support are as follows:

- "Letters to the Editor" page of newspapers: these letters will notify the community that an important issue of consumer interest is before the legislature and is intended to enlist other supporters in the lobbying cause.

- "Opinion Page": the group may submit an article to the newspaper's opinion section to catch public interest.

- "Radio and Television Talk Shows": most stations have talk shows that deal with items of public interest. Nurses should approach the directors of these shows to schedule programming on their issues.

- "Editorial Stances of Media": nurses should write to editors and columnists of the local press and managers of local stations pointing out the public interest in nursing issues and encouraging them to take a public stand on an issue. Legislators are extremely sensitive to editorial comments of the media from their local area.

- "Equal Time": if any channel of the media takes an editorial position contrary to nursing's stance, nurses should demand equal time to disagree. It is required by law that the media grant such time.

- "Call-in Radio Shows" provide nurses with an excellent opportunity to state political positions and to educate the public on present and potential legislation that will affect health care (U.S. Government, 1979).

Utilizing Influential Individuals and Groups

Nurses will occasionally find that the most successful contact with a legislator can be through a third party or third group that has influence with the legislator. But first, you must identify those people and groups that actively supported the legislator in the election campaign. In addition, the nurse must look to community leaders who personally know the legislator, such as party leaders, merchants, mayors, and county officials. When selecting the influential person or group, the nurse should provide them with a simple and basic explanation of the cause and ask them to speak to a legislative contact on behalf of nursing. It will be helpful to give the third person background sheets and examples of news to study. The same strategies should be used in approaching this third person as those used with the legislator.

COALITION BUILDING

In planning for a successful conclusion to a legislative issue, nurses may feel they do not have the stamina, manpower, or resources to independently carry out their plan. At this point they should consider coalition building, a growing concept and practice in politics. A coalition is a conglomerate of groups whose overall goals are different, but that share a common interest in a single issue or in achieving a special project. Nurses who believe that the state law should be changed to allow nurse practitioners to provide primary care in employment settings may, for example, form a coalition with a group of unions that want more accessible health care for their members and certain large oil companies that see the issue as a way to cut costs of employee health care. Even though the overall purpose of the various groups are different, they can form a successful coalition if they support the fundamental issue of changing the law to allow the nurse practitioner to provide care in the employment setting.

A coalition can be generated by the various groups' mutual need for different legislative contacts, finances, staff support, expertise, or greater numbers of participants. But nothing is as important to the groups as the *mutual benefit* each will receive. It is therefore vital that each member group understands what the coalition can realistically do for it.

The most obvious potential coalition member is a group that has had similar interests with nursing in the past or groups that would profit from the succesful outcome of an issue. For example, school nurses who want to see junk foods removed from school grounds and cafeterias might do well to contact the PTA for support in lobbying and education.

To start a coalition, the nurse would approach the identified groups and call a meeting. The nurse will find that patience and group-dynamics tips will make the outcome of the coalition meeting more positive. Each group member participating should have something to contribute, such as political influence, strategy skills, valuable contacts or large memberships. Of course, the nurse must ascertain what each group expects from the coalition for if the member group does not have some of its needs met, it will not function at maximum capacity. Coalition members who are flexible and open minded should be sought because you may be bringing together people who are extreme adversaries on another issue (U.S. Government, 1979).

In conducting the first meetings of the coalition, the nurse should make sure that ground-rule decisions are made, such as how will decisions be made, who will decide when the group uses the media for the cause, and all other decisions on operation. This is a temporary organization that will need to know how it will operate.

ACTION IN THE
LEGISLATIVE PROCESS

At first glance, the legislative process may seem confusing, but in actuality it is a well-defined process totally governed by rules. Nurses would do well to learn the common abbreviations for terms of the process, to familiarize themselves with its steps, and to become aware of major parliamentary rules that govern these steps. The process is quite similar at the national and the state level of government. However, the nurse should know the peculiarities of each process. Copies of each state legislative process may be obtained from the public library.

Ideas for new laws may originate from a number of sources: citizens, nurses, governmental staff, elected officials, and special interest groups. National and state governments have specialists called "legislative counsels" who perfect the drafting of bills and assist congressmen with the legal technicalities.

Bills usually resemble any legal document and may be difficult to understand. A bill will have a title or caption that identifies the subject it addresses; its content will usually be the text of the proposed law.

In order for a bill to be introduced as a subject in Congress, it must be sponsored by a member of the House or Senate. By "sponsoring" the bill, congressional representative acts as its primary spokesman or advocate. Other representatives may cosponsor the bill and provide support. Bills may be introduced in either the House or the Senate. The sponsor introduces the bill by giving it to a clerk in the House who reads the title of the bill and assigns the bill a number for identification.

The Speaker of the House acts as the presiding officer and assigns the bill to a committee for study. The House usually has a number of permanent committees to handle

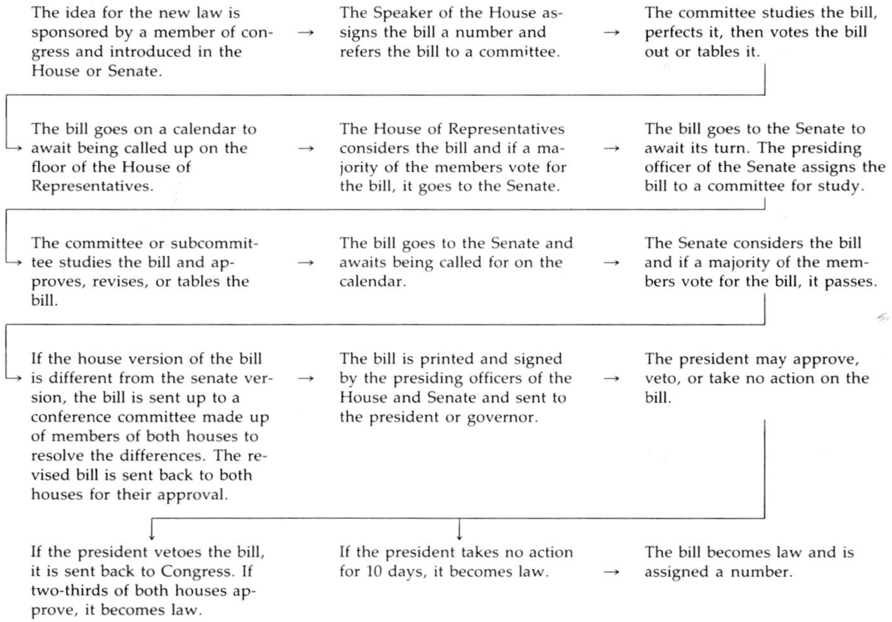

The idea for the new law is sponsored by a member of congress and introduced in the House or Senate. → The Speaker of the House assigns the bill a number and refers the bill to a committee. → The committee studies the bill, perfects it, then votes the bill out or tables it.

The bill goes on a calendar to await being called up on the floor of the House of Representatives. → The House of Representatives considers the bill and if a majority of the members vote for the bill, it goes to the Senate. → The bill goes to the Senate to await its turn. The presiding officer of the Senate assigns the bill to a committee for study.

The committee or subcommittee studies the bill and approves, revises, or tables the bill. → The bill goes to the Senate and awaits being called for on the calendar. → The Senate considers the bill and if a majority of the members vote for the bill, it passes.

If the house version of the bill is different from the senate version, the bill is sent up to a conference committee made up of members of both houses to resolve the differences. The revised bill is sent back to both houses for their approval. → The bill is printed and signed by the presiding officers of the House and Senate and sent to the president or governor. → The president may approve, veto, or take no action on the bill.

If the president vetoes the bill, it is sent back to Congress. If two-thirds of both houses approve, it becomes law. If the president takes no action for 10 days, it becomes law. → The bill becomes law and is assigned a number.

Figure 4.2
Basic Steps in the Legislative Process

specific subjects. The committee studies the bill by holding hearings and soliciting testimony. With some large or controversial issues, it may be necessary to appoint a subcommittee of the committee to study the bill comprehensively. After studying the bill, the committee has three options: they can vote the bill out, revise the bill and vote it out, or lay the bill aside. This is the way hundreds of bills die in legislative sessions. If the bill is voted out of committee, it goes to another committee that schedules bills to be heard by the House. Again, bills may never make it past this process.

The House considers the bill when it is read for the second time. This is the point at which major debate and discussion of the bill takes place. The third reading is usually just a title reading, which comes after the majority work on the bill has been accomplished. The bill will pass

Table 4.1
STRATEGIC POINTS FOR ACTION
IN THE LEGISLATIVE PROCESS

Steps in the Legislative Process	Strategic Action
The surfacing of a concept that suggests changes may be needed in the law; the issue is researched and a bill is drafted.	The nurse may be the catalyst that brings the issue to the legislator's attention. If the nurse receives information that a certain issue is already being researched, the nurse should offer her expertise to the legislator and staff.
The bill is introduced and assigned to a legislative committee.	The nurse may contact the elected official and request him or her to cosponsor the bill. At this time, if the legislator will not cosponsor the bill, the nurse will alert the legislator to nursing's interest in the particular piece of legislation.

Table 4.1 (*Continued*)

The legislative committee holds hearings and takes action on the bill.	The nurse may be requested to testify and bring nursing's viewpoint to the committee hearing on the bill. In addition, nurses may be called on to personally visit each committee person to brief them on selected issues.
A vote is taken on the bill by either the House or Senate.	Nurses will be called upon by nursing leadership to contact their representative or senator to vote in support of the nursing position.
President or governor takes action on the bill.	Depending on the bill, nurses will be asked to communicate their desire with high-ranking officials that either the bill be signed into law or vetoed.

through the House if a simple majority—one more than half—votes for it.

The bill then proceeds to the Senate and goes through a similar process, with committee hearings and senate floor debate. If the senate version of the bill differs from the house version, the bill is referred to a conference committee made up of members of both houses. This group works out language differences and sends the bill back to the House and Senate for final approval.

When both houses have completed work on the bill, it is referred to the highest official, either the president or governor. The president has 10 days to sign the bill into law or veto it. The president may also let a bill become law by letting a certain number of days pass without any action.

Nurses may be called upon by their professional leadership or through their own convictions to intervene at any point of the legislative process. Table 4.1 represents strategic points at which nurses can wield the most influence for a profitable outcome.

NURSING PRACTICE ACTS

The best example of the nurse's perpetual ties to politics is the nursing practice act. Every registered and licensed vocational nurse practices under a public law of the individual state. This state law is the legal document that permits a nurse to offer to the public skills and knowledge in a particular area where such practice would otherwise be unlawful without a license.

Under the police power reserved to each state by the United States Constitution, each state has the legislative authority to regulate the practice of nursing to secure the people from incapable, deceptive, and fraudulent practitioners. This state legislative authority to regulate nursing was first exercised around 1910 in New York, New Jersey, and North Carolina (Sarner, 1968). Since that time, all 50 states have adopted nursing practice acts, which have been modified and rewritten over the years to keep the law in step with nursing practice. Each time these acts have been opened to change, nurses have been called upon by their leadership to enter the political process to influence the laws that govern their practice.

Many nurses first become politically involved because of a desire to influence a legislator in regard to the nursing practice act. Since it is imperative to be aware of the content of the state's nursing practice act, the following actions can be taken by the nurse:

1. maintain individual nursing practice within the boundaries of the law;

2. identify new nursing practices that do not fall within the boundaries of the law; and

3. address the sections of the act that need to be rewritten with legislators.

The American Nurses' Association has published a model nursing practice act to encourage continuity and direction in revising state laws on nursing. Figure 4.3 summarizes the elements of *nursing practice acts.* Many of the states' nursing practice acts resemble this model act and have common sections. Before practicing in a state, nurses should review thoroughly a copy of the state's practice act. A nurse may obtain a copy of the state licensing act by writing to the Board of Nurse Examiners. One of the most important components in a nursing practice act is the definition of nursing. This definition usually is important for two reasons: (1) it delineates the area of professional nursing for which a license is required, and (2) it protects the nurse from charges of the unlicensed practice of medicine. This is the legal boundary in which a nurse performs services.

The definition section will usually speak to limiting the act to those individuals providing nursing care "for compensation." Usually this section will also separate the acts a nurse may perform independently from areas of dependent functions. In addition, certain acts may be clearly labeled as "prohibited acts for nurses" in the definition.

A definition of professional nursing.
A definition of practical nursing. (In a few states, the definition is
  in a separate law.)
The creation of a board of nursing examiners.
Responsibilities of the board of nursing examiners.
Requirements for a license to practice professional nursing.
Exemptions from licensing requirements.
Grounds for revocation of a nursing license.
Requirement that a nursing license be registered.
Fee for licensure and license examinations.
Section dealing with temporary license or reciprocity.
New sections dealing with specialty practices.

Figure 4.3
Elements of a Nursing Practice Act (Source: H. Sarner. *The Nurse and The Law.* W. B. Saunders, Philadelphia, 1968.)

These usually include writing prescriptions or making medical diagnoses.

The majority of states have a combined practice act for both registered nurses and licensed practical nurses. Some states still have separate acts and boards that function independently. All acts have separate definitions of practice.

Some part of the law will deal with the creation of a board of nurse examiners. This section of the law provides for the appointment of a board to oversee the enforcement of the act. Usually, the board is appointed by the governor of the state and may consist of nurses, consumers, and other health professionals.

One section of the act is devoted to responsibilities of the board of nurse examiners. This section of the law usually sets out the board of nurse examiners' responsibilities which frequently fall into three categories:

1. to determine the qualifications of those applicants to take the exam;

2. to select and administer the nursing examination; and

3. to administer the law, which customarily includes maintaining the listing of nurses and policing of the law.

Requirement for a license to practice professional nursing is an important component. Generally, this section of the law will speak to the education, age, citizenship status, good moral character, and the examination score of the nurse applicant as criteria for licensure.

Most professional licensing acts have a section that deals with exemptions from licensing requirements. While most nursing acts provide that it is unlawful for a person to practice nursing without a license, many of the acts also exempt categories of individuals from the act. Common exemptions to acts are: physicians and dentists; employees of a federal agency; unlicensed persons in emergencies; student nurses; spiritual nursing; individuals awaiting licensure; a person who does not identify his or her work as nursing; nurses aides and others.

A section on grounds for revocation of a nursing license usually gives the board its needed authority to revoke or suspend nursing licenses. The most common grounds are: fraud in licensing, criminal or immoral acts, negligence and malpractice, and intemperant use of drugs or alcohol.

Registration of a nursing license is required by some nursing acts. There may be a requirement that the nurse register her license in the county in which she practices.

Fees for licensure and licensure examinations usually fall at the end of the act so this part may be dealt with without reviewing the entire act. There is usually a separate section of the law that sets acceptable fees the board may charge in its operations. (Creighton, 1970).

Additional sections may speak to a nurse practicing under temporary license or about reciprocity for persons licensed in other states. In more updated acts, there are new sections dealing with specialty nursing practice.

SUMMARY

The nursing profession has survived many years of conflict. Most senior leaders of nursing agree that it will continue to survive in some format. The question that younger leaders in the nursing profession will have to address is, "Will the format in which the profession survives be one the profession wants?"

The greatest way to shape that final form will be through the political process. In the coming years, nurses will have to surpass the basic knowledge of politics of their older peers and move into the highest level of the political game—that of holding public office. Ultimately, nursing's political power will determine the quality of its survival.

Nurses slightly awed of the political process should move ahead armed with information. Remember that all that is necessary for the destructive forces in the health care system to win out in this nation is that enough good nurses do nothing.

BIBLIOGRAPHY

Abalos, D.T.: Strategies of transformation in the health care delivery system. *Nursing Forum, 17*:285–316, 1978.

Archer, S.E., & Goehner, P.A.: Acquiring political clout: Guidelines for nurse administrators. *Journal of Nursing Administration 11*:49–55, 1981.

Creighton, H.: *Law Every Nurse Should Know.* Philadelphia, W. B. Saunders, 1970.

French, J.R.P., Jr. & Raven, B.: The bases of social power. In Cartwright, D. (ed.): *Studies in Social Power.* Ann Arbor, University of Michigan, 1959, pp. 150–167.

Johnson, C.: *Legislative Advocacy Manual.* Austin, Legal Services Center, 1979.

Kalisch, B.J. & Kalisch, P.A.: A discourse on the politics of nursing. *Journal of Nursing Administration 6*:29–34, 1976,

Merriam-Webster: *Webster's New Collegiate Dictionary.* Springfield, Mass., G & C Merriam, 1977.

Sarner, H.: *The Nurse and the Law.* Philadelphia, W. B. Saunders, 1968.

Shorr, T. (ed.): Nurses politically concerned and active, study of voting habits reveals. *American Journal of Nursing 79*:1181, 1979.

Texas Nurses' Association: *TNA Constituent District Handbook on Legislation,* 1980.

World Book-Childcraft Internationl, Inc.: *The World Book Encyclopedia.* Chicago, 1979.

U.S. Government: *People Power*. Washington, D.C., Office of
Consumer Affairs, 1979.

RECOMMENDED READINGS

Kalisch, B.J. & Kalisch, P.A.: A discourse on the politics of nursing. *Journal of Nursing Administration* 6:29–34, 1976.

This brief article cites the importance of political activity to nursing
and the consequences of political neglect. A summary of nursing's
problems with presidential vetoes on the nurse training act is provided. The article points out the similarities between governmental
and institutional politics.

Stevens, Barbara J.: Power and politics for the nurse executive.
Nursing and Health Care 1:208–212, 1980.

This article's content and information could be of value to *any* nurse.
Political power is defined and sources are identified.

Capuzzi, Cecelia: Power and interest groups: a study of ANA and
AMA. *Nursing Outlook* 28:478–481, 1980.

This article reviews in depth the ten factors that affect the strengths
of organizations and relates them to the American Nurses' Association and the American Medical Association, allowing the reader to
draw conclusions about the political effectiveness of each group and
the underlying reasons.

HEALTH CARE
AGENCIES AND
POWER

HARRIETT S. CHANEY
ELIZABETH A. KNEBEL

Health care agencies have become increasingly important to millions of Americans who receive or administer health care. As service organizations, health care agencies contribute to the fastest expanding portion of the gross national product. This trend, which is expected to continue, places increasing importance on the role of the professional who delivers health care.

Health care is a labor intensive industry rather than capital intensive or product oriented. As such, the health care agency is concerned with people. Delivery of services by and to people requires the professional administering these services to be skilled in human relations management. An integral component of this skill is insight into and competent application of power in health care agencies.

Power in health care agencies is both unique and in certain respects similar to power in other organizations. Expert power, for example, is the base from which physicians practice medicine in most hospitals. Physicians are the true consumers of hospital services, as these services are used by them to benefit their patients. The physician's competence and expertise can only be verified by another expert in the field. Now, it is true that the physician's expert power and subsequent relationship with the hospital is unique and profitable, but it is also potentially troublesome to both himself and the health care agency, as well as to other professionals within the agency.

The demonstration of expert power among nurses is more consistent with the common understanding of expertise and power. Critical care nurses, for example, have achieved colleagial relationships with physicians, and frequently higher pay for increased expertise. Both rewards are potent and reinforce feelings of power and elitism among these nurses. Expert power may also be garnered by nurses who develop skill and expertise in the operating room, labor and delivery areas, and hemodialysis units.

Because health care agencies are labor intensive, they are fertile grounds for the exercise of reward power. Most people tend to think only of tangible rewards such as money, promotion, title, private office, etc. However, intangible rewards are not only more accessible to all individuals, but facilitate remarkable results in terms of productivity. Recognition, opportunities for achievement and advancement, in addition to personal growth are the important elements of intangible reward power. Research indicates that the contemporary worker no longer subscribes to the traditional work ethic, but instead views work in more personal terms. The nurse manager who understands this phenomenon will incorporate the liberal use of intangible rewards in professional practice as well as recognize their use by others.

Power in health care agencies is supported not only by expert and reward power, but also by legitimate or positional power. The nurse needs to know and to be able to recognize appropriate situations in which to use all of these forms of available power in developing an effective professional practice.

LEGITIMATE POWER

It should be noted that legitimate or positional power may or may not be earned, but is merely the result of an individual holding a specific position. Positional power, unlike authority, need not be legitimized by subordinates to be exercised.

Legitimate or positional power is generally prescribed by organizational design. In basic terms, organizational design describes how the organization hierarchy is put together. This is schematically depicted in the organization charts of this chapter. Organizations are designed with varying degrees of complexity, depending on the mission and size of the agency.

Figure 5.1
Line Organizational Design

Line Organizational Design

The line design is used in organizations that have a simply-stated mission and minimal technology. As depicted in Figure 5.1, the mission is accomplished by a small group of individuals performing a diverse set of tasks. The school health nurse or the home health nursing agency may function well within a line design. Power is derived from position in this design, and is straightforward and simple.

Line-Staff Organizational Design

The line-staff organizational design is used frequently by medium-to-large health care agencies. This design can be quite complex, as depicted in Figure 5.2. Line departments are generally those departments related directly to the mission of the agency; for example, the nursing service department. Line departments have a greater power posture than staff departments, such as personnel, housekeeping, and maintenance which supply support services to departments related directly to the agency's mission. Combining the power of a line department with the fact that hospital nursing service departments hire up to 85% of health care

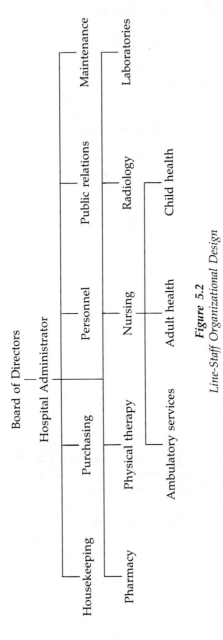

Figure 5.2
Line-Staff Organizational Design

126

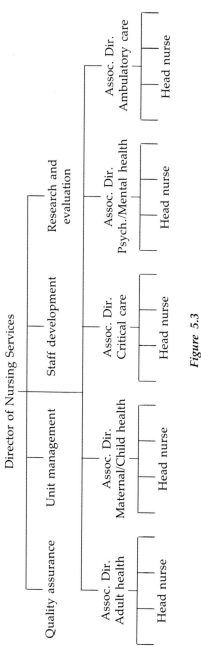

Figure 5.3
Nursing Service Department

agency employees makes nursing a power to be reckoned with. It is thus apparent why the individual in charge of nursing services should have direct access to the person administratively responsible for the agency's mission.

Line departments can be considered isolated entities that possess both line and staff functions. Figure 5.3 provides examples that make this point more understandable. Supervisors, head nurses, assistant head nurses, and charge nurses perform line functions as their work is directly related to the agency mission of delivering health care services. Departmental secretaries, staffing clerks, researchers, educators, and clinical nurse specialists perform staff functions that support line personnel. Staff functions generally do not include policy development and enforcement, or departmental decision making and planning. This illustrates the relative power positions of staff function employees as compared to line function employees. Many clinical nurse specialists have expressed intolerable frustration in their positions which may be the direct result of holding a position with staff functions. It is also interesting to note that, generally, staff functions receive the "budget axe" before line functions when the agency needs to tighten its economic belt. Yet the power outlook for the staff position or staff function is not totally dismal since power in these positions must be derived from the nurse's ability to project a positive image, self-confidence, and professional competence.

Project Matrix Design

Large health care agencies frequently incorporate aspects of the project matrix design within the line-staff design. Briefly, the project matrix combines agency projects with agency employees representing multiple departments within a matrix format as illustrated in Table 5.1. Projects are generally temporary and may include accreditation preparation, expansion projects, and organizational safety practices programs. Basically, this design tends to defuse

Table 5.1
PROJECT MATRIX DESIGN

Departments Represented	Project Title				
	Expansion	Awards Banquet	Grounds Improvement	Safety Exercises	Accreditation Preparation
Nursing, adult health					X
Nursing, child health				X	
Nursing, ambulatory care	X				
Nursing, maternity	X				
Physical therapy				X	X
Occupational therapy	X	X			X
Dietary					X
Personnel		X			
Maintenance			X		
Housekeeping				X	
Clinical laboratory					X
Grounds			X		

or minimize legitimate power. Since project members have multiple bosses, and projects may be of varying importance, the project matrix design can be a source of frustration and the cause of unachieved goals.

BUREAUCRACIES

Most health care agencies function as bureaucracies, a word that now carries a negative connotation although it was originally a specific type of organizational design constructed to produce a particular effect. Max Weber studied and analyzed this organizational structure and identified as its major purpose the ability to assure predictable employee behavior and a standard of product output within the organization. He compared the bureaucracy to other organizational forms, as mechanized production compares to other nonmechanized forms of production (Gibson, Ivancevich, & Donnelley, 1979).

In its ideal form, the bureaucracy is designed to increase production by identifying the major focus as the job to be done, with personnel, as people, considered only secondarily. Tasks are divided according to specialization and are performed within specific guidelines. Authority rests within a vertical hierarchy and is delegated downward. Impersonal management style is encouraged and work routine is emphasized.

Today, most organizations possess one or more of these bureaucratic characteristics to the extent that they have some system for division of labor, involve superior-subordinate relationships, and operate according to procedures. Necessary as this may be, the term "bureaucracy" has come to mean administrative padding with excessive layering of personnel, many levels between the line employee and the administrative decision maker, slowness to respond to change and suggestion for change, operating procedures mired in "red tape," and employees who have only a narrow perspective of the mission of the agency and thus decreased motivation for productivity.

Health care agencies as a whole function within this design for a number of reasons. Much of their funding comes from sources far removed from the agency itself, such as state and federal government programs or large insurance companies. This funding process is administered within a bureaucratic system and thus imposes and perpetuates the system. The health care agency hierarchy places power at the top of the organizational design and within the ranks of the medical staff. The power that rests with the physician is often wielded in a paternalistic and authoritarian manner. Jobs within the health care agency tend to be divided according to specialized function with many employees performing small parts of patient care, the major task.

For the employee working within this design, several strong messages are communicated that mold his or her performance. Above all, this system promotes the status quo with its ponderous approach to change. It encourages concentration on the task at the expense of the person, both worker and patient, and places formal authority at the top with unidirectional communication, primarily downward, to the worker. Power within this design is usually centralized and of the legitimate type, based on position.

At the same time, bureaucratic design discourages individual initiative and creativity. There tends to be a great deal of time between cause and effect in change, little opportunity and reward for independent decision making, and a minimal focus upon the employee as a person.

For the nurse working within this setting, there is often conflict between what the bureaucracy supports and promotes, and what is taught as professional nursing practice. The nurse has been taught to function independently and encouraged to make decisions, to work for change and to be concerned for others, both patients and health care workers. When attempting to practice in this manner within a system that encourages and rewards opposite behaviors, a tremendous amount of energy must be expended, and the results are often frustration and discouragement. Aspects of this professional-bureaucratic conflict are discussed in Chapter 10.

ASSESSING ORGANIZATIONAL POWER

It is important to assess and identify power in an organization in order to predict what is likely to occur as well as for the development of supportive or counterstrategies. The presence of legitimate, expert, and reward power may be obvious while other power entities are more subtle and elusive. Regardless of these difficulties, all power sources must be identified.

How Decisions Are Made

Organizational design does not prescribe how decisions are made. Instead, decision-making processes spring from the basic philosophies held by the managerial group. Certain beliefs about people, work, and productivity will contribute to how a manager goes about making a decision. Generally, the more a manager thinks people need direction, the more directive or autocratic he or she will behave. Conversely, the more a manager thinks people can contribute, the more he or she will encourage participative or democratic behavior. Thus the autocratic manager will exercise centralized decision making while the democratic manager will employ decentralized decision-making strategies. In the case of centralized decision making, power resides with the autocratic manager. Under a participative or democratic manager, it is defused to the subordinates. It should be noted that the astute manager can employ centralized or decentralized strategies depending on the situation, the time available to make the decision, and the magnitude of the issue.

To assess how decisions are made in an organization, one should begin by analyzing the job of the first line nurse manager. Generally this will be the head nurse or assistant head nurse. The first line nurse manager will have the following functions with regard to subordinates: hiring, firing, promoting, suspending, counseling, scheduling, and evaluating. If the first line nurse manager does not perform these tasks, then decision making and its associated power is probably centralized at a higher management level. If the first line nurse manager does perform these tasks, then several other performance areas should be investigated. Does he or she plan, execute, and evaluate service activities as well? That is, is the nurse manager accountable for the quantity and quality of the nursing services delivered, special projects and/or research, and the budget for the area of control? If these areas of accountability are within the scope of the first line nurse manager, then the best possible potential exists for satisfying employment and high productivity. In reality, however, the scope of responsibility for the first line nurse manager will fall short of complete service, resource, and fiscal accountability. Some of these functions may be performed by the nurse manager, or he or she may only participate in certain parts of the functions while major decisions are made by another nurse manager at a higher level. Both of these situations are unfavorable and a source of frustration.

While administrative nursing power and decision making tends to be centralized, on the clinical level, it is almost totally decentralized. In other words, the clinical practice of nursing is conducted by individual professionals making independent judgments, decisions, and subsequent actions which are rarely challenged by others. This is a major untapped source of power for nurses that warrants further consideration and investigation.

In addition to assessing *how* power and decision making occur in an organization, it may be worthwhile to assess *where* it occurs as well. It is somewhat naive to assume that all decision making occurs exclusively in an administrative conference room or office. Other possible sites include the cafeteria, health spa, vacation resort, restaurant, club, or gym. If one is aware of the modus operandi favored by a particular manager, this information may be put to good use at the appropriate time.

Who Is Reputed to Have Power

There is no doubt that within organizations individuals possess power despite the fact that they do not hold a formal source of power such as a significant position or degree of expertise. The exact genesis of this power reputation may never be known. Perhaps the individual is a college friend of the boss, or has performed some act or service for which there is indebtedness, or deserves the reputation but does not wish to rise in the ranks. Whatever the reason for this informal or referent power in the organization, it should not be ignored.

How do you find out who has informal power? Ask. Generally everyone within the organization is knowledgeable about the people with power and is willing to divulge what is known. To transmit this knowledge is itself a use of informational power. Once the informal or reputed sources of power are known, the next strategy is to observe the powerholder to ascertain how and under what circumstances he or she exerts power.

Reputational power, which rarely occurs by accident, can be acquired by most competent individuals. A nurse, for example, may consciously generate such power by selecting an unusual or unique area in which to excel; by informing the boss, colleagues, and subordinates of achievements; or by arranging press coverage to highlight achievements or special interests. These activities take planning and to some degree should be employed by every assertive professional nurse.

It should be noted that reputational power can also be attributed to an organizational department in addition to individuals. The reason for this power may be equally vague, but an awareness of its existence can minimize unfortunate encounters.

Where Are the Symbols of Power?

People rarely hesitate to use the symbols of power. They merit attention not only because they derive from power but because they connote its essence. Certain common organizational symbols of power are assigned parking places, office size, office view, special eating facilities, private restrooms, and office furnishings. Health services agencies have acquired some unique symbols of power. For example, an office, a typewriter, a secretary, or a telephone are highly valued by nurse managers. While such symbols distinguish between vertical levels of power, they may also differentiate people who appear to be on the same hierarchic level.

Dress has been an interesting manifestation of power among nurses. In the past, the nurse's cap symbolized knowledge, authority, and commitment. As increasing numbers of individuals with less education and responsibility began donning the cap, its power was defamed. Many nurses now resist wearing the cap and do not acknowledge its importance.

The laboratory (lab) coat or jacket is currently worn with the traditional white uniform or over street clothes. This practice has been recommended by fashion experts as it mimics the dress of physicians whose power is irrefutable.

A more recent symbolism of power through dress is demonstrated by the business uniform or skirted suit. Before one criticizes this attire as male-imitating, we should note that research indicates that the skirted suit is perceived as communicating power, authority, and efficiency. Therefore it is only prudent that nurses in appropriate positions should extract the power associated with wearing the skirted suit. For a more detailed discussion of dress, see Chapter 8.

To survey the symbols of power may seem crass and mundane. However, to the shrewd nurse these symbols of power are hallmarks of the profession and their skillful use may serve as entrée to future professional growth and advancement.

What Committees Possess Influence?

Committees in general frequently have obnoxious reputations, perhaps because their tasks are not perceived as meaningful, the group is not efficiently directed, or an individual may prefer to work alone. Health care agencies do have a number of committees, some of which will incorporate nursing personnel.

Committee membership is a source of power because participation provides access to information, resources, and decision making. Any one of these entities can be a compelling source of power. Further, membership allows for both internal and external personal visibility to the committee.

Some of the most influential committees generally deal with policy making and planning. The membership of these committees will represent major agency departments as well as physicians and consumers. Committee tasks generally focus on organizational direction and efficiency.

Any committee that incorporates physician membership should be viewed with interest because of the physician's unique relationship with hospital administration. Since committees are generally concerned with problems associated with the quantity and quality of clinical services, committee membership offers an excellent opportunity for the nurse to articulate nursing concerns as well as to hear these concerns expressed from a medical point of view.

Most health care agencies view community service as a primary goal. Therefore committees that address community service needs are keenly important. The obstetrical service committee, for example, may plan and evaluate prenatal community education programs. This is an important organizational marketing strategy, of interest to the nurse employed in that area. The active involvement of the nurse at the committee level is important because it is a power base for all nurses who participate in any aspect of community service.

Power is also attributed to committees that produce outstanding achievements. Benefits of committee success are accrued by each member just as if the result had been achieved by one individual alone. Compliments such as "you did a good job" indicate that individuals are viewed separately over the committee as a whole. Therefore, membership on a highly productive committee is worthwhile to consider and pursue if time is available.

POWERLESSNESS AND NURSES

Nurses feel powerless as the result of several types of experiences. Clinical situations such as patient death, suffering, deterioration or pain can make any practicing health professional feel helpless. A sense of powerlessness is also the result of organizational and personal circumstances. The following describes some of the reasons for these feelings.

Unity of Command Violation

Unity of command is a management principle that prescribes that an individual should have only one boss. While a boss may have numerous subordinates the reverse should not be true. That is, a worker should not be accountable to numerous supervisors. If the worker has more than one boss, the resulting violation of the unity of command principle produces role ambiguity and conflict for the worker.

Nevertheless, the nurse is obviously accountable to several people: the physician and agency management personnel. Every practicing professional nurse is required to follow the orders of the physician which are generally clinical in nature and require nursing judgment in order to apply them. Since judgments differ just as people do, there is a potential for conflict. Further, the physician's orders are so compelling that they are mentioned in the Florence Nightingale pledge as well as every nursing job description. Failure to appropriately carry out a physician's order can result in financial and professional liability.

Now, enter the other boss, the agency manager. Remember that the agency boss is responsible for hiring and providing financial remuneration for the nurse's services. Should the boss expect and receive quality nursing services? Yes, because management's prerogative is to set care standards and insure subsequent achievement through agency personnel. So here, the nurse is obligated to follow the direction of still another boss.

The fact that the two bosses, physician and manager, have no authority over each other further compounds the difficulty of this situation. In fact, the physician and agency manager have a mutual need for each other because without the agency, the physician cannot obtain services for patients, and without the physician the agency cannot offer services to patients. Thus the nurse's "two-boss" problem becomes a much greater dilemma. It is apparent that when conflict involves the nurse with the agency manager and the physician, the outcome is not likely to favor the nurse. Within this trio, the nurse is more dispensable than the issues and needs shared by the other two actors. This brutal fact renders the nurse powerless to improve many conditions of employment.

Certain circumstances can moderate the powerless posture of the nurse in the manager/physician/nurse triangle.

If the physician is employed by the organization, then there is some authority relationship between the manager and physician and their mutual needs are altered by that fact. A second circumstance is that corporate hospitals seem more concerned with corporate goals and achievements than with placating physicians. This milieu benefits the nurse since there is a tendency to focus on problems instead of personalities and idiosyncratic behavior. A third means of moderating the powerless position of the nurse is to maintain constant vigilance over potential areas of conflict that would place the nurse in direct opposition to either boss, physician or agency manager. This is a phenomenal task that is partially achieved once the nurse understands the unity of command principle and its violation.

Sexual Relationships and Behaviors

Sexuality has been juxtaposed with professional nursing for as long as the profession is old. There are countless reasons for this perception that need not be detailed here, but the fundamental issue is that nurses are predominantly female and work in a male-dominated environment.

Organizations generally do not have a written policy regarding the volatile issue of sex. However, they do have an unwritten code that requires that all sexual affairs be conducted with discretion and decorum. If the code is violated, the female will be the one removed from the position. While this practice may not be lawful, it nevertheless exists. Even if it is not the practice, in all job-related affairs the female is in the inferior position, is vulnerable to exposure of the relationship and, as a consequence, is deemed unable to carry out job responsibilities.

As long as females and males work together there will always be a potential for sexual relationships. Of course, this is not without good reason since men and women are accustomed to acting as parent, spouse, or lover with the opposite sex. Learning to work with the opposite sex in a collegial relationship can be a new experience and appropriate behavior must be learned. Some people, however, do not achieve this maturity easily.

Nurses and physicians function within a unique set of circumstances. The interdependent roles within medicine and nursing can frequently force a man and a woman to experience together life, death, disappointment, success, joy, and failure. These shared experiences require mutual understanding and support. The mere fact of being available on a personal level in combination with other personal factors can propel relationships beyond professionalism. Again, regardless of position or status, the female, is considered the inferior or less powerful partner. Remember, too, that the interpretation of a relationship by others is not restricted to true facts and incidents.

Behavior that signals sexual availability also diminishes power. Sexual signals include leaning, stooping, staring with fixed and rapturous attention, fingering jewelry around the neck, placing a pencil or pen between the lips, allowing the skirt to be above the knee, touching with sexual intent, talking with a weak or soft voice, and using the sociosexual arm around the shoulder.

Sexual behaviors occur for a variety of reasons. The person may fear failure or lack self-confidence. Or the person may need social approval or reinforcement that he or she is doing a good job. Research suggests that women tend not to be aggressive, competitive or possess achievement motivation. The absence of these qualities may contribute to some female nurses' use of, or failure to reject sexual signals.

Sharing the Room Rate Revenue

The most financially profitable health care services are those that are delivered on a fee-for-service or product basis. In other words, there is a direct relationship between a specific health product or service and what the patient pays. Examples include the physician's office visit, physical therapy treatment, oxygen, drugs, intravenous solutions, heat lamp treatment, and x-ray films. The patient charge for a product is determined by the original wholesale price of the item, labor and processing costs, and the predetermined profit margin. Professional service charges such as physical therapy are based on the amount of professional time used, the equipment required and, again, the profit margin.

The work of the nurse is not performed on a fee-for-service basis. Instead, charges for nursing services are included in the room rate or bed charge. This room rate or bed charge also includes the maintenance service, housekeeping, dietary service, and the services of departments concerned with business and administration. It is indeed extraordinary that one of the major services offered in most health care agencies, nursing care, is not directly charged to the patient. Consequently, nursing is definitely in a less powerful posture as there is no visible evidence of the financial value of its services.

To rectify this problem will require arduous investigation into the services delivered by nurses. These services must be identified, time and motion studies conducted, and a relative value assigned to each service. This is a monumental but critical task that will significantly abate the powerless status of nurses.

THE USE OF POWER IN HEALTH CARE AGENCIES

Nursing's power is presently limited by barriers such as the predominance of females in the profession, a work setting that is controlled by predominantly male physicians and hospital administrators, the violation of the unity of command principle, and a lack of unity within the pro-

fession itself. However, there is still power available for
use even within these constraints. It is imperative that the
nurse recognize this, and develop and use strategies to
maximize the power present within each nurse's working
environment. Power is a tool for accomplishment, and
should be used to the advantage of every nurse, and the
profession of nursing.

Strategy Will Get You Somewhere

In developing or expanding a power base it is important to
proceed in a planned and systematic manner. When identifying and formulating strategies to be used, the nurse
must consider the results desired, the work situation, and
those methods most appropriate to use within that particular situation to achieve the desired results.

It is important that the nurse develop and maintain a
strong personal position of power in the work setting. This
can be accomplished in several ways. Increased competence is a strong developer of expert power. As others
recognize a job well done, recognition of the doer increases
accordingly. A greater degree of skill and expertise increases the nurse's self-confidence which in turn will allow
for better job performance. This is a positive feedback
mechanism that also builds credibility with others which in
turn leads to more opportunities to function from a position of power.

Risk taking is an essential element in any strategy for
increasing power. But it is not synonymous with taking
chances, where the results depend more on circumstances
than on individual responsibility. When deciding to take a
risk, it is important to evaluate the pros and cons according
to their relative magnitude, the implications for that particular situation, and the possible payoffs. The alternative
selected should be the one that carries the greatest degree
of control over the outcome, and it should be structured to
minimize possible negative consequences. After the risk-
taking decision is made, it should be carried out with self-

confidence which will increase the probability of a positive outcome.

When functioning from a power position, another strategy for increasing the power is to share it with others. Personal monopoly of power, or autocracy, results in diminishing that power. The potential for increasing power is greater where there are opportunities for others to participate in activities that will build power for them. Good will and cooperation is a mutual process so that benefits accrue in both directions as the parties support and strengthen each other.

A strong support base is important for maintaining and expanding power. This support base must be cared for and nurtured. It can be developed in several ways. One way is to identify and obtain a mentor. For the first line nurse manager, the mentor could be a nurse manager at a higher level who is willing to share information about how progress in career advancement has been made. People are generally happy to help others in this way unless they are insecure and perceive the other as a threat to their own position.

Networking is another way in which to build support. This involves identifying a group, or groups, that will support each other, primarily at the peer or colleague level. These groups may be formed within the work setting, or across work settings where positions and duties are similar. The major purpose of the groups is to share experiences, to offer suggestions and resources, and to serve as a nonthreatening audience for venting feelings and problem solving. A network might be formed by nurses who work in a small agency, or in several small agencies of the same type, who decide to meet regularly to share ideas and expertise.

To operate from a power position, personal visibility is essential and the nurse must be aware of ways in which this visibility can be heightened. For example, you must know where and how the informal social system functions, in addition to the more formal organizational system, and gain entrance to this group, perhaps by taking coffee breaks or lunches in particular places at particular times, or by offering assistance with specific projects, committees or activities. Another way to increase visibility is to develop innovative ways of getting the job done rather than relying on old routines. This takes skill and planning, but is worth the effort in terms of recognition from others and the payoff of a higher level of task performance.

Because most nurses are women who function in a male-dominated work environment, it is important to keep this dimension in mind when planning power strategies. Behavior in the work setting always should be professional. When interaction falls into the sexual arena the power position is weakened. Responses to those who attempt interaction at this level should be kept direct and objective. The nurse's particular response pattern should be premeditated and should be one consistent with his or her basic personality. It might be the use of humor, or ignoring the sexual level of the interaction while responding on the task level, or the straight retort or calm confrontation of the other's motive. It is important to use the same response patterns with males at all levels in order for the professional position to be maintained at its strongest point.

The way in which a nurse responds to any interaction within the work setting can strengthen his or her power position. A framework that is helpful for analyzing response patterns is Eric Berne's transactional analysis as discussed by Thomas Harris (1969). Appropriate interactional patterns within the work world are those of adult to adult, or those that focus upon facts and information. The nurturing and support level is important too, but the nurse must be careful not to move into the less positive parent-child pattern of interaction that emphasizes unequal positions between two people.

Using Power When You Get There

Control over allocation of resources such as money, space, materials, or people, is a method of increasing the amount of power available for use. The nurse manager who has control over budget, personnel, services, the supplies used in delivering these services, and the space within which these services are delivered is in a strong position of power.

Another effective method of using power is the management of information. The nurse who takes the initiative in developing or revising job descriptions or performance evaluation tools, or suggesting the possibility of new positions or different uses for current positions will increase the power of her position.

An additional facet of managing information is knowledge and skill in the conduct of meetings. The nurse manager needs to be familiar with parliamentary procedure and "Robert's Rules of Order." These are valuable tools and meetings should be conducted according to these rules for they will insure that the decisions made have been appropriately processed and considered. It is also important to remember that the meeting should move at the optimum pace that allows time for discussion and presentation of major points, but not allowing for time to get bogged down in any person's special pleading or filibustering on a single issue. Even such details as the seating arrangements could have an impact on the outcome of the meeting and they should be structured to produce the desired results.

Managing information can also include monitoring the timing of information flow. The nurse needs to be aware of task deadlines, of meeting them, and of insuring that others adhere to them as well. This will avoid the problem of immobility so often found in bureaucratic systems. It takes persistence, but it is an important way to increase power.

The scope of the information should extend beyond the immediate work setting. The nurse should be aware of broader issues, both in health care and in the larger economic and political arenas, for this can help in interpreting implications for the work setting and in anticipating directions for change.

When using power it is important to gain access to others who also occupy power positions, and to use what they have to offer. For the nurse manager, this will mean getting to know other people in positions of power and their areas of control, as well as working with them on mutually beneficial activities. It will involve give and take in asking for and granting help when it is needed to accomplish these activities. For example, the nurse manager could initiate a project with administrative personnel in physical and occupational therapy to develop components of a new charting system. At a later time, the nurse manager may be asked to work with these people again to identify the best time schedule for patient activities on the care unit. Prior relationships allow for give and take to occur and also stimulate support on issues from either side.

It is also advantageous to build a pool of outside support, and to call upon this source of support to strengthen the power position. One area available for support is the literature of nursing. The nurse manager should select, subscribe to, and read several professional journals that are especially helpful to the specific job area. This information can then be used to support and document what is done on the job while placing these activities within a broader professional framework. When appropriate, outside experts in particular areas may also be called in as consultants to lend credibility and support to the nurse manager's plans and activities.

WHEN ALL ELSE FAILS: COLLECTIVE BARGAINING

Nurses have endured frustration and powerlessness for a very long time. While the genesis of powerlessness is deeply ingrained in social tradition and practices, some responsibility for it must be assumed by nurses themselves. Possessing knowledge and skills in business, management, assertive techniques, and change processes will help nurses to claim their rightful legacy. In the event that the acquisition of all this knowledge and skills are not enough, bargaining as a collective body may be the final alternative.

Collective bargaining or labor unions have been a part of the American scene for over fifty years. However, not until 1974 did Congress provide for collective bargaining in non-public, nonprofit health facilities. Even then, special regulations were developed to assure the continuation of health care services regardless of labor union activities.

Labor unions have experienced variable success rates throughout the country. Generally, economic conditions are usually better in unionized as opposed to nonunionized agencies. Further, the nurse's control over issues that affect clinical practice has been a continual source of strife and these issues have become part of collective bargaining.

Collective bargaining is extremely complex and is not an undertaking for the inexperienced nurse. Agencies spend a great deal of money and energy in attempting to keep unions out of the organization. Therefore, all nurses must be knowledgeable about collective bargaining and if they are interested in forming a collective bargaining unit, they must consult nursing colleagues experienced in union activities. The law is quite clear regarding the formation of a union and nurses must be informed of the personal and professional liabilities arising from unionization. In addition, nurses must recognize unlawful agency acts and deal with them appropriately.

SUMMARY

Power in health care agencies is both traditional and unique. Legitimate power operates through several organizational designs: line-staff, project matrix, and bureaucracy. While the design specifies the formal use of power, informal power may be demonstrated by decision making patterns, the symbols of power, reputation, and achievement.

The professional nurse experiences numerous sources of powerlessness. The violation of the unity of command principle—or the fact that nurses have more than one boss—places the nurse in a powerless position when dealing with both the physician and the agency administrator. Other sources of powerlessness include the inability to identify chargable nursing behaviors, and the female nurse's tendency to use—or not to reject—sexual signals.

The effective use of power in health care agencies requires the identification of power and its appropriate use through personal visibility, by establishing expertise, by taking appropriate risks, and by establishing a strong base of support. Networking within the work setting or across work settings can provide needed support, power, and problem-solving ability among nurses.

Collective bargaining is an option available to nurses in the event that other strategies are unsuccessful in solving professional problems. This alternative requires the consultation of an expert in labor relations.

BIBLIOGRAPHY

Fenn, M.: *In The Spotlight: Women Executives in a Changing Environment.* Englewood Cliffs, New Jersey, Prentice-Hall, 1980.

Gibson, J., Ivancevich, J., & Donnelly, J., Jr.: *Organizations.* Dallas, Business Publications, 1979.

Harragan, B.L.: *Games Mother Never Taught You: Corporate Gamesmanship for Women.* New York, Warner Books, 1978.

Harris, T.: *I'm OK—You're OK.* New York, Avon Books, 1969.

Marriner, A.: *Guide to Nursing Management.* St. Louis, C. V. Mosby, 1980.

Molloy, J.: *Dress For Success.* New York, Warner Books, 1975.

O'Rourke, K. & Barton, S.: *Nurse Power, Unions and The Law.* Maryland, Prentice-Hall, 1981.

Stead, B.: *Women in Management.* New Jersey, Prentice-Hall, 1978.

Werther, W. & Lockhart, C.: *Labor Relations in The Health Professions.* Boston, Little, Brown, 1976.

RECOMMENDED READINGS

Marriner, A.: *Guide to Nursing Management.* St. Louis, C.V. Mosby, 1980.

This book offers one of the most comprehensive discussions of *nursing* management, and applies organizational and behavioral theories to the nursing management setting.

O'Rourke K. & Barton, S.: *Nurse Power, Unions and The Law.* Maryland, Prentice-Hall, 1981.

This book provides some poignant reasons why nurses might select unionization as a method for professional problem resolution. In addition, it explains the lawful basis for unions and union formation, and presents contractual elements and language.

Stead, B.: *Women in Management,* New Jersey, Prentice-Hall, 1978.

A collection of articles selected to provide advice, sources of information, and professional encouragement for women interested in pursuing careers and moving into management positions. Although not written from a nurse's perspective the book is an excellent source for examining the individual woman in management and the organization's response to women managers.

PUBLISHING AS A
SOURCE OF POWER

SUZANNE HALL JOHNSON

Publishing is powerful! It provides an opportunity to influence the thinking of others through sharing research, clinical suggestions, opinions, and other ideas. It is written communication that can influence the thinking of not only other nurses but of other health professionals and the public.

Authors are seen in a prestigious light and are given legitimate authority to influence others through their writing. Consequently, publishing is an influential and legitimate source of power. By developing this source of power, nurses can advance nursing practice and enhance the quality of patient care.

NURSING PUBLICATION—
SLOW TO DEVELOP

Nurses have gained the skills of publishing slowly because of factors present in nursing's developmental history. Some of the factors that have hampered the development of publishing as a common power source for nurses are their lack of confidence, feeling of powerlessness, lack of experience in the publishing game, and the narrow focus of nursing responsibilities. Since the nurse has felt that she or he was not "the expert" and had "nothing to say," the result has been to delay the development of strong publishing skills in the profession.

Although nursing has emerged from the shadow of medicine into a unique and valuable profession, the absence of a strong and independent identity still creates a lack of self-confidence in nurses. Nurses often hold three common misconceptions about their ability to publish: that their ideas are not good enough, that their journalistic skills are inadequate, and that their peers will ridicule their writing.

Many nurses have avoided writing altogether by saying, "I do not have anything important enough to write about." This author, however, has helped many nurses develop unique ideas that have resulted in publication. Many of the authors of those ideas were surprised to discover the value of their contributions. Nurses have excellent ideas worth sharing through publication, yet few of them identify the importance of their ideas.

Another misconception is expressed in the often-heard statement, "I am not good in journalism." The feeling of "I can't" is more detrimental than the lack of writing skills itself. Advanced journalism skills are not necessary in professional publishing and can sometimes even interfere with writing for a nursing publication. Nursing journals and newsletters prefer clear, readable writing rather than metaphors and similes (Brogan, 1975).

The third misconception is a fear of undue criticism from peers which results in a writing block. Many nurses have expressed to the author that they were afraid to write because of this fear. They were afraid that they would be embarrassed seeing their own writing or having others read it. It is true that publications are open to criticism from many others and subject the authors to disagreement or even attack. This can be very frightening to a professional person who lacks confidence. Yet most authors receive praise rather than ridicule for their writing.

An historical aspect of nursing that has delayed the development of publishing is the feeling of powerlessness which has and still afflicts nurses. In Chapters 1, 2, and 5, powerlessness is described as a characteristic trait of the profession. Nurses who feel they have no power and have no hope for changing their situation are not likely to put any energy into publishing. While they often think that the public should respect nurses, many do not know how to develop this respect. To tell the public that they *should* respect the nurse is not as powerful as to do something for the public that will command respect. For example, an article sent to a local newspaper explaining why the public should respect the nurse is not likely to be printed. On the other hand, an article written by a nurse that lists helpful hints on ways to reduce blood pressure is not only likely to be published, but will actually show the nurse's value in patient education. Fortunately, an increasing number of such articles are being written by nurses. Eventually, as nurses feel more powerful and influential, more articles will be written for the public and the public image of the nurse will be enhanced.

Another inhibiting characteristic of nursing's history is that the profession is comprised mainly of women who, as a sex, have traditionally been left out of business and political games. Until recently, women were less able to identify and use the rules of the publishing game to their benefit. Some of these rules are crucial to gaining the respect of editors and hence the opportunity to continue publishing. For example, one strict and sometimes-ignored rule is that a manuscript may be sent to only one journal at a time. The publishing process and its rules can be easily learned once one recognizes the importance of playing the game as it has already been established.

A final aspect of nursing history which has slowed the development of publishing skills is the narrow definition of nurses' responsibilities in the past. Many nurses simply do not see publishing as a part of their responsibility, while in many other professions, such as medicine and business, writing has long been identified as a major profession responsibility. Some nurses will even accuse nurse authors of abandoning nursing. Yet publishing in nursing can help develop many innovative nursing techniques. There is evidence, however, that publishing is gaining some acceptance among nurses as a necessary nursing function. In addition, there has been an increase in publishing courses in graduate programs and in continuing education for nurses.

As nurses increase their confidence, recognize their power, learn the publication game, and recognize the publishing process as a legitimate and vital function, this source of power will grow. Activities that increase the nurse's confidence and ability to use the rules in publishing lead to more positive results than mastering journalism styles. Nurses already possess most of the necessary tools for publishing, yet many have not yet discovered them. In the following pages, we describe the steps to be taken to develop publishing as a source of power.

PUBLISHING AND POWER

Publishing includes writing, editing, printing, and distributing information to others. The ability to influence others through the printed word is what gives publishing its power. Published material can circulate farther, to a larger number of people, and has a more longlasting effect than a verbal presentation.

In addition to being a strong source of influence, publishing is directly related to another type of power: authority. Authors are often deemed to be authorities or experts by the reader. As authority is one of the most reliable and stable sources of power, publishing is one of the most definite and consistent techniques of increasing power.

Publishing is one of the most legitimate sources of power available to the nurse since society attributes legitimate power to authors. Acknowledgement of this power and authority is reflected by the number and popularity of authors on radio and television talk shows. One example of the amount of power that authors can exercise over the public is the publishing of various fad diets. Within only a few months of the publication of a book on a new fad diet, people all over the country will be talking to each other about the new diet and altering their eating behavior.

When used ethically, publishing deserves this legitimate power. Unfortunately, however publishing can be unethically used and abused as is true of all sources of power. The very few authors who report fictitious experiments or information can mislead the reader and can create a dangerous situation if the reader acts on this incorrect advice. Although infrequent, reports of publications of illegitimate information hurt the credibility and authority of all future publications. Most nursing journals prevent misrepresentation and abuse of publishing power by having all manuscripts read by at least three reviewers before they are accepted for publication. As with any other source of power, nurses must oversee the use of publishing power to prevent its abuse.

Publishing may be chosen over other sources of power for several reasons. First, it encourages continual development within nursing since new topics are sought to expand nursing theories and repetitive manuscripts are rejected to avoid redundancy. Second, it is an efficient source of power for influencing large numbers of people in a relatively short time as compared to travel and audience size for oral presentations. Third, publishing greatly increases the accountability of the nurse. A written presentation implies that the information can be checked at a later date and that the author can be held accountable for it. Fourth, a publication can reach and influence people in rural settings who otherwise would be difficult to contact. And last, publishing may be one of the cheapest sources of power. The cost of a publication is often covered by the publisher so that nurse authors can publish and disseminate their ideas with little or no personal cost. In some cases, they may even be paid for their articles.

Publishing can be beneficial not only to the individual nurse but also to the profession. It can help the individual nurse to be more visible since the author's name appears on published material. The names of many nurse authors are associated with their contributions, such as Marlene Kramer with *Reality Shock* (Kramer, 1974).

The second benefit to the profession is that nurses can use publishing to actually guide the direction of the profession. For example, in the last several years many nursing publications have described the need for a college degree to be the prerequisite for nursing practice.

The third professional benefit is that nurses can use their publications to develop their identity as nurses. Nursing literature emphasizes family teaching, clinical technique, behavioral assessments, and other nursing activities that help the nurse to identify a strong image of nursing that is unique among the professions.

Fourth, publishing can enhance the image and reputation of the nurse in the eyes of the public. Articles in non-nursing magazines or newspapers can emphasize the important contributions of nursing to patient education.

Fifth, publishing also enhances the nurse's image among those in related professions. Among other professionals, nurses help to evaluate the status of nursing by writing for hospital administration, physician, and other professional journals.

Lastly, publishing increases the professional status of the nurse since professionals are expected to continue to develop, refine, and share new innovations within their profession. Thus, publishing can be the choice power source for directing the nursing profession as well as for enhancing its reputation with the public and among professional colleagues. Remember that publishing is a legitimate source of power that increases the nurse's authority and influence over others.

TECHNIQUES IN DEVELOPING PUBLISHING POWER

The publishing process is similar to the nursing problem-solving process. In publishing, the nurse identifies the problem that needs to be solved or investigated, develops a solution, tests it, and communicates the findings through publication. Through its widespread circulation, a publication can influence other nurses, health professionals, and the public. The following techniques will help the nurse to develop these written communication skills.

Identify What Needs Changing

Most ideas for publication start with the identification of a problem. A difficulty that occurs in one hospital or community health setting is frequently shared by other agencies. For example, retention problems for staff in one hospital will often be representative of similar problems in other hospitals. Similarly, patient or family problems may be equally widespread. In one situation, a family with children at risk experienced guilt. When the nurse found guilt to be common to many families in this situation, her observations resulted in an article (Johnson, 1979). Any problem or difficulty can be the point of departure for article, and the nurse may want to use publishing to offer solutions and reduce a specific problem.

ACTIVITY

1. Consider your own nursing practice and answer the following questions:
   - What difficulty has the nursing staff had with a patient?
   - Are there any organization or management difficulties at work?
   - Have patients shown concern by asking questions or by asking for help?
   - Have other colleagues been asking you for help with a problem?
   - Have you asked others for help with a new difficulty or technique?
   - Have the family members demonstrated concern about a problem?
2. List any of these problems, concerns, or difficulties that you may want to influence.

3. Select one of these problems or difficulties to be the focus of an article.

Investigate the Problem

After identifying the difficulty, the next step is similar to the problem-solving process: you investigate the problem. However, in publishing, this means gathering information in three ways.

First, search the literature to find past references related to the idea. The two main nursing indexes are the written index, *Nursing Index*, and the computerized index, *MEDLARS* (Medical Literature Analysis and Retrieval System). In addition, there are several written and computer indexes available such as the *Bioscience Retrieval System*, which contains psychological abstracts, and *COMSEARCH* which lists grant project topics and funders. You must be very clear about the specific topic for the search before starting the review of literature to avoid becoming overwhelmed with too many references on a general topic. In the course of the search, you will assess the literature to support the ideas and address those aspects of the topic that are not discussed in the existing literature. Another outcome of the literature search could be to challenge the existing literature. Knowledge of the present literature and the experts in the field will help you to gain credibility and to develop a unique slant on the topic for the article.

A second way to investigate the problem is through clinical study. Various facets of the target problem can be studied, perhaps by interviewing colleagues or patients on their viewpoint. This informal type of study will provide clinical examples and specific information as a basis for your reporting of the problem. For example, one nurse recognized the problem of a father who wanted to be present during the cesarean birth of his son. At that time, fathers were not allowed in the delivery room during the surgical procedure. The nurse interviewed ten fathers to determine their desire to be present at such a birth. With this information, she published a report using actual quotes from the fathers which helped her to influence the administration. As a result, the policy was changed, allowing fathers to be present during deliveries.

The third way to investigate a problem is through a controlled research study, using both a study group and a control group to compare results. The investigator must employ valid and reliable instruments for investigation as well as an appropriate statistical analysis to analyze the information. The results should be very specific in describing new information about the initial target problem.

With supporting literature, clinical examples, or research findings, you should be able to develop your idea which may have a major influence on others. Three types of support can be used in combination or separately. Literature support is a very strong method of demonstrating that a problem has been occurring or has roots in past difficulties. Clinical examples are very effective in motivating others since they have human appeal. Research information can be the most convincing since it is probably the most objective information.

ACTIVITY

For the problem you selected in the activity above, describe any support you have that shows this is a problem.

1. Literature support

2. Clinical example support

3. Research support

Develop and Implement
a Solution

The nurse can influence others through publishing a manuscript that will help the reader to identify a problem. At times, professionals are helped by the identification of a problem that they did not know had existed. Since identification of the problem is the first step toward solving it, such manuscripts are helpful in themselves. However, the most influential articles are those that suggest solutions for they are concerned with actually changing behavior.

After identifying the problem, the nurse author must identify, develop, and suggest possible ways to implement its solution. While testing the solution, the nurse collects more clinical examples and information on its success. Examples should show real clinical application, while data should show an evaluation of the project. This kind of information is more powerful than reasoning alone in convincing others of the need for a change and in guiding them toward changes.

For example, one nurse who identified the problem of retention of staff in a hospital, set up and studied the effects of a day-care center that cared for the nurses' children during their shifts. After implementing her solution, she interviewed the nurses who used the day-care center to find out how they liked the program—her examples. She also gathered information on the long-term effects on the retention rate at the hospital. In this case, the examples, plus the retention rate, would be persuasive information that could influence other hospitals to try a similar program.

ACTIVITY

For the problem that you have identified, describe a possible solution you may want to try.

Identify what clinical examples or data you could coll ct that would show the results of your solution. (With a positive result, this data will make your publication more powerful.)

Identify the Target Audience

After identifying the problem, implementing a solution, and obtaining support for the suggested solutions, the nurse author is ready to draft this information with the intent of influencing others. But first the target audience must be identified. The nurse has three basic target audiences: nurse colleagues, other professionals, and the public. The author must ask which audience she or he would really like to influence.

If the nurse decides to influence other nurses, further narrowing of the target audience is still necessary. That is, the nurse author will need to identify as specifically as possible what types of nurses should be the target of the communication. Or, who would have the greatest interest in the problem and who would be the most likely to carry out the solution? For topics where staff nurses would be the most likely target audience, the author could create more specific subdivisions such as pediatric, psychiatric, medical, surgical, obstetric, or other type of nurse (Mc-Closkey, 1977; O'Connor, 1976). Even more specifically, the author could identify the target audience as the school nurse, the infection control nurse, or the enterostomal therapy nurse. The more specific the target audience, the easier it will be to write a manuscript that maximally communicates the message and therefore has the most influence on the audience.

The author may decide to influence other health professionals and choose them as the target audience for an article. They may be physicians, physical therapists, respiratory therapists, social workers, dietitians, or hospital administrators. Nurses are knowledgeable about many topics and can write on topics that are of interest to other professionals. For example, one nurse developed a picture chart to use in isolation rooms to help health professionals and families to don the right clothing for the isolation case. This subject was clearly of interest to more health professionals than nurses alone, and the article was written for hospital administrators and published in the journal, *Hospitals*.

The nurse can also write for professionals outside the health field like another nurse who was concerned about educating high-school students interested in entering the profession. In a high-school counseling journal, she wrote about counseling students for careers in nursing. In this way, a nurse can demonstrate standards of excellence to other professionals with the likely result of gaining their respect. But in order to win r spect from other professionals, nurses must do work deserving respect.

The nurse who wants to influence the general public should carefully choose a topic appropriate to this audience. In daily practice, the nurse works closely with the health consumer and is almost always involved in patient education. However, because nurses have had less experience in verbal presentations to a large public, ironically, they are less likely to provide patient education through published materials. In reality, nurses are ideally suited to write health articles of public interest because of their close dealings with patients, their knowledge of the public's point of view, the vast choice of actual life examples available to them, and their understanding of the patient's perspective.

In the past, many health-related books sold to the public have been written by physicians. Yet the public is asking for more concrete and humanistic help. Nurses can answer this need by writing influential articles on many topics in which they are uniquely qualified. Indeed, it is only recently that nurses have become aware of the role they can play in writing for the public. Even in the academic setting, where publishing is stressed, articles written for the general public—as opposed to those written for professional journals—are given very little weight and credibility as standards for faculty merit or promotion. Yet, writing for the public probably holds the greatest potential for impact on patient education and for developing the reputation of nursing. Topics such as parenting in high-risk situations, changing unhealthy life-style habits, caring for the elderly at home, and similar subjects are of concern to the public and ideal for nurse authorship (Spikol, 1979b).

The nurse author must specifically select the target audience for any one manuscript; however, after completing that manuscript, she or he may want to develop the same topic for a different audience. The same topic may be developed for more than one audience provided that none of the same terms, charts, or pictures are used, and that the organization is not the same. For example, one author who had excellent clinical experience with anorexic adolescents wrote a manuscript on anorexia for a nursing journal, a dietetic journal, and is working on a manuscript for the general public. This author had little difficulty reslanting the topic to different audiences or using different terminology. When the manuscript is tailored to the needs of a specific audience, the wording, organization, and illustrations should follow naturally.

ACTIVITY

1. For the idea you have selected, describe at least one type of person in each of the three areas of readership who might be interested in your topic. Be specific in your description of each type of person.
   - List at least one specific type of nurse.
   - List at least one specific type of other professional.
   - List at least one specific type of person in the public.

2. Select one of the specific audiences you have listed above to be the single target audience for your publication. This is the audience that you would most like to influence. It is best to have only one target audience in mind so that your manuscript can be written to their needs. Combining too many possible audiences in one manuscript often results in an article that is too broad and too general to meet the needs of any audience.

Reach the Target Audience

After determining the target audience, the nurse author should select the best vehicle for reaching this group. The first questions to ask are, "Where are these people?" and then, "How can I reach them?" The nurse can ask some people from the target audience what type of publications they commonly read. This will give the nurse author a personal indication of what journals may be the most influential and powerful.

JOURNALS

There are many publication indexes that list journals by their specialty areas. The nurse author can use these to identify appropriate journals for the article. Three sources that list journals in the health field are *Medical Books and Serials in Print* (Spikol, 1979a), *Markets for the Medical Author* (Deaton, 1977), and *Writer's Guide to Medical Journals* (Lane & Kammerer, 1977). These three publications list journals in many medical specialities and are especially helpful in identifying journals with readerships from nursing as well as from other health professions. Two indexes that list many of the journals that circulate to nurses are *Lippincott's Guide to Nursing Literature* (Binger & Jensen, 1980) and *Author's Guide to Journals in the Health Field* (Ardell & James, 1980). Both list many nursing journals. One index that is especially useful to the nurse author who would like to write for public journals is the *Writer's Market* (Koester & Hillman, 1979). It indexes many public magazines under popular topics such as women's magazines and fishing. It also includes information about the amount of payment for manuscripts and whether or not the editor is willing to work with the author through letters before the final manuscript is submitted.

PUBLIC NEWS AND INFORMATION

In addition, the nurse who would like to influence the public through sharing information may find several other appropriate formats. Newspapers are widely read by the public and are an excellent vehicle for carrying information to the consumer. The public is very interested in many health topics including the prevention of illness, involvement in health decisions, family stresses, and other topics in which nurses have expertise. The nurse can share this information through editorials, letters to the editor, and feature articles for newspapers. Letters to the editor and some editorials can be submitted individually; however, for larger features the nurse should contact and work with the editor. In addition, the nurse can write and send a news release to a newspaper to describe a special service, an upcoming presentation, or any other information of public interest.

In a news release, the nurse author first writes the heading material which includes the nurse's name as a contact person, address, and telephone contact (Kelly, 1981). Then, a title similar to a descriptive title in a newspaper is added, along with the date for release of the information. The body of the news release begins with noting the city of the news release. This informs newspapers of the origin of information. In the body of the news release, the author uses descriptive words, quotations, and actual examples to convey the message. Very concrete images have popular appeal and should be selected for newspaper publication in preference to a more conceptual format. The news release should be sent to the publication that circulates to the target audience. This may be a small-town newspaper or a large metropolitan one. The newspaper will make the decisions on editing and printing the material.

The most important element of all publications for the public is the "human interest" angle. The public is interested in information that both entertains and informs. Examples of actual people, their problems, and the realistic ways in which they solve their problems hold the public's interest. Topics such as the birth of a premature infant, weight loss, heart attack, and job burn-out are familiar to a majority of the public. They have experienced these problems firsthand, or they know someone who has, or they are afraid they "might be next." When the topic is one that interests the public, the likelihood of having the article published is very good. When the writer's examples include actual families, the article will have even more public appeal and the chances of publication will increase accordingly.

For example, a news release written about "High Risk Parenting" described the counseling of families of children at risk. The release was placed on the Texas news wire. Even when edited, all the actual quotations and family examples in the news release were retained and the story was published in four newspapers. In addition, one newspaper sent a reporter to interview the author for more background information, which was recorded and subsequently broadcast on radio. On the same subject, another newspaper sent a reporter and photographer, which resulted in a news article about the author's specialty. Notice the positive nursing image in these articles addressed to the general public.

NURSE OUTLINES PROCEDURES FOR HIGH RISK FAMILIES

Parents of premature babies, hyperactive children or children with genetic birth defects, sons and daughters with alcoholic parents or parents who are terminally ill -all those persons have something in common, according to a neonatal clinical nurse specialist who spoke recently at the University of Texas in Austin.

Those groups can be labeled "high risk" families, Suzanne Hall Johnson said.

Johnson is the author of *High Risk Parenting,* a book which was given the American Journal of Nursing "book of the year" award in 1979. She is founder and head of Health Update, a consulting firm for health professionals based in Denver, Colo.

With a master of nursing degree from UCLA, Johnson also works as a private consultant with high risk families. She defines high risk families as those with a parent or child at risk due to a long-term medical condition, usually one which is not preventable.

Johnson believes high risk families need extra attention, because "parenting is already difficult" in the best of situations.

Although health professionals tend to look at each situation individually, the nurse said it is useful to look at the problems common to all high risk families.

Guilt is one emotion almost everyone feels is a high risk situation, she noted. A normal reaction is, "Why did it happen to me or my child?" Families also experience grief as they mourn the loss of a normal parent or child, Ms. Johnson added.

Financial pressure resulting from high medical bills and physical exhaustion "from trying to work, run a house and make trips to the hospital" are other problems families must face, she continued.

Emotional exhaustion is found frequently among high risk families who may feel drained after worrying day after day.

"The best example of emotional exhaustion are the hostage families," the nursing specialist observed, referring to the Americans recently freed from captivity in Iran.

Families should understand that feelings of grief, guilt and exhaustion are all normal reactions, Johnson said. To help her clients deal with guilt feelings, she sometimes asks them to list all possible causes of the medical condition. With 10 or 12 possible causes, it becomes harder for the family member to believe he or she is to blame. Johnson also asks her clients to list their problems, then identify the one they wish to work on first. She has found that most people choose physical exhaustion as the most critical problem.

Families under stress may do well to make lists of persons who are sources of strength, as well as lists of those who are to be avoided, the nursing specialist said, since often neighbors and relatives can cause more harm than good.

The mother-in-law who said, "I'll bet you'll go to a real doctor next time" after her grandchild was born dead, delivered by an osteopathic physician, is a good example of someone to be avoided, Johnson said.

Johnson suggested people seek out specific solutions to specific problems, such as finding someone to transport children to school while one parent is at the hospital or consulting the hospital's financial person for help with high medical bills.

"These families tend not to ask for help," she cautioned.

Because, in many cases, high risk families have problems which will not go away, those problems should be examined and discussed, Johnson said.

"There are some families where the major problem is not

medical," she continued, as she discussed a client whose child had been under observation in intensive care for jaundice.

"After the child was discharged, the father kept saying his son was going to be retarded," she said. "He thought the intravenous fluid going under the skin of the child's head was going into the child's brain. Here's this family really worried for four to six months after the medical crisis. Sometimes problems don't come up during the crisis itself."

Johnson's visit, as a consultant for two nursing workshops on high risk parenting and developing consulting skills, was sponsored by the UT School of Nursing.

Permission to reproduce by *Everywoman*, February 1981, and the University of Texas Newscenter.

NURSE TEACHES PARENTS TO HANDLE ADJUSTMENT TO CARE OF 'RISK' INFANT

Sometimes parents are scared to death of the infants they bring home from the hospital when they are at last pronounced well after treatment for prematurity, cardiac, digestive or other problems.

That's where Suzanne Hall Johnson, a Denver clinical nurse specialist, steps in, working with parents and with nurses who assist such parents.

"The babies are all well, and the families are afraid they can't take care of the well baby at home 24 hours a day.

"They actually can," she said at the Crippled Children's Division of the University of Oregon Health Sciences Center in a recent interview. She was in Portland participating in a seminar for professionals sponsored by the Crippled Children's Division and the university-affiliated Maternal and Child Health Program. Approximately 120 attended.

Of the families she works with, the clinical nurse says, "Sometimes their fear will go on for six months. The first pitch is to find out from them what their experiences are, what their fears are and their hopes for the baby.

"I also try to find out what they think caused the difficulty (for the infant). They always experience guilt. Finding the answer helps keep the family together. If the mother says she shouldn't have done something, and the father says, 'Yes, you should not have,' they always think there is one cause.

"Always there are many causes. I try to help them not feel guilty or not feel too guilty.

"I emphasize for them that whatever are their ways of handling the baby, it's OK. Guilt is natural, Grief is natural."

Mrs. Johnson said that it is also important to look at the interaction among the mother, the father, their infant and any other sibling to see how they adapt to the new situation.

"Sometimes there is a financial problem, and the father has to take a second job. I'm concerned about how this is influencing the mother and the child. I'm trying to see how they change all their roles to cope."

Mrs. Johnson, a Philadelphia native, has a bachelor's degree and began in neonatal nursing at Stanford University's neonatal intensive care unit. She now has her own consulting service in Denver, "Health Update," and works with families, although she is concentrating more and more on training nurses in her field.

She had additional training at the University of California at Los Angeles. She wrote a recently published book aimed at nurses, "High Risk Parenting" (J.B. Lippincott), which won the nursing book of the year award.

She said she does not want parents to watch her demonstrations and copy her exactly: "I want it varied. I want them to find their own way by watching their baby. If the baby smiles, coos, sleeps and gains weight, they're doing it right. The idea is, I want their baby to tell them they're doing things right.

"We teach them how their baby is a person. They should learn he is a person in the hospital. Sometimes they like their head stroked or their feet. He sucks strong. Or he kicks. He likes noises. Or he doesn't.

"We really do stress that even the high-risk babies have personalities, and parents need to get to know them."

By Ann Sullivan of *The Oregonian* staff.
Reproduced with permission of *The Oregonian*. © 1980.

Similar releases about significant topics of public interest can be directed to television stations. A report on unusual nursing innovations in any specialty may result in a television interview, or a news report or documentary. In one case, I was interviewed for television, with the broadcaster asking clinical and human-interest types of questions. The interview was broadcast on the prime-time evening news by WKBT-TV in La Crosse, Wisconsin.

Remember to use examples and clear, concise descriptions of nursing innovations when communicating with those in the media. Such stories are likely to be published or broadcast to the public and this public exposure is invaluable in enhancing the image and credibility of nurses. One resource for identifying local newspapers is your public library's file of newspapers; most libraries take all local and regional papers. In addition, there is a listing of news bureaus that are news centers in *News Bureaus in the United States* (Weiner, 1981). In large cities, the Chamber of Commerce also lists the available newspapers and broadcast media.

In writing for journals, newspapers, or getting presentations on radio or television, the nurse must first prepare the content in a clear, concise, descriptive fashion. First, study the publication to determine the usual format, number of case examples, length, and other styles that have been used in the past. This will usually be the preferred style and format for that newspaper or program. To reach your target audience, remember to use descriptive and human-interest examples.

ACTIVITY

1. List at least one specific publication or broadcast station which may be interested in the topic which you have chosen, in each of the formats below.
   - Specific nursing journal
   - One other professional journal
   - One public magazine

- One public newspaper
- One radio station
- One television station

2. Select one of these as the target journal or station for your topic. (*The journal should have readers in your target audience.*)

3. Write a summary of your topic, aimed at the one target journal or broadcast station you selected. Include a description of your background, your topic, a quote about the topic, and a real example. (*Keep in mind what your target audience wants to know about this topic.*)

4. Now edit the above summary so that it is clear and concise. Send in your summary as a letter to the editor of the target journal or the manager of the broadcast station, asking if he or she would be interested in more information on your topic.

Write the Manuscript

After selecting the idea, identifying the target audience, and selecting the format, the nurse author writes the manuscript. Remember that it must focus on a central idea: it should start and conclude with the same idea and all parts of the article should relate to the central topic. Two mistakes to be avoided are rambling away from the topic and using vague ideas that are not clearly related to the main idea. In the organization, writing, and editing stages the nurse author should aim for a final draft that is clear and concise with one central theme.

Should you need assistance with the writing steps, this is available from several sources. Many workshops and seminars on writing are conducted for both professionals and the public (Hodgman, 1980). The American Medical Writer's Association (headquarters in Bethesda, Maryland) is an organization that focuses on writing medical manuscripts. In addition to holding meetings, the organization has a journal called *Medical Communications* plus a newsletter called AMWA News. The *Writer's Digest* is a monthly magazine published in Cincinnati which can help the nurse author to gain insight in writing for public magazines. It often describes priority topics needed by different magazines as well as tips for writing for the public.

In addition, there are many references to help the nurse author develop a clear writing style. One of the best sources is *Clear Technical Writing* (Brogan, 1975), which includes activities for the reader rather than only presenting editing points. Two other books that are clearly written and easy to apply in developing a writing style are *Why Not Say It Clearly?* (King, 1978) and *The Elements of Style* (Strunk, 1979). The latter is one of the classics in journalism.

Although there are many sources of assistance in publishing, the nurse author must recognize when to stop reading about publishing and start writing. Writing requires both an organization of ideas as well as writing skills. Both are learned best through practice.

In addition to focusing on writing style, the nurse author who would like to use publishing to influence others must also recognize the importance of accuracy. A manuscript whose content is inaccurate reduces both the credibility of the author and the influence on the reader. Therefore, the nurse author closely check for accuracy of all ideas, theories, references, and any numerals that are used in the text. In every stage of writing, from developing the idea through writing the draft and approving the final page proof, an error may slip into the manuscript. For the most powerful manuscript, accuracy of content must be checked at all steps.

ACTIVITY

Review the news release or other draft that you developed in the preceding activity. Answer the following questions to determine your style and need for rewriting the manuscript.

Is your writing clear?

Does each paragraph have one main idea?

Are a few main points emphasized?

Is the writing concise?

Is there information that rambles off the topic?

Are there any unnecessary words that add little meaning?

Is the information accurate?

Are all numerals correct?

Are all references to others or past literature correct?

Know the Rules

There are several formal and informal rules in publishing that, when followed, will make the manuscript stronger and the author more respected by the publisher. Ignorance of these rules can result in a rejected manuscript and the publisher's loss of respect.

USE THE PUBLICATION'S GUIDELINES

Journal and book publishers usually print "Guidelines for Authors" that describe how the manuscript should be developed for the particular publisher. Some guidelines include only basic material on how to type the manuscript while others include guidelines on the format and audience of the journal. Note the guidelines shown here for the journal, *Dimensions of Critical Care Nursing*, which include information on the development of the manuscript as well as on the typing and final copy.

DIMENSIONS OF CRITICAL CARE NURSING AUTHOR GUIDELINES

Define the idea. Develop your manuscript around *one* main idea stated clearly in the beginning and summary of your manuscript. Please notify the editor of the topic you are developing for more suggestions before writing the manuscript.

Use headings. Organize your paper with headings and subheadings.
DCCN is a clinical journal so the headings should focus on nursing decisions, actions, and strategies, not medical aspects. Fit the medical aspects in under the nursing decisions or actions requiring this information or place in charts or drawings. Please send your basic outline to the editor for early feedback on developing your topic for the *DCCN* audience and format.

Write for the DCCN audience: The *DCCN* audience is made up of critical care nurses in many subspecialties. Mention how your ideas might be applied in several subspecialties. The depth of the material should be for advanced nurses; not too easy to insult the reader or too complex to confuse the reader. Describe *how* the nurse can do something rather than just that she or he should. Use examples to help the reader identify the application to clinical practice.

Develop your ideas. Develop *your* ideas around a topic. The main headings should be your ideas supported with reasoning, literature, or research; whichever is available. Blend the literature and theory into your main ideas rather than placing all the literature in one section of the paper. Avoid a long review of the literature and many quotes as they overshadow your expertise.

Use pictures and illustrations. Emphasize your visual ideas with pictures, draw an important concept in a model, and list information in a chart. Refer to the illustration in the text, but place it in the back of the manuscript as an appendix. Pictures should be 5 x 7, or 8 x 10, black and white glossy. Models and drawings should be in black ink on white paper. Place the illustration number and caption below each illustration. Use illustrations wherever possible.

Permissions.   Obtain permission "to photograph and use the photograph in a professional publication" for all people in pictures. For reproducing copyrighted material such as other people's pictures, charts, or quotes of 30 words or more, obtain copyright permission. Send the editor a copy of the permission and ask for help if needed.

Abstract.   Include a one-page abstract in the front of your manuscript.

Author's background.   Describe your background as the author, attached to the front of the manuscript as the first page.

Accuracy.   You are responsible for the accuracy of the manuscript. Ask colleagues for a review of your draft before submitting it. Ask for feedback on accuracy, organization, and clarity so you can revise it before submitting to the *DCCN* Editorial Board.

Typing.   Type the manuscript using wide margins, double spacing, and black ink. Type the bibliography in the order in which it is referenced in your paper, including only the references actually used in the paper. Include author(s), and page numbers. Target manuscript length is 10 to 20 pages, for most formats.

Submission.   Send the original and three copies. Keep a copy yourself. We will notify you of receipt. Submit the manuscript to us for sole consideration. If we reject it, we will give you suggestions and the original for you to submit elsewhere, if you would like.

Questions.   The Editorial Board Members of *DCCN* are committed to helping you to develop a high quality article for the *DCCN* format and audience. Please feel free to ask questions and we will give you suggestions. All manuscripts will be reviewed by several reviewers since we are a refereed journal.

Contact. For sending manuscripts or for queries or questions contact Suzanne Hall Johnson, *DCCN* Editor, 9737 West Ohio Avenue, Lakewood, CO 80226. 303-988-0056 (Mountain Time Zone). Please include both your home and your work phone numbers on all correspondence.

Reprinted by permission of DCCN: Dimensions of Critical Care Nursing. © 1981.

Too often, manuscripts sent to the publishers do not follow the publisher's guidelines for authors. The publisher is uncertain as to whether the author did not read or just ignored the guidelines. Either will lower the respect of the publisher for the author. Guidelines for authors can be obtained from most journals and publishing houses when querying them on a possible topic. But the nurse author must ask for their guidelines, read them carefully, and follow them in developing the manuscript.

RESPECT THE EDITOR AND PUBLISHER

The editor and publisher have experience in the developmental, copy editing, typesetting, layout, and design of the publication. Authors who work closely with the editor will find that he or she can help in developing the manuscript. A query letter sent to journal editors to ask if they are interested in a topic will help the author identify which journals are the most suitable for their topic before the manuscript is developed. This approach helps the author to quickly find an interested journal without the delay that results from the manuscript review process. If an editor makes a suggestion at any stage in the manuscript development, the author should seriously consider it, for it will probably strengthen the accuracy, clarity, or conciseness.

A manuscript should result from the coordinated efforts of the author and editor. The editor knows the rules, readership, and format of the journal. Authors who take advantage of the editor's role and experience will increase the quality of the manuscript and their own reputation.

MEET DEADLINES

Deadlines are essential for the editors to do their work. The editor needs to consider a combination of topics, the layout of the publication, and other publication preparations. The author will gain respect from editors by meeting deadlines. In addition, deadlines are very important for the nurse author who needs help to avoid procrastination.

SEND YOUR MANUSCRIPT TO ONLY ONE PUBLISHER AT A TIME

Because the publisher spends a great deal of time in manuscript review, development, and other publishing steps, it is usually the publisher's requirement that the nurse author send the manuscript to only *one* publisher at a time. Sending multiple copies to several publishers is time-consuming and expensive for the publisher and shows the author's lack of respect for the publishers. The nurse author who has determined the best target audience and who has decided what editor seems the most interested will easily be able to select one publisher. If the manuscript is rejected, the nurse author may obtain the original and then resubmit it to another publisher. The author who determines why the manuscript was rejected can then revise the manuscript to avoid the same difficulty before sending it to the next publisher.

TRANSFER THE OWNERSHIP TO THE PUBLISHER

The author writes the manuscript for the journal where it will be published (Lieberstein, 1979). Most journals will ask the author to transfer the rights of copyright to the journal. The journal or book publisher will then register the copyright on the material. Many journals require that the nurse assign the copyright rights to them. Some authors confuse copyright with authorship. When the publisher copyrights the material, they own the material, but the author is still credited with authorship. Copyright actually fixes the author's name on the manuscript. Therefore, the copyright protects the author's credit but prevents the author from using the exact wording in the same format for another publication.

This restriction does not interfere with the nurse author who continues to develop ideas. Creative nurse authors would never want to use their old slant in another publication because the reader would lose interest in the author who merely repeats information. A creative author who continues to develop new aspects of an idea is more likely to be respected by others.

ACKNOWLEDGE THE USE OF OTHER'S MATERIAL

The nurse author who would like to influence others must carefully acknowledge any other people whose original ideas have been the basis for the author's work or ideas. In addition, their material such as quotes, charts, or pictures are used, the author should obtain official permission from the copyright holder to use this material and should include an acknowledgement of the source in the manuscript. Respect for the work of past authors will result in increased respect for the new author.

USE FAIR PUBLICATION CREDITS

The respected author will determine who should be considered a coauthor and the ordering of the authors' names. Some authors suggest that the first author on a manuscript be the person most responsible for the manuscript. With an equally shared responsibility, flipping a coin may be appropriate to select the order of names. The coauthors should determine this even before the manuscript is written and should not leave the choice of ordering names to the editor or publisher. Anyone who has been actively involved in the project or the writing should be considered as a possible coauthor. In a research study of past authors, it was found that most experienced authors believe that the order of the names in a publication should reflect the significance of the contributions from the greatest contributions to the least (Spiegel & Keith-Spiegel, 1970).

The nurse author who wants to retain the respect of his or her professional colleagues should identify any colleagues who are involved in the project or the writing, and discuss either acknowledgement or coauthorship with them. This must be done before writing and submitting a manuscript because the credits cannot be changed after the manuscript is printed. It is then too late for the nurse author to change the names or order of names, and anger and disrespect could follow any disagreement on these questions. The nurse author who discusses credits in advance will gain pleased and honored colleagues by recognizing their work as well as opportunities for power through publishing.

SUMMARY

Motivation is the key to the use of power through publishing (Diers, 1981). A nurse who is motivated will find the publishing process exciting. Publishing is a strong power source that can greatly influence others and also gain respect for the nurse author. Used wisely and appropriately, publishing is a legitimate and efficient power source in nursing.

BIBLIOGRAPHY

Ardell, D. & James, J.: *Author's Guide to Journals in the Health Field.* New York, Haworth Press, 1980.

Binger, J. & Jensen, L.: *Lippincott's Guide to Nursing Literature.* Philadelphia, J. B. Lippincott, 1980.

Bioscience Retrieval System. Latham, NY, Bibliograph Retrieval Services Inc., 1982.

Brogan, J.: *Clear Technical Writing.* New York, McGraw-Hill, 1975.

COMSEARCH: New York, The Foundation Center, 1982.

Cumulative Index to Nursing and Allied Health Index. Glendale, CA, Glendale Adventist Medical Center, 1982.

Deaton, J.: *Markets for the Medical Author.* St. Louis, Warren Green, 1977.

Diers, D.: Why write? Why publish? *Image* 13:3–6, 1981.

Hodgman, E. C.: On writing and writing workshops. *Nursing Outlook* 28:366–371, 1980.

International Nursing Index. New York, American Journal of Nursing Co., 1982.

Johnson, S.: *High Risk Parenting.* Philadelphia, J. B. Lippincott, 1979.

Kelly, K.: Publicity basics for the entrepreneur. *Executive Female* Jan/Feb, 23–26, 1981.

King, L.: *Why Not Say It Clearly?* Boston, Little, Brown, 1978.

Koester, J. & Hillman, B. J.: *Writer's Market.* Cincinnati, Writer's Digest Books, 1979.

Kramer, M.: *Reality Shock: Why Nurses Leave Nursing.* St. Louis, C. V. Mosby, 1974.

Lane, N. & Kammerer, K.: *Writer's Guide to Medical Journals.* Cambridge, Ballinger, 1977.

Liberstein, S.: *Who Owns What Is in Your Head?* New York, Hawthorn/Dutton, 1979.

McCloskey, J. C.: Publishing Opportunities for nurses: a comparison of 65 journals. *Nurse Educator* 2:4–13, 1977.

MEDLARS (Medical Literature Analysis and Retrieval System). Bethesda, MD, National Library of Medicine, 1982.

O'Connor, A. B.: *Writing for Nursing Publications.* New Jersey, Charles Slack, 1976.

Spiegel, D. & Keith-Spiegel, P.: Assignment of publication credits. *American Psychologist 25:*738–747, 1970.

Spikol, A.: *Medical Books and Serials in Print: An Index to Literature in the Health Sciences,* 7th ed. New York, Bowker, 1979a.

Spikol, A.: *Magazine Writing: The Inside Angle.* Cincinnati, Writer's Digest Books, 1979b.

Strunk, W. & White, E. B.: *The Elements of Style, 3rd ed.* New York, Macmillan, 1979.

Weiner, R.: *News Bureaus in the U.S.* New York, Public Relations Publishing, 1981.

RECOMMENDED READINGS

Ardell, Donald B. & James, John: *Author's Guide to Journals in the Health Field.* New York, Haworth Press, 1980.

This book adds tremendous breadth to nurse authors' possible publication audiences. Journals in many aspects of health are included along with their preferred content areas, publication lag time, and acceptance rate.

Clayton, Bonnie C. & Boyle, Kathleen: The refeered journal: prestige in professional publication. *Nursing Outlook 29:*531–534, 1981.

The reader will gain a greater understanding of the meaning of "refereed" and its implications. In addition, the results of a survey indicate which of 25 current nursing journals are and are not refereed.

Diers, Donna: Why write? Why publish? *Image 13:*3–6, 1981.

This article encourages you to write in order to reach wider audiences with your innovations, for self expression, and for enjoyment. Excellent in convincing you that you can and should write.

Johnson, Suzanne H.: Nurses' writing blocks. *The Journal of Continuing Education in Nursing 12:*14–17, 1981.

This article helps you to identify and reduce writing blocks of self-confidence, how to start, select a location and time, priority, style, and perfection.

Johnson, Suzanne H.: Selecting a journal for your manuscript. *Nursing and Health Care* 3:258–263, 1982.

This article describes seven criteria for selecting the target journal for a manuscript. These are the journal's audience, format and topics, circulation, acceptance rate, referee status, payment, and editor's interest. A chart on the referee characteristics of 71 nursing and related journals is included.

McCloskey, Joanne C. & Swanson, Elizabeth: Publishing opportunities for nurses: A comparison of 100 journals. *Image* 14:50–56, 1982.

This study of 100 journals helps the author decide between many nursing and health related journals. A valuable chart on the time for acceptance, word length, number of manuscripts published, and acceptance rates is included.

CAREER
DEVELOPMENT AS A
POWER STRATEGY

KATHERINE W. VESTAL

Career planning is an important source of power for nurses. As a nurse moves through a series of positions requiring increased skills and knowledge, the ability to succeed is clearly based on expert power. Expert power is based on the special expertise that an individual is perceived to possess. Thus, career planning has numerous positive results for both the individual nurse and the nursing profession collectively.

The results of successful career planning include the nurse's opportunity to realize personal and professional success as well as the profession to benefit from having self-fulfilled and creative members. Nurses who make informed career decisions have an awareness of career pathways and display a commitment to personal growth. This permits them to achieve a degree of career autonomy that results in success as they define it. On the other hand, failure to define career routes may result in investing great quantities of energy into superficial activities rather than into systematic growth.

The dictionary provides a broad, but accurate, picture of planning. A *plan*, according to Webster's New Collegiate Dictionary, is a "method for achieving an end," or an "orderly arrangement of parts of an overall design or objective." *Planning*, Webster's goes on to say, is "the act or process of making or carrying out plans." These fundamental activities are of necessity, part and parcel of every nurse's career. A career by definition is "a course of continued progress." Thus the interpretation of a career plan can easily be construed.

It is clear that to *not* have a plan, is in fact, having a plan—and the consequences of that kind of career planning would be tragic indeed. It is rare that a person can achieve career success without planning.

Successful careers seldom happen by chance. With few exceptions people who really get what they want in a career do so because they define clear objectives, assume personal responsibility for implementing and following these plans, monitor their progress regularly, improve their plans when they aren't getting the desired results, and persevere in the face of frequent setbacks until their objectives are achieved. They do not wait for things to happen to them—they take charge. They do not spend all their time responding to unanticipated events not of their making. They find ways to anticipate future events and influence them in advance. They have learned how to escape a purely reactive mode of living and become more proactive. (Weiler, 1977, p. 105.)

The nurse who understands that it is possible to control one's own professional destiny holds a key to power and success. Aimless moving from one job situation to another in pursuit of an employee utopia will prove that such a mecca does not exist and will emphasize the need to define the elements of a career that one regards as successful.

Nursing as a profession has the distinction of having numerous job options in a variety of settings. The potentially limitless number of positions serves as a catalyst to movement so that many nurses equate a "move" with career advancement. This may or may not be true. The need for the professional nurse to develop a sense of "career" versus "job" is essential to the attainment of career success. Career planning enables the nurse to realistically match the opportunities that exist with personal and professional goals, thus insuring that the individual has the power to become successful in the profession.

DEVELOPING A PLAN

Three tasks must be accomplished when developing a career plan or when revising the plan. These are determining a direction, assessing organizational fit, and finding career opportunities.

Determining a Direction

The process of moving up the career ladder can be exciting and challenging but is seldom without frustration. In reality, career progression will involve both success and failure, so the *commitment* to persevere toward an ultimate goal is often more important than the triumphs and the setbacks.

In order to determine a direction for growth, the nurse must make the fundamental decision of whether or not he or she desires a series of jobs or a true career. While a "job" can be construed to consist of a number of assigned tasks that result in meeting a specific role expectation, the term *career* implies upward mobility through a succession of positions requiring increasing levels of skill, expertise, and knowledge. The scope of a position broadens as additional responsibilities are assumed. Career building implies that one has a goal in mind, which when reached, signifies success to that individual. Most people do not apply any strategy to their own personal growth and satisfaction, so it is not surprising that few people achieve a career that meets their unique personal criteria for success.

There is nothing wrong with wanting a job rather than a career. Not all nurses are career oriented and it is important to recognize that fact. Just as nurses' values differ, so do the individual's reasons for working. For the career-minded nurse, the path must be identified and both the nurse and the institution must participate in nurturing professional growth. On the other hand, the nurse who desires to have a job that meets her personal need for work, can be supported in such a way that she derives satisfaction from her role without undue pressure to progress to roles she does not want to pursue. Thus, it is clear that the ability to clarify one's own goals is vital.

The clarification of goals requires a written plan. Unwritten plans are only dreams, and it is difficult to operationalize a dream. A written plan serves as a guide, is available to discuss with others, and can easily be altered. A dynamic career will probably necessitate changes in the plan, but the ability to systematically map a plan increases rational career decision making. A written plan serves several basic purposes:

1. It defines the ultimate goals to be accomplished.

2. It provides a clear picture of qualifications needed to achieve the selected career.

3. It enables careful strategy and conscious thought of how to market one's strengths to get the types of jobs that will result in the most valuable experience.

4. It introduces the element of time as a reminder to progress.

The plan is a guide that enables the nurse to round out her career. To begin, it is important to look to someone who others regard as successful in nursing. How did they round out their career experiences to qualify for the position they currently hold? An analysis of their career progression is likely to show that they have had a variety of experiences in several areas—clinical, education, administration, and research. As one progresses upward, positions become broader in scope, requiring a variety of skills to be successful. The notion of a "pure" role such as only an educator, or only a clinician is seldom possible. In reality, an administrator must teach, and a teacher must administrate. So the development of a career plan must provide for a variety of experiences that will ultimately form a firm foundation for success.

Student nurses often do not know what their career goal is when they begin to work. But everyone must start somewhere, so selection of a job that will support personal and professional growth is critical. Programs such as nurse internships provide a system for new nurses to function in a variety of settings before making a permanent selection. Many organizations also support career growth by providing mechanisms for transferring personnel who request a new opportunity.

Nurses, like other professionals, often avoid working in their preceived areas of weakness. Thus, the area of weakness always remains. Mastery and competence precede self-actualization, so it is important to consider the weaker areas as well as those of strength. By developing the requisite skills and promoting self-reliance, the nurse will be rewarded through the power to respond effectively to nursing challenges.

When a career opportunity arises that appears valuable, examine it from the point of view of what can be learned that will ultimately contribute to one's career plan. Goals can be accomplished in a variety of settings, so there is no need to wait years for an opportunity to arise in a specific area. Be flexible and ready to progress—the opportunities are there.

A sample career plan can be seen in Figure 7.1. A new graduate can broadly define a plan that will result in identification of goals. A comparison with the actual pathway shows that while revisions were made in the plan, the ultimate goal was met. It is important to be open to alternatives as long as they contribute to growth and to realize that career control is personal. No one has the power to dictate another's career unless that person lets them. Taking charge of one's own career is a powerful motivator, and will result in enormous professional satisfaction. So feel free to redefine goals, revise time frames, or change directions completely, but base decisions on sound rationale and data. Stop to decide where to go next; taking the time now to plan may save frustration later.

While reaching the goal is important, beware of moving too fast to develop a good foundation. Career success is not a quick or easy process, so the fastest way to the top may not necessarily be the best. To go quickly into a complex position without the necessary knowledge and skills to be successful may result in failure. It is one's own expert power that will ultimately provide the tools for success.

Initial Career Plan with Timetable Made in 1972

Year 1	Year 2–3	Year 3–5	Year 5–6	Year 6–8	Year 8 GOAL
Student: BSN pediatric clinical experience	Staff Nurse pediatrics	Head Nurse pediatrics	Education MS pediatrics	Practice pediatric clinician	University instructor
	(clinical)	(administrative)	(educational)	(clinical)	

Actual Career Path

Year 1 1972	Year 2–3 1973–74	Year 4 1975	Year 5–7 1976–78	Year 6–8 1978–79	Year 8 1980	Year 9 1981 GOAL
Student BSN	Staff Nurse nursery	Head Nurse nursery	Medical-Surgical Staff Nurse with critical care	MSN Pediatric nursing	Pediatric Nursing as clinical specialist	University instructor
	(clinical)	(administrative)	(clinical)	(educational)	(clinical)	

192

Assessing Organizational Fit

One of the most important aspects of career building is to find opportunities in an organization that will support the accomplishment of its members' goals. In order to predict potential success or failure in a job, the nurse must take the time to consider details of how the organization functions. Some people who are unsuccessful in a particular job will later say that they knew an untenable situation existed when they took the job, but thought they could "change the system." The likelihood of changing the entire system to suit personal needs is slim; it is better to assess organizational factors prior to accepting a job. The decision to be made is whether or not it is possible to live with both the positives and negatives of the situation, and be successful in a given role.

A good "job fit" is the result of several factors including whether or not one feels competent, enjoys the work, and perceives that work and personal values and interests coincide (Fox, 1979). Labor experts estimate that tomorrow's workers, seeking the elusive job fit, will change careers three times during the course of an ordinary work life.

In order to systematize your assessment of job fit, you can ask the following questions. The answers provide data from which to make a decision.

1. Is the field right for your interests? Do you want to work in a hospital, school, public health organization, etc.?

2. Is the size of the organization right? Is it too big, too small, or comfortable for you?

3. Is the location suitable?

Figure 7.1

Sample Career Plan. The actual career pathway shows that the goal was ultimately met within a reasonable time frame, although the route was somewhat different than originally planned.

4. Do you like the job content? Is it a people-oriented or task-oriented position? Is it too stressful, too boring, or too easy?

5. Do you feel comfortable with the people you would work with? Are they supportive, competitive, indifferent?

6. Are the opportunities for advancement clear and attainable?

7. Are the financial and benefit packages suitable?

8. Is the job compatible with your personal plans and responsibilities? Is it too time-consuming for your family obligations at this point in your life?

There are certainly other questions that can be asked. The resulting answers form a data base from which to derive an informed decision. The answers can be used to picture the negative and positive aspects of the job in terms of a force-field analysis diagram. (Figure 7.2) The force-field analysis provides a pictorial review of the considerations to be weighed. By consolidating the positive factors on one side of the line and the negative factors on the other, it becomes clear how the person weighs the decision. In the example shown, it is apparent that the negative factors outweigh the positive ones. This does not necessarily mean that the nurse should not take the job, but rather that the opportunity needs to be explored further for possible outcomes before deciding to make a career move.

Once enough information about a job has been collected to make an informed decision, the job opportunity may not show the potential for a genuine promotion, increased responsibility, new opportunities, or may not meet personal needs that are deemed important. In such a case, the individual would benefit from exploring other career options that are more consistent with your defined needs.

The need to assess the organization, just as employers assess candidates for jobs, cannot be overemphasized. Organizations differ vastly and the ability to feel comfortable

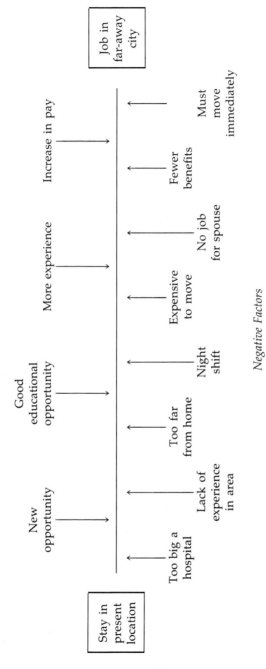

Figure 7.2

Force-field Analysis. This sample indicates that there are more negative than positive factors related to this nurse's move to a specific new job. It is easy to see pictorially that the negatives outweigh the positives.

and the room to grow must be present. Select a workplace for what it can offer to you, the employee, as well as for what you can offer the organization. The result of a good "fit" between employer and employee is a high level of productivity and mutual support—clearly an ideal environment for career growth.

Finding Career Opportunities

The current national shortage of working nurses has created a wealth of career opportunities for both new graduates and experienced nurses. With such a demand in the job market, the nurse must assume the responsibility to define what job is best for his or her career development. If the individual does not determine the experiences that are needed to expand her career foundation, then the temptation to accept the first reasonable offer will be strong. In other words, the nurse's personal and professional goals must serve as a guide to selecting a job.

Career opportunities can be found by exploring many sources, which include, but are not limited to, the following:

1. Written advertisements in newspapers, journals, and newsletters.

2. Word of mouth through collegial networks, recruiters, professional associations, etc.

3. Local and national seminars and conferences.

4. Contact with professional recruitment agencies.

The more specialized the opportunity sought, the greater the need to consult specialty information channels such as professional organizations and specialty groups.

Career opportunities in nontraditional settings or remote locations are somewhat more difficult to locate and may be best found through state or local placement agencies. In addition, the World Health Organization, the American Hospital Association, and the American Nurses' Association can often refer nurses to appropriate resources.

SEEKING A POSITION

Positions are sought through two methods: writing and interviewing. The applicant's written and personal presentations must be well planned and executed.

Presenting Yourself in Writing

Identifying available career opportunities is only the beginning of career building. The next logical step is to market one's strengths to the employer. Marketing strategies will usually include both written and personal contact with a representative of the organization. The written contact is important because it serves as an introduction to one's assets and may well be the key that opens many doors. A nice feature of the written personal summary, or resumé, is that it is possible to take the time to produce a professional document that represents the strengths possessed by the individual. It is a history of professional experiences that can be continually amended to include recent accomplishments. Thus, the written resumé is an extremely valuable tool for presenting one's self in a positive light to prospective employers. It is also useful for providing a summary of accomplishments for other professional activities.

PERSONAL DATA RETRIEVAL SYSTEMS

In order to be able to easily compile and update a resumé, it is essential that the individual maintain a data file on a yearly basis. A system as simple as filling all evidence of professional activities in a special manila folder each year, will soon create a source for data retrieval that is readily available. By filing important professional documents such as brochures from programs attended, letters of commendation from patients or colleagues, and data on committee or organizational responsibilities, it will be possible at any time to revise or amend a resumé with accurate information.

A data retrieval system that depends on memory alone is risky. Much valuable data can easily be lost in time; thus, the ability to revise the resumé based on facts will be limited. The best advice to give a new graduate nurse embarking on an exciting career is to maintain good professional records to serve as a data base for future career building.

THE RESUMÉ AND CURRICULUM VITAE

Both the resumé and curriculum vitae (CV) serve as a summary of one's educational and professional experiences, but the CV is regarded the more stylized version. The resumé is used primarily for presenting one's self in health care organizations, while the CV is customarily reserved for presenting one's self for an academic position, committee, honor, or consultant activity (Newcomb & Murphy, 1979). The CV is intended to chronical scholarly achievements such as degrees earned, publications printed, and professional experiences. The resumé, in addition to degrees and professional experiences, can encompass a broader arena of activities such as special interests, skills and personal accomplishments. In nursing, the resumé is used when seeking a position in a clinical or service setting; the CV is used for the academic setting. Indeed, the nurse may find a dual position in education and service necessitating the development of both a resumé and CV. Samples of both a resume and a CV are found in Figures 7.3 and 7.4.

The style of a resume or CV can vary, depending on the individual developing it. The only constant requirement is

SUSAN MARKS

1402 Elm Street	Born: June 27, 1955
Houston, Texas 77024	Health: Excellent
(713) 668-7485	Married, one child

Career Goal: Management position in nursing administration
                  in a large teaching hospital

EXPERIENCE

Staff Nurse: Westside General Hospital, Houston, Texas.
1979-1981   Responsible for patient care as a primary
                  nurse on a 35-bed general surgery unit.
                  Relief Charge Nurse on 3-11 p.m. shift, and
                  unit teacher for new employees.

Graduate Nurse: University Hospital, Dallas, Texas.
1979   Responsible for patient care as an Associate
                  Nurse on a 20-bed pediatric unit. Delivered
                  total patient and family care.

Student Nurse: University Hospital, Dallas, Texas.
1977-1979   Worked as part-time Student Nurse/Aide
                  during the school year and summer. Delivered
                  patient care on various units; assisted the
                  Registered Nurse in unit activities.

EDUCATION

BSN: 1979   University of Dallas School of Nursing,
                  Dallas, Texas

EXTRACURRICULAR ACTIVITIES

Officer: Vice President, Student Nurses' Association
1978-1979

Volunteer: Health Counselor, Dallas Youth Association
1978-1979

Member: District Nurses' Association, Houston, Texas
1979 to present

CONTINUING EDUCATION

Seminar: 1980   "The New Nurse Manager," Houston, Texas

Seminar: 1981   "Caring for the Neurosurgical Patient,"
                  Houston, Texas

References upon request

Figure 7.3
Sample Resumé.

199

Name: Date:

Present Position(s):

Biographical: (Date and place of birth, marital status,
                         children, home address.)

Education: (Dates, field of study, degrees, location for:
                         undergraduate, graduate, and postgraduate
                         training. List most recent first.)

Experience: (Dates, positions, locations. List most
                         recent first.)

Committee
Responsibilities: (Educational and scientific. List current
                         and past five years. Include national and
                         local.)

Membership
Scientific Societies: (Note those whose membership is on an
                         elective basis.)

Honors: (Scientific and educational, research and teaching.)

Additional
Information: (Continuing education and community activities.)

Research Projects,
Publications:
(Use the following style)

   Professional article

     Author(s), "Title of Article," Name of Journal. Volume, page
       numbers, date of publication.

   Book

     Author, Title of Book. Publisher's location (city): publisher's
     name, date of publication.

Figure 7.4
Curriculum Vitae.

that the written document be accurate and professional in presentation.

Writing the Resumé

You are the best person to construct your professional resumé. Having invested time and energy into your career advancement, you can probably best define your marketable strengths.

The basic purpose of the resumé is to provide information about an individual's qualifications and experience and to create an image that is attractive to employers (Dale,

1977). The image created results from including information that describes your strengths and qualities.

The format of the resumé can vary but should include information in the following areas:

1. Full name, address, phone

2. Professional goals

3. Personal information (optional)

4. Education

5. Job experience (may include responsibilities)

6. Honors, awards, publications, research activities

7. Professional involvement (committees, organizations, etc.)

8. Extracurricular activities and special interests

While the length of the resumé will vary from one to several pages, an excessively long resumé is not desirable in most cases. The resumé should be edited to result in a descriptive, concise document that presents the desired image.

It is absolutely necessary that the resumé be accurate in both grammar and style. Grammatical or typographical errors are inexcusable, and may cause the reader to question the nurse's attention to detail. It is often a good investment to have the resumé professionally typed so that it has a good appearance. It is possible to have the typing done on a word processor. This has several advantages, including the ability to produce multiple original copies, ease in revising and updating content, and the professional appearance that automated typewriters provide. The cost of superior typing is money well spent. Figure 7.5 gives practical tips for resumé development.

Distributing the Resumé
When seeking a job the resumé is a valuable tool for presenting yourself to potential employers. The process for getting a resumé read by the correct person in an organiza-

- Do not use exotic paper, fancy typography, or creative gimmicks on a professional resumé.

- Use standard 8½ × 11-inch bond paper and a clear typeface.

- Do not send photographs with a resumé.

- Absolute accuracy is required in both grammar and spelling. Small errors are extremely distracting and spoil the impression of the resumé.

- Be honest about all information in the resumé. It is easily checked, and falsified information would be grounds for dismissal.

- The best order is to give personal information first, then education, and job experience data. Other information such as hobbies, club affiliations, and outside activities may be of interest to some employers.

Figure 7.5
Practical Tips for Resumés.

tion requires as much planning as writing the resumé. Resumes sent with little forethought frequently result in no response, and little is learned about opportunities in that organization.

As a basic rule, it is not impressive to an employer to receive a photcopied resumé. The impression created by a photocopy is that like copies have been sent across the country in an effort to elicit responses. Since the employer assumes that you are interested in a particular job or organization, the personal touch of sending an original copy is far more impressive. Indeed, the "original" may be from a multicopy word processor or an offset printer, but the image created is worth the extra effort. An "original" resumé accompanied by an appropriate cover letter will attract the attention needed to solicit further communication from the prospective employer.

The cover letter to accompany the resumé has two basic purposes: (1) to solicit interest in the resumé enclosed, and (2) to identify the job the applicant desires (Dale, 1977).

The letter should express interest in the organization and the position, and should draw attention to the qualifications specified in the resumé. It can also request further information or an interview, either of which require a response by the employer. Figure 7.6 is a sample cover letter for a resumé.

As with the resumé, the cover letter should be a typed original, addressed to the appropriate person. If an applicant does not know who will be interviewing or hiring, it is often best to call the organization to obtain the name of the

```
328 Thompson Lane
Chicago, Illinois
January 1, 1983


Dr. Sandra Smith
Vice President for Nursing
Greendale Hospital
Houston, Texas 77030

Dear Dr. Smith:

I am interested in joining a progressive nursing organization
that has a need for my skills and can provide opportunities
for my further professional growth.  I understand that the
nursing service at Greendale Hospital has a career plan that
can meet my interests as a pediatric nurse.

I have a BSN from New York University.  The attached resume
further outlines my qualifications.

As you will note, I am presently a staff nurse in a large
pediatric hospital in Chicago.  My experience includes three
years as a primary nurse with frequent charge nurse responsi-
bilities.  I would like to progress to a nursing management
position that will enable me to broaden my managerial and
budgeting skills.

If you would like to discuss my experience in greater detail,
I would be glad to come for a personal interview.

Sincerely,


Jane Walker, R.N., BSN

Enclosure
```

Figure 7.6
Sample Cover Letter for Resumés.

person, so that a more personalized cover letter can be designed.

Remember that the letter should be designed to present a professional image. Stick to the point and structure the letter to show interest in the job or organization. Proofread the letter and revise it until the copy is perfect. This may be your only opportunity to make a good impression on the employer, so make the best of it!

Personal Presentation in Interviews

Resumés create interest in the applicant, but only the successful interview will result in being hired. The personal interview provides a forum for presenting oneself in person to a potential employer. It gives the applicant the opportunity to market her or his special skills and background and to obtain information about the organization and people who work there (Lee, 1980).

Because of the importance of the interview, it is self-defeating to be unprepared. An applicant who has no knowledge of the organization, no enthusiasm for the job, and no expressed goals to share with the interviewer will fare poorly in an interview. The responsibility to be prepared for an interview rests with you.

First impressions should never be underestimated. Presenting yourself well, in appearance as well as by your preparation, says something positive about your character, maturity and interest in the job. Dress should be neat, clean, and conservative, presenting an image of a professional business person. (Chapter 8 discusses dressing for success.) Greeting the interviewer with confidence, introducing yourself with a firm handshake and using good eye contact indicate a confident composure. Responses to questions should be well thought out and examples of previous accomplishments may be helpful to the interviewer when choosing between several potential employers.

Perhaps the easiest way to feel at ease in an interview is to be well prepared before the actual meeting. Preparation involves several important steps.

1. Make an appointment for the interview to allow sufficient time for preparation. Dropping in unexpectedly to interview will usually result in a rushed meeting that will not provide a receptive atmosphere. At the time of arranging the appointment, request that an application, job description and information about the organization be sent.

2. Gather as much information as possible about the organization so that informed questions can be formulated. Specific information can be obtained through current employees, published reports, and community referral agencies. Write questions down so that the approach in the interview indicates systematic preparation. Figure 7.7 lists essential questions.

3. Analyze the needs of the job being sought to determine what strengths and weaknesses you have in relation to the position. Stress experiences that indicate expertise for the job and avoid calling attention to the negative. Be honest, but remember that the purpose of the interview is to market your positive attributes.

4. Arrive early for the interview to allow time to fill out any necessary forms.

5. Relax and let the interviewer initiate the conversation. Questions that will be asked are largely predictable, allowing formulation of answers before the meeting. Expect questions related to experience and qualifications for the job, availability, career plans, personal and professional interests, strengths and weaknesses, and monetary requirements (Lee, 1980). It is helpful to determine the salary range for the position, but the initial

1. Job description: Ask for a written description of the position for which you are applying.

2. Organizational chart: Review the organizational plan to determine the chain of command and where you will fit.

3. Orientation: Determine the type of orientation that you will be given, including didactic and clinical instruction. How formal or informal is the orientation? How long will it be?

4. Transfer/Promotion/Career development policies: What is the organization's commitment to internal transfers and promotions? What programs are available to provide career advancement?

5. Malpractice insurance: Does the hospital or organization provide coverage, and if so, for what?

6. Compensation: Determine the wage and benefit package that you would receive. Are shift differentials paid, overtime, etc.? Are there additional benefits such as tuition reimbursement, pharmacy discounts, child care facilities, parking provisions?

7. Staffing and scheduling practices: What are the patterns in the area you will work in, provisions for meeting peak demands, and policies for providing adequate staff coverage?

8. Philosophy of nursing care delivery: What philosophy of care delivery is practiced—primary, team, functional—in the area you will work in? Tour the unit and judge for yourself the nature of the services, staffing, and morale.

Figure 7.7
Questions To Ask The Interviewer.

interview is not the time to negotiate for specific dollars. Such negotiations should take place after the organization has indicated which applicant they want to hire for the job; then the selected applicant is in a position to negotiate.

One thing that can be said about job interviews with some certainty is to expect the unexpected. Be well prepared for the interview, but at the same time be flexible in response to the interviewer's approaches. Unsuccessful interviews are often characterized by the applicant's inability to project a sense of competence for the job, a history of frequent job moves with no evidence of promotion, aggressiveness or verbosity in the interview, poor communication skills, or overcriticism of past employers. The successful interview reveals an applicant who is aware of past accomplishments, clear about his or her potential for the job, able to discuss learning experiences in past jobs, prepared to share career goals, and able to ask pertinent questions about the organization. An applicant who establishes initial rapport with the interviewer sets a positive tone for the meeting and consequently projects himself or herself as the right person for the job. Even with preparation and practice, there are times when interviews do not go as planned. Realize that no interview is perfect, so there is always a need to review the interview carefully. Reconstruct the events and evaluate the outcome. Find better ways to conduct future interviews and practice approaches with a friend until the process feels comfortable to you.

It is always reasonable to inquire when the decision for offering or not offering the position will be made. It may be necessary to contact the interviewer in the specified time to inquire if there is any further information needed or just to indicate a continued interest in the job. Often, you will have to be persistent since organizations tend to become bogged down in the hiring process, leaving applicants wondering about the outcome.

A final follow-up to an interview is crucial. Take the time to send a letter to the interviewer thanking him or her for the interview and tying into the previous conversation. Even if you do not accept the position explored, there may well be other opportunities there in the future, so take the time to conclude the interview process in a professional manner.

NEGOTIATING OPTIONS

Probably every decision a person makes involves negotiation. Cohen states that negotiation is a field of knowledge and endeavor that focuses on gaining the favor of people from whom things are wanted. Such things include prestige, money, justice, status, security, and recognition. People who acquire such intangibles possess the ability to negotiate to get what they want (Cohen, 1980).

Negotiations related to career development are varied, and take place continually on both a formal and informal basis. Negotiation is necessary so that people can contribute to the organization's goals and at the same time continue to achieve their own goals on a reasonable timetable. Negotiations in nursing careers may be related, but not limited, to types of responsibilities, titles, hours of duty, scheduling, salary, and benefits. The reality of a structured organization may limit the opportunity for formal up-front negotiations: that is, the job description is explicit, the benefits are set for all employees, and the salary structure is fixed. Such explicit conditions of employment often characterize entry-level positions; however, the opportunities to negotiate these items increase as one moves upward in an organization.

Nurses do not have a professional history of being good negotiators for themselves. Possibly because of the paternalistic health care system and the female dominance of the profession, the opportunities for negotiation by nurses were never made available. Negotiation is a skill that nurses must begin to develop and use effectively. Fortunately, it is a talent that can be learned and practiced without undue stress and, if developed, will enable the nurse to tap other sources of power.

All negotiations involve taking a risk. Therefore, you must know what you want in order to bargain successfully. If you have a clear picture of your goals, you can confidently ask that they be met. Keep in mind that negotiations for career building are more easily accomplished before accepting a new job. This is the time to clearly set out the arrangements so that all parties have an understanding of one another's commitments. After hiring, negotiations can be more difficult unless the individual has demonstrated a series of accomplishements and successes in the organization to form a firm base for further negotiations.

One important area of negotiation for nurses is compensation. Nursing salaries have risen dramatically during the last ten years but continue to lag behind other professional groups. In order to negotiate higher salaries, nurses must become more knowledgeable about financial compensation. As with any negotiation, there is a need for data to support the request. To gather information related to financial compensation in nursing, the nurse should consult local and national survey results, talk with colleagues about salaries in comparable positions, keep abreast of advertised salaries, and request information from specific health care organizations.

Salary plans frequently include incentives for education, experience, specialization, and responsibility. While the employer may not volunteer such information, the nurse can ask direct questions that clarify the salary plan and set overall financial goals for negotiations. Obviously, asking for a salary that far exceeds the market seldom produces positive results, but if the nurse can justify the request through supporting data, there will be a better chance for a negotiated compromise. Likewise, the nurse who undervalues his or her professional worth will surely receive lower compensation than should be expected.

The nurse must accept the responsibility for determining her compensation requirements. Be realistic and reasonable when negotiating because there are always limits on what the market will bear. At the same time, the nurse is entitled to feel good about the agreement that is made.

Determine when and how future raises and promotions are obtained, and ask for the criteria that are used to make these decisions.

There are times when you will accept a job that does not meet all of your requirements. For example, if the job provides a valuable and necessary experience for career growth but less compensation than you desire, a compromise is acceptable. The trade-off may be necessary to build a solid experience foundation for later career moves. It is important to realize that, while fair compensation is important, job decisions cannot be made solely on money issues, but rather must be decided within the context of one's projected career plan.

CAREER MOVES

Career growth depends on career moves. These moves can be made by either changing positions within an organization or resigning the position for one in another organization.

Changing Positions

A predictable phenomenon in any job is that the longer one stays in a position the more comfortable the role becomes. The risk of failure is reduced proportionately to one's success in the job. Consequently, the easiest thing for an employee to do is to remain in that safe position, dependent on the status quo to maintain his or her role. While this is obviously a low-risk situation, it is also the basis for a stagnant career. Career growth depends on continuous learning and the acquisition of increasingly complex skills.

For example, a nurse must assume responsibility for continuous assessment of her or his role behaviors and compare them with the skills needed to advance. Eagerness, talent, and hard work do not guarantee upward mobility; rather, upward movement must be built into career plans through careful assessment, planning, and the flexibility required to take advantage of new opportunities. Frequent career assessment will help one to determine where she is now, where she wants to go next, and the preparation that will be needed to achieve the next step.

An important part of a nurse's career assessment and planning is to let other professionals know the nature of his or her interests, ambitions, and skills. Successful people in the organization may be in the position to promote one another's talents if the expectations are articulated and understood. No one should depend on the system to advance his or her career. You must take charge yourself and make supervisors and managers aware of your goals. Too often, people assume that others understand their career plans, only to find later that others were advanced ahead of them.

Changing positions can be a positive way to advance a career if new roles are assumed to add skills and learning experiences. Job changes can occur within the organization through promotion or transfer, or may require changing organizations to take advantage of a good opportunity. Talking with others inside and outside the organization to stay current on new opportunities. One can also pick up clues to career options by keeping track of expansion in services, realignment of jobs, availability of qualified nurses, and movement of people within the field. At the same time, discuss ways to broaden job responsibilities with your supervisor who may be able to give you the opportunity to be considered for jobs that become available in the future.

Resignation

Resigning a position is an important aspect of career development. When should you consider resigning your current position? If you are contemplating a job change, ask yourself the following questions.

Have you had praise or a raise in the last year?

Has your area of authority expanded or eroded?

Have you and your supervisors discussed future opportunities?

Have you been passed over for a raise or promotion?

Are you bored with your job?

Whether you are considering a move either inside or outside the organization, the resignation process should be handled in an impeccably professional manner. In either case, it is usually wise to inform your immediate supervisor of the opportunities that you are seeking before you resign. In this way, the supervisor will know that you desire professional growth options and may be able to assist you in finding a new role in the organization. Even if you are looking for a position in a different setting, you will still have given the supervisor the opportunity to help you explore possibilities before leaving.

Once you have decided to leave your job, you should discuss your resignation *first* with your immediate supervisor. Discussion with peers may case the rumor mill to distort your plans, which will inevitably create unnecessary conflict. Give adequate notice according to the personnel policy guidelines, both verbally and in writing. Failure to give adequate notice may result in forfeiture of benefits, such as accrued vacation pay and the possibility of becoming ineligible for rehire. Such an unfortunate end to a job can create an enormous barrier to future career plans, as a poor job reference can follow an individual for years. It is

April 30, 1982

Ms. Sue Smith, R.N.
Head Nurse
Hermann Hospital
Houston, Texas 77030

Dear Ms. Smith:

This letter is to notify you of my resignation as Staff Nurse,
effective June 1, 1982. As we have discussed, I am interested
in pursuing management opportunities in nursing and have accepted
a position as Head Nurse on a surgery unit at this hospital.

I have enjoyed my three years as a staff nurse on your unit and
appreciate the opportunities you have provided for me.

Sincerely,

Kay Brown, R.N.

Figure 7.8
Sample Letter of Resignation.

unfortunate when an employee with a good employment
record resigns improperly and thus creates a negative exit.

The letter of resignation should be clear and to the point;
it should include a reason for resignation and the date for
the last day of employment in that position. (See Figure
7.8) Remember that the letter of resignation should not be
used to fight a war. If there is a conflict, handle it separately, either in an exit interview or in another letter. In
any case, burning bridges as one leaves a job may result in
limiting future opportunities for employment. All institutions grow and change, and there may well be a later time
when your return would be desirable. In short, the resignation process should be handled maturely and professionally.

CAREER EVALUATION

It will be rewarding for you to look at your career and feel good about the accomplishments and about yourself. The opportunities that you pursued as well as the hard work and experience have hopefully provided a solid base from which you can advance professionally. A variety of experiences form a foundation leading to multiple career options. Naturally, professional actualization is gratifying and your path to a successful career can be made smoother by following several basic guidelines:

1. Set goals and find ways to continually move toward them.

2. Seek and accept increasing levels of responsibility and experiences.

3. Continue learning to acquire the skills and knowledge necessary to advance.

4. Present a positive work image. Be involved, confident, prepared for tasks and properly groomed. Above all, be on time and productive in the work setting.

5. Learn to view risks as a positive challenge. The risks involved in a new job, new location, new colleagues can be a positive growth experience.

6. Display excellent communication skills, not only to achieve the work but also to build bonds with colleagues and peers.

7. Do not be afraid of success. All new experiences may be frightening, but by reexamining strengths and identifying ways to get assistance with weaknesses, there is probably no job that cannot be done well!

SUMMARY

Success is the product of many things including education, experience, hard work, and discipline. It is not always easy to achieve, but if the motivation to succeed is strong, there is always a way to arrive there. The key to success is to start out with a plan and have a steady, consistent organization. Successful executives create priorities, are always ahead of schedule, and keep a calendar of deadlines. They always set aside time to examine progress and reexamine aims.

The nurse who is beginning a new career has numerous exciting opportunities to create career autonomy. A systematic, open, and productive approach to career planning will provide an avenue for personal and professional power. As the profession of nursing matures, the wealth of opportunities will steadily increase, thus providing options for career planning for every nurse. Each must decide between a "job" and a "career." If the career climb is chosen, the future is indeed exciting. The rewards of surpassing goals, reaping rewards and feeling great about professional accomplishments is self-perpetuating, and the height of the ladder to be climbed is an individual choice.

So decide on your personal definition of success, and design a career plan to fit it. The rewards will far exceed the efforts, and the end result will be power that you have created for yourself as a professional nurse.

BIBLIOGRAPHY

Cohen, H.: *You Can Negotiate Anything.* New Jersey, Lyle Stuart, 1980.

Dale, A.: *Change Your Job, Change Your Life.* New York, Press Paperbacks, 1977.

Fox, M.: *Put Your Degree to Work: A Career Planning and Job-Hunting Guide for the New Professional.* New York, W.W. Norton, 1979.

Lee, N.: *Targeting the Top.* New York, Doubleday, 1980.

Newcomb, B.J. & Murphy, P.A.: The curriculum vitae: what it is and what it is not. *Nursing Outlook* 9:580–583, 1980.

Weiler, N.W.: *Reality and Career Planning.* Baltimore, Maryland, Addison-Wesley, 1977.

RECOMMENDED READINGS

Bolles, R.: *What Color Is Your Parachute.* Berkeley, Ten Speed Press, 1980.
A very clear guide for individuals seeking job or career changes. This book is full of examples and provides an organized route for the reader to follow when considering a change.

Cohen, H.: *You Can Negotiate Anything.* Secaucus, New Jersey, Lyle Stuart, 1980.
This book deals with practical aspects of negotiation. It describes the skills and approaches needed to negotiate and addresses issues of power.

Komar, T.: *The Resume Builder.* Chicago, Follette, 1980.
This book explains how to develop "career documents" that effectively represent an individual. It gives many examples of resumes as well as tips on job searching and interviewing.

Lee, N.: *Targeting the Top.* New York, Doubleday, 1980.
This book is a complete handbook for exploring basic management know-how, and is a resource book on planning career strategies. It is directed toward women in management.

Weiler, N.W.: *Reality and Career Planning.* Mass., Addison-Wesley, 1977.
This book discusses personal values as they relate to today's organizations. It tells how to apply transactional analysis to career planning or career counselling to develop a clear awareness of how most organizational systems really operate, and then how to design personal programs for dealing with these realities.

PERSONAL EFFECTIVENESS AS A POWER SOURCE

KATHLEEN R. STEVENS

When it comes right down to it, influence is an outcome of a one-to-one interaction between two people. The direction of the outcome is a result of two factors: the power available to either party and the persuasive abilities of either one. This is true whether considering political coalitions, publishing, the workings of a bureaucracy, or any of the other power sources described in this book. For example, the legislative sponsor of a health-related bill is influenced by a nurse during a one-to-one interaction whether the communication takes place in a group or is written or verbal. The person who possesses power must also possess some degree of pursuasive ability in order to influence the behavior of another. Power—whether legitimate, reward, referent, expert, informational, or coercive—is close to being ineffective when used without persuasion. When it is coupled with persuasion, the ability to influence increases dramatically. The nurse representing a 1,500-member coalition possesses a tremendous base of power derived from numbers. But it is the nurse's personal effectiveness exhibited during the interaction with the legislator that ultimately brings the power to bear on the legislator's decision.

The objectives of this chapter are to describe personal effectiveness as a component of persuasion and, therefore, to highlight two facets of personal effectiveness: personal image and responsible, assertive communication.

PERSONAL EFFECTIVENESS DEFINED

Personal effectiveness is the impact one has on producing a definite or desired result. Within the context of power, personal effectiveness is one's ability to bring power and persuasiveness together to influence the behavior of another person. The essence of personal effectiveness is that it is a representation of one's self-esteem and positive self-image. It can be viewed as the energy or enabling power one can concentrate on the task of influencing others.

Personal effectiveness has many facets: content of the verbal message, structure of the verbal message, tone and inflection of voice, body and facial movements, and clothing—yes, clothing. The verbal message, or the actual words, are but a minor part of the total message communicated. The complexity or simplicity of the words and sentences can enhance or detract from this impact. For example, although the content of a head nurses's verbal communication to a subordinate may be decisive, faltering speech flow and downturned eyes will detract from the message and decrease the nurse's effectiveness. By way of contrast, erect posture and direct eye contact will confirm the nurse's confidence in a managerial decision or in a conclusion drawn about a patient's change in condition.

Self-confidence must be felt before personal effectiveness is present, but the relationship between the two is indirect and circular. The link between the two is self-esteem which is described as "evaluation of the self by the self" (Greenleaf, 1978). A person has high self-esteem when the evaluation is positive and low self-esteem when the evaluation is negative. Figure 8.1 shows that high self-esteem leads to energy and an enabling power. This energy is the personal effectiveness that results in our accomplishing the task of influencing others. That is, it is power applied. Successful task accomplishment leads to increased confidence and pride. Such confidence makes self-evaluation more positive and, as a result, self-esteem increases. The final result of this cycle is increased personal effectiveness. The self-esteem of a new nurse in terms of skill competence is enhanced when, for example, she or he successfully gives tracheostomy care. The nurse's self-confidence increases when the task is accomplished and the nurse feels proud of her or his ability to give patient care. The resulting personal effectiveness would enable the

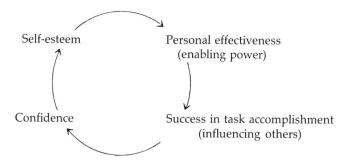

Figure 8.1
The Cycle of Personal Effectiveness

nurse to convince the head nurse to assign more independent care of the tracheostomy patient. As we shall see
later, self-esteem is also related to two facets of personal
effectiveness: assertiveness and anxiety. To exhibit personal effectiveness—to be persuasive—two conditions must
exist: (1) you must present the appropriate personal image,
and (2) the content of the message must be direct. The
following section deals with personal image and the re-
mainder of the chapter focuses on the basics of assertiveness as one form of direct communication.

PERSONAL IMAGE AND
NONVERBAL BEHAVIOR

Personal image is the reflection of one's self-esteem, self-
confidence, and power in his or her appearance and man-
nerisms. Without a word, it conveys a clear message about
one's power. In communication, the major part of the total
message is conveyed through nonverbal communication
(Mehrabian, 1972). Clothes and hairstyle, voice inflection,

facial expressions, hand movements, and body position are all part of the image that one presents to another person during an interaction. To be persuasive, personal image must communicate strength and conviction. A person is much more readily influenced by one who demonstrates self-confidence and certainty than by one who wavers.

While verbal behavior is a conscious attempt to communicate a message, nonverbal behavior is not as much under the control of the individual, but communicates nonetheless. Nonverbal behavior is learned and used in an almost subliminal fashion. Because nonverbal messages are not usually consciously controlled by the sender, the tendency is to trust the nonverbal message more than the verbal message (Dennis & Knapp, 1974). As you develop and acquire more power and wish to influence another person, it becomes critical to send verbal and nonverbal messages that are in harmony. If, for example, you wish to influence another person by saying, "It is my decision that this action will be taken," the verbal and nonverbal messages must agree in order to convince the other person of your conviction. When there is disharmony between the two, the nonverbal message will be trusted. Consider the statement again: "It is my decision that this action will be taken." Now picture the speaker with downturned eyes and a hesitating, almost inaudible voice. The verbal and nonverbal messages do not agree and the most likely interpretation is that the speaker is actually unsure.

Awareness of nonverbal behavior can create greater control over the total message communicated. While the message communicated by a given nonverbal behavior may vary from culture to culture, within a culture its message is relatively consistent. The power of nonverbal behavior is derived from control over the messages one sends and from more accurate interpretation of the messages sent by others. Once you understand the meaning of specific nonverbal behaviors, you will be able to use them to amplify the verbal message you are sending. Remember that when your verbal and nonverbal messages agree, your communication will be accurate and clear. If you choose to apply your power to influence another person, your communication will be more persuasive if you are aware of your nonverbal behavior. Likewise, an understanding of nonverbal messages will assist you in "reading" another person's total message. Thus, cognizance of nonverbal behavior facilitates effective communication.

When you choose to exhibit strength and conviction to be influential, you must be aware of both your verbal and nonverbal messages. What do strength and conviction look like? A person who is self-assured usually exhibits a pattern of nonverbal behavior that conveys the message, "I am confident." The nonverbal behavior of this person is reflected in wearing apparel and hairstyle, voice modulation, facial expressions, hand movements, and body position.

Dress and Personal Image

The function of wearing apparel has evolved into a complex statement about one's social status and role. Originally, apparel was donned for one purpose: protection from the elements. Today, one's apparel may denote authority, life-style, wealth, and social role. Because clothing has such a significant social meaning, it can be skillfully used to elicit from others a desired response. Among other things, it can signify authority. Clothing is a facet of personal image to combine with your drive, ambition, and education so that you convey the message that you are to be taken seriously, that you are trustworthy, and that you are not frivolous.

The dress of women has been particularly reflective of their role in society. Although this role is changing, the clothes are not. Women, by and large, dress to attract men, not to be successful in a career (Molloy, 1977). Moreover, the selection of clothing available to women is dictated by the fashion industry which is controlled by men with old prejudices who are interested in fashion frivolity to maintain a rapid turnover of merchandise (Molloy, 1977). Witness, for example, the rapid altering of hemlines from very short to very long and back up again. Clothing styles are not designed to promote a woman's career.

Therefore women, more than men, must scrupulously select a career wardrobe. But pitfalls for men exist, too. For both, the programming into social roles must be overcome so that each can dress for success. The image-building approach to dress follows a few basic rules and several specific ones. Generally, a career-oriented person should dress conservatively—not fashionably, not frilly. In addition, the clothes selected should reflect an upper-middle-class background (Molloy, 1977).

Since most of the readers of this book will be women, and because women have a particularly difficult fashion problem to overcome, the following discussion on dress will be limited to women's dress.* The guidelines for dress presented here are based on the research of John T. Molloy (1977). While he studied women's dress in the business world, his findings are relevant to the wardrobe of the nurse, especially the "street clothes" worn by nurses in situations such as job interviewing.

BUSINESS APPAREL

The reader is forewarned that the most exiciting prospect of Molloy's recommended business apparel is that it can give you an impressive career image. Intriguing as this may be, it does not mean that you will be donning high-fashion clothes. Actually, the career outfit is the antithesis of a woman's usual orientation to clothing. Recall the previous statement that the fashion industry reflects women's social role in the styles it produces. Even today, women in the home and in business are viewed in predominantly traditional, dependent roles. The fashion industry reflects this role-oriented viewpoint, accentuating the femininity of the woman, which is associated with emotionality and depen-

*Information about men's dress is available in John T. Molloy's *Dressing for Success* (see Recommended Readings at the end of this chapter).

dency. While there are many positive facets of the feminine role, a career orientation and success are not traditionally part of being feminine. Fashion, therefore, reflects the weaker traits of femininity: frivolity, sexuality, emotionality, and dependency. High fashion does not create a power image. Reflect momentarily on the image created by a woman in a sheer, pastel dinner dress, low-cut neckline, rustling skirt, frilly cuffs, and open-toed, high-heeled shoes. The image does not promote a belief in her stability, straightforwardness, and rational thinking! Or consider the collegelike image projected by a woman wearing a turtleneck sweater, blazer, plaid skirt, and high-heeled boots. Again, the image is not one of power, but one of youth and naivete. This woman would certainly not sit on a board of directors.

The most effective business dress for a woman is the skirted suit (Molloy, 1977). Through his research, Molloy found that the skirt suit projected an image that afforded the woman greater recognition, more credibility, and more influence when dealing with others. Surprisingly, the man-imitating clothes, such as vested pantsuits, neckties, and grey, pinstripe skirt suits drew a negative reaction from both men and other women. As a result, he suggests that women adopt a business "uniform" that will communicate positive business qualities. Although specific variations of the "uniform" exist, it is basically as follows: a navy blue or grey skirted suit (blazer-cut coat) with a conservative blouse (usually white, light blue, or tan) that is devoid of lace or ruffles and is not low cut. Accessories should include low-heeled, plain pumps, neutral hose, and an attaché case in lieu of a purse. Some variations and accessories have an unexpected negative impact on the business image. For instance, a vest added to the skirt suit decreases the business tone of the outfit because most men find a vest "sexy." All clothes and accessories must be of good quality or, at least, excellent imitators. For example, polyester may be acceptable if it looks and feels like wool or linen. Various color combinations have been shown to produce different effects. For instance, a red blouse worn with a grey suit will increase the woman's presence; a light blue blouse will make her more likeable. Hairstyle must be conservative. Long hair or very curly hair decreases the status of the woman in business relations (Molloy, 1977).

THE NURSE'S UNIFORM

The conclusions that can be drawn from Molloy's findings on apparel that favors women's success in business relations are that (1) the conservative skirted suit decreases the traditional femininity of the image projected, and that (2) it increases the impression of stability, sensibleness, rationality, seriousness, and credibility. This conclusion can therefore be used when examining the image projected by the apparel of the nurse.

Nursing is in a curious position with regard to dress. Most nurses wear white uniforms in their work and have a limited choice of wardrobe possibilities. In spite of this limitation, some choice does exist. Unlike the suggestions on business dress, the suggestions presented here are not research based. Rather, they are extrapolations from Molloy's research (1977), combined with the author's observations.

Although the nurse's uniform has had a long and interesting history, a uniform serves mainly three basic functions: (1) to endure frequent washings to insure the necessary cleanliness; (2) to allow physical activity necessary in nurses' tasks; and (3) to make a statement about the wearer's identity. The first two functions are relatively straightforward. The third is more complex.

Consider for a moment the uniform's function of identity and two specific items of the nurse's uniform: the cap and the pantsuit uniform. While the nurse's cap serves to identify the role of the wearer, many contemporary nurses have chosen to leave theirs on the shelf. The identity the cap offers is one that was associated with apprenticeship and a phase of nursing that did not reflect professional status. In addition, the cap no longer provides a clear identity: all levels of registered nurses, licensed vocational nurses, hospital aides, and cafeteria workers wear caps. Still, the question of whether or not nurses should wear caps is a live issue, whether or not the cap adequately fulfills its function of identity.

On the other hand, a very functional uniform—the pantsuit uniform—has in the recent past been the subject of controversy among nurses, hospital administrators, and others. While it was clear at the time the pantsuit was introduced that it was ideally suited to the requirements of the nurse to bend, stoop, and reach, adoption of the pantsuit into hospital uniform policy was slow and, in some instances, controversial. It is the author's experience that as late as the early 1970s, some hospitals were tangled in heated debate over whether or not to "allow" the nurses to wear pantsuits. The significance of this issue did not lie in whether or not the pantsuit "looked professional"; any uniform can be worn to look tasteless and unprofessional. Rather, its significance lay in the fact that so much control over what the nurse wore was in the hands of others. The dress uniform was seen as the "proper" uniform for the nurse, perhaps because of the association of the skirt with women's role in society. With the example of this controversy, the nurse who seeks to build her image through dress should be aware of the significance the uniform holds for others—others who can exert control over uniform policies.

The existence of uniform policies is the loudest testimony to the fact that nurses have not done an adequate job of building their image through dress. The fact is that the nurse *can* select uniforms that communicate a professional image and the status of the nurse. Although more research would offer additional guidance to selecting uniforms, some guidelines can be suggested. Selection of a nurse's uniform should follow the same principles as selection of business apparel, with a few additional considerations.

1. Be conservative.

2. Be functional.

3. Show good taste, not high fashion.

4. Do not "go casual."

5. Do not "go cute" or "sexy."

Remember, what is sought is apparel that signifies authority and that you are to be taken seriously. A quick glance through a uniform catalogue reveals that the choices that meet these criteria are limited, but are available. What is found in abundance are uniforms that send strongly female messages—puffed sleeves, ruffles, and curvy lines. Many nurses yield to the temptation to dress youthfully because of the societal emphasis placed on being young. But youth does not have power. The nurse who chooses these uniforms is falling into the male-female-game trap instead of building a career image. Remember, if you want respect, dress the part.

Voice Inflection and Modulation

The voice not only expresses the words of the verbal communication, but also conveys other nonverbal messages through tone, loudness, fluency, and inflection. If an influential role is desired, the voice should be well modulated and distinctly audible. An awareness of your inflection may lead you to discovery that your voice pitch goes up at the end of a declarative statement, making it a question. This would lead the listener to believe that you are unsure of your statement. By contrast, a statement that is made with confidence is stated directly and in a matter-of-fact tone. If you need to hold another's attention while talking, your voice should not be held to a monotone; inflection helps the other person listen. The inflection of the voice can also show whether the statement, "I like your idea" is meant sincerely or sarcastically. The emphasis placed on words, as well as the loudness of the voice, communicate as much as the actual words do.

Knowing your subject well and having predetermined what your convictions are will enable you to speak fluently and without hesitation, hence giving an image of self-confidence. An interesting research finding is that emergent leaders of a group talk more than nonleaders (Reynolds, 1980). As you interact in a group, notice who speaks and who listens to gain an understanding of the leadership and influence.

Facial Expressions

The face is the greatest source of nonverbal messages. The eyes, mouth, brow, and nose communicate the gamut of emotions: happiness, sadness, fear, anger, surprise, pain, pleasure, and more. The eyes alone can communicate a wide range of complex emotions.

Eye contact is powerful in conveying messages. Adequate eye contact is required for communicating one's confidence or determination. Through eye contact, we communicate involvement, willingness, and some degree of trust and absence of hostility. No eye contact signifies that the person is not willing to maintain social contact or that he or she is withdrawing from the message, be it a suggestion, a command, or an expression of affection. For example, you may notice the staff nurse glance away while you are reviewing the care needs of a patient. This glance could tell you that the staff nurse does not understand how to do that particular procedure or perhaps does not agree with the suggestion. The meaning of that glance would be worth clarifying.

On the other hand, too much eye contact may make someone uncomfortable. The cliche, "the eyes are the windows of the soul" says that our innermost thoughts are expressed in our eyes. If we feel vulnerable, too much eye contact is threatening. Dominance, too, is communicated through eye contact and is indicated when, during mututal eye contact, one person continues to look and the other glances away. The first to look away has been dominated.

In addition, followers tend to look more at the leader than at others (Argyle, 1975).

Ego is also involved in eye contact. Threatening communication will lead to one's avoiding eye contact to reduce involvement, thereby perserving ego. Spatial distance, of course, affects eye contact. As spatial distance decreases, the proximity will maintain the involvement with less eye contact. However, as spatial distance increases, more eye contact is needed to maintain involvement.

Smiling is a societal mask which can express humor, pleasure, apology, defense, or excuse. The significant point about smiling and power is that a great deal of inappropriate smiling is done by the subordinated person. While smiles communicate warmth, pleasure, and welcome, too many smiles say "I'm not sure of myself" or "I am submissive."

Control of facial expressions is possible through developing an awareness of what your face is "saying." Do you maintain eye contact? Do you smile appropriately? Is your face tense and your brow furrowed? Become aware of facial expressions—yours and others'—and use them to convey your sincerity and determination.

Gestures

Gestures made with the hands are extremely expressive of a wide variety of messages; they can emphasize, punctuate, and assist verbal communication. However, too much gesticulation may actually detract from the message, reducing its impact. Although gestures have not been standardized as to meaning, some do communicate specific messages. For example, spreading the hand across the chest is done at a time of stress (Fast, 1970), and may indicate helplessness. The hands of the speaker can also communicate the conviction of belief in his or her words. For example, in "steepling," the speaker's hands are comfortably clasped, palms inward, with fingers intertwined. The index finger may form a "pointer" or "steeple" which is moved in rhythm with the speaker's main verbal points.

Other hand gestures may reveal the listener's thoughts. For instance, when the listener disapproves, she or he may rub the back of the index finger under the nose. The same gesture performed by the speaker, however, means that the speaker's utterances are not quite true (Argyle, 1975). Another hand gesture worth noting is the hand covering the mouth. The message implied here is that the speaker is attempting to monitor what he or she is saying as though it should not be said.

Body Posture and Spatial Distance

Two other aspects of nonverbal communication are body posture and spatial distance. Pride and confidence is expressed through erect body posture with the chin out and shoulders back. Conversely, low self-esteem is communicated by stooped shoulders and downturned head. Specific messages may also be conveyed by certain postures. The message conveyed by crossed legs and crossed arms is "I am closed"; perhaps because of defensiveness, vulnerability, or prejudice. By contrast, a message of self-confidence is sent by the person who places both feet on the floor and positions one or both arms away from the center line of the body (Argyle, 1975). A message of attentiveness and interest is conveyed by leaning forward when seated and tilting the head slightly to one side.

Examine your body position when you feel tense or anxious. Compare it to the posture you assume when you feel proud and confident.

Three zones for spatial distance have been defined as: (1) intimate, (2) personal, and (3) public (Argyle, 1975). These zones are culturally defined and are expected norms in the Western world. If the spatial distance is violated, the person feels uncomfortable or threatened. As the term indicates, the intimate zone is the distance within which easy eye or physical contact may be made, to about three feet. The personal zone, a bit more distant, is still within handshaking distance—from about four to ten feet. Most of our business interactions are carried on in the personal zone. The public zone begins at about 12 feet and is used, for example, at lectures or in large group meetings. The importance of the zone lies in the reaction of people when a zone is inappropriately entered. For example, research has shown that a subordinate who enters the office of the boss by just entering the door and then stopping is perceived as having less status than the subordinate who walks up to the front of the desk. Also, the time that elapses between knocking and entering is related to status: the less time elapsed, the higher the status (Argyle, 1975). Consider the status of the person who (if he or she knocks at all) enters before the knock is answered, walks up to the desk, and looms over the seated person. This is clearly a dominating act. Dominance is also conveyed through height. A prominent leader is often placed on a raised platform. Also, the head of the table is a point of domination; for example, the committee chairperson who sits at the head of the table.

All aspects of nonverbal communications should be examined when the desired personal image is one of power and influence. Nonverbal behavior can be studied to make social interaction more effective, to understand the messages being received, and to make clear the messages being sent. If you practice nonverbal behaviors which convey self-confidence, you will begin to feel more self-confident.

RESPONSIBLE ASSERTIVENESS

As we have seen in the previous discussion, the image that one projects is an important facet of personal effectiveness. Another vital facet of personal effectiveness is responsible assertiveness. Assertiveness is a communication style and is actually more than putting together certain words in specified ways. It is a total approach—a philosophy that supports the values of the self and the values of others—which then leads one to communicate in such a way that indicates respect for both the rights of self and those of others. In the responsible, assertive approach, one's own thoughts and feelings are valued and acted upon after considering the rights of others. One outcome is greater self-esteem. Again, increased self-esteem will raise personal effectiveness, thereby enabling the person to command more influence. An additional result is that those who interact with the assertive person will trust that their rights are also being considered. When this occurs, they will be more willing to follow the lead or to allow themselves to be influenced, and will respect the ideas and feelings of the leader. In this way, responsible assertiveness is a safeguard against the misuse and abuse of power and influence and can increase power through sharing power.

Benefits of Assertiveness

Every nurse can recall at least one situation in which she or he felt used or frustrated but said nothing. Or perhaps a situation comes to mind in which the nurse felt particularly proud of an accomplishment but said nothing. In both of these situations, assertiveness is lacking. We have all experienced the frustration of being unappreciated, "walked on," or "put down." When a nonassertive or an agressive response is used, guilt and anxiety result. However, the guilt and anxiety we experience when we deny our expression of feeling is decreased by using an assertive response. Assertiveness reduces the fear of sounding boastful, as in the statement, "I did a good job"; and it decreases the guilt experienced by saying, for example, "I choose to spend my time in another way." The most powerful and influential response is the assertive response because it reduces both anxiety and guilt. The connections among assertiveness, self-esteem, and anxiety are depicted in Fig-

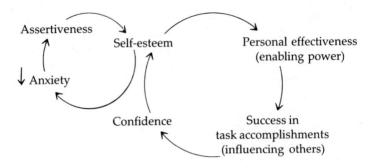

Figure 8.2
Assertiveness as part of the Personal Effectiveness Cycle

ure 8.2. The circular connections are shown in relation to the cycle of personal effectiveness discussed earlier in this chapter. Self-esteem is the common factor in these two cycles. Assertiveness enhances self-esteem as people's rights are respected. Increased self-esteem in turn leads to a decrease in anxiety and reinforces subsequent use of an assertive approach (adapted from Greenleaf, 1978). Since assertiveness increases self-esteem, it is a powerful communication style to use when appropriate.

ACTIVITY

Recall a situation in which you thought your efforts were unappreciated. What did you do? What did you say? What were the results? How did you feel?

Beyond the personal benefits gained from assertiveness, the nurse is in a position to assure benefits for patients and the health care system through using assertiveness. Clearly, physicians and hospital administrators need help from nurses in revising the health care system into a more humane and caring system. When nurses speak up assertively and share their expertise, the system of health care will become more responsive to the client's needs.

Assertiveness Defined

Assertiveness is a type of interpersonal behavior—a social skill. "Acting assertively means standing up for your assertive rights and expressing what you believe, feel, and want in direct, honest, appropriate ways that respect the rights of the other person" (Jakubowski & Lange, 1978). Assertion encompasses the honest expression of a range of feelings, including justified anger, caring, and affection (Galassi & Galassi, 1978). It is expressed in both verbal and nonverbal behaviors.

Since assertiveness involves the direct expression of your thoughts or feelings, an assertive statement usually begins with "I"; for example, "I don't agree with you" or "I like what you did." Assertions can be expressions of (1) positive feelings or thoughts, as in "I want you to know how much I enjoyed this meeting"; (2) negative thoughts or feelings, such as "I want you to stop. I don't like what you are doing"; and (3) setting limits on how others act toward you, for example, "Sexist language bothers me and I perfer not to hear it." In all three cases, the statement is a direct expression of the thought or feeling.

Assertiveness as an Option

Assertive behavior is an option available to all of us who take the time to learn to be assertive. It is one of three options, the other two being nonassertive behavior and aggressive behavior (Jakubowski & Lange, 1978). Perhaps you have found yourself in one of the following situations:

- You have difficulty expressing your opinion during a multidisciplinary team conference about your patient. Although you have suggestions, it is difficult for you to be direct.

- You need to correct the nurse aide's technique of measuring urinary output, but you ignore the situation, hoping it will take care of itself.

- The head nurse compliments your performance but you respond with a humorous remark that diminishes the compliment.

- You are verbally abused by a person and passively accept the abuse or put the person down.

- You avoid asking a coworker not to smoke during a conference by convincing yourself that it is only for a short time.

Most people who have had to deal with situations similar to these feel trapped or think they have only two options: to be passive or to be aggressive. The decision to be passive results in saying nothing. Such a response denies one's thoughts and feelings, while the resulting feelings of helplessness, of being exploited, and of anger lead to disappointment and lowered self-esteem. Tension may then mount to the point of overreacting to a minor circumstance. That is, the person may "come on too strong" or "blow up" when he or she finally does express the thought or feeling (Jakubowski & Lange, 1978).

Aggressiveness is the other commonly known option. Demeaning, angry, or accusing behaviors are sometimes used to accomplish an end. But the other person's response to such an attack most likely will not be the response desired. For example, the supervisor will most likely respond unfavorably if you place blame for a schedule mix-up by saying, "You could have posted this schedule on time and avoided this mix-up." Aggressive behavior rarely accomplishes anything except feelings of guilt later because of its irrationality. Self-respect is lost and self-esteem is lowered as a result.

Personal Rights

The basic issue in these three behavior options is *personal rights*. When people act assertively, their personal rights and the rights of others are respected. In aggressive behavior, the rights of the first person may be respected, but the rights of the second person are clearly violated or ignored. When the nonassertive option is used, the rights of neither party are considered.

Recall that assertiveness means standing up for your assertive rights and, at the same time, respecting the rights of the other person. Standing up for our rights does not mean that we may be obnoxious in expressing our rights. To the contrary, responsible assertiveness is respecting the rights of others. "One of the ultimate goals of assertion is developing caring, honest, and accepting relationships with others" (Jakubowski & Lange, 1978).

What are your assertive rights? Jakubowski and Lang have identified the following as the most basic ones:

1. The right to act in ways that promote your dignity and self-respect as long as others' rights are not violated in the process.

2. The right to be treated with respect.

3. The right to say no without feeling guilty.

4. The right to experience and express your feelings.

5. The right to slow down and think.

6. The right to change your mind.

7. The right to ask for what you want.

8. The right to do less than you are humanly capable of doing.

9. The right to ask for information.

10. The right to make mistakes.

11. The right to feel good about yourself.*

In addition to these rights, you may have other personal rights you wish to list. Consider, for example, the addition

*From Lange, A. J. & Jakubowski, P.: *Responsible Assertive Behavior*. Campaign, Ill., Research Press, © 1976. Reprinted with permission.

of "the right to choose not to be assertive in a situation."

It is important to list those rights you believe in as *your* personal rights. An awareness of your rights is requisite to your assertiveness because assertiveness is an expression of personal rights. For example, the nurse who has not identified the right to say no without feeling guilty may either fulfill every request made or may feel guilty when turning down a request. In either case, the nurse will experience anxiety and will probably be uncomfortable. By fulfilling every request, the nurse may come to feel like a doormat for others, and resent being used and exploited. If the nurse denies the request and feels guilty, the feeling of guilt may cause fewer refusals in the future. By claiming the right to say no without feeling guilty, requests can be refused in a humane manner without loosing self-respect and without violating the rights of others. This is not to say that the person making the request will *like* the refusal; it may be that the person will *not* like the refusal. This is okay, for that person, too, has a right to experience and express feelings. However, the mutual respect of each other's rights will lead to an assertive interaction which could sound like this:

Jamie: I'm presenting a patient case study at the conference down on my unit in a few minutes. I'd like for you to come.

Pat: I appreciate the invitation and I think it would be interesting. But that is not a priority for me at this time.

Jamie: Oh, come on, whatever you are doing can wait.

Pat: Jamie, I choose not to go.

Jamie: I don't like your choice, but you do have the right to make it.

Pat: Yes. And I understand that you don't have to agree with it.

Pat believes in the right to say no without feeling guilty and Jamie believed in the right to express feelings. Both people gave themselves permission to act assertively, respecting their rights and the rights of the other.

ACTIVITY

Recall a situation in which you were not assertive. Your reaction may have been nonassertive or aggressive. What is the personal right that you had *not* claimed? If you had been consciously aware of this right, how might your behavior have been different?

Assertiveness as Learned Behavior

Assertive, nonassertive, and aggressive behavior are social styles learned largely through socialization. The socialization process has taught us our personal rights and concomitant assertiveness. If few personal rights are taught, then little assertiveness is demonstrated. Many people are socialized to suppress personal rights. For example, the child who quite naturally says "Didn't I do well!" is quickly cautioned against seeming too boastful.

To some degree, we are all socialized to be nonassertive. However, this socialization seems especially disadvantageous for women. In the recent past, success and independence were not acceptable for girls and women. If a girl showed signs of being successful, independent, self-assured, and competitive, she was labeled "unfeminine" and the fear was that boys would be repelled by such behavior. Consequently, girls learned to influence others through indirect routes such as subtle manipulation, for example, crying or coyness. Such nonassertive approaches are still evident in the daily interactions of many women.

Nurses have exhibited nonassertiveness as a result of two situations: (1) 98% of nurses are women, who have learned nonassertive interaction patterns; and (2) in the past, the role of the nurse has been subordinated to and dependent on those of physicians and hospital administrators. Nurses are socialized into this role and, again, nonassertive behavior is reinforced. Nurses learn to be compassionate, tender, caring, supportive, and nurturing—putting "all others before self" (Heide, 1973; Muhlenkamp

& Parsons, 1972; Minnigerode, Kayser-Jones, & Garcia, 1978). While most of these qualities are virtuous, the more important point is that the nurse never learns what her or his personal rights are. The nurse is socialized to suppress feelings and to avoid expressing thoughts. The author believes that now is the time for nurses to move beyond this aspect of their socialization—to move on to assertiveness.

Assertiveness as a Skill

Just as nonassertiveness is learned, there is evidence that assertiveness can be learned (Galassi & Galassi, 1978; Jakubowski-Spector, 1973; Manderino, 1975). Assertiveness is a skill that can be developed by any nurse. But because it is a skill that may be a new behavior, assertiveness requires concentration and practice. Later, it will come quite comfortably. The benefits of learning assertiveness are well worth the effort required.

POSITIVE SELF-PRESENTATION

To this point, we have defined assertiveness, distinguished it from nonassertiveness and aggression, identified personal assertive rights, and discussed three types of assertive statements (positive assertion, negative assertion, and limit setting). The next step in developing assertiveness is to present yourself proudly. If you are to assert yourself convincingly, you must develop an awareness of your positive traits. Such self-enhancement has been shown to be an effective strategy for building a more positive self-concept (Harnden, 1979). When we appreciate ourselves, self-esteem is high and even problem solving can be fun.

Self-enhancement, or positive self-presentation, is powerful in convincing yourself *and others* that you do not depend on them for a feeling of self-worth, that you are self-confident, and that you are personally effective. However, because you have been taught to downplay yourself, to concentrate on your weaknesses, positive self-statements may be uncomfortable at first.

ACTIVITY

Develop a positive self-portrait. Begin by recognizing that parents, teachers, and others have sought to help you grow by pointing out areas in need of improvement. Now look at your *positive* traits. Make a list with two columns: (1) My Strengths (2) My Accomplishments. List only positives. Avoid using "qualifiers" such as "sort of" or "sometimes": these qualifiers downgrade the strength or accomplishment you are describing. Examine the list and practice positive assertions by stating "My strengths are . . . ." and "I have accomplished . . . ." *Remember, the point is to make your strengths productive and your weaknesses irrelevant!* Here are two examples of positive self-presentations: "I did an outstanding job with this patient and family." "I am a dependable and skilled member of the nursing staff and I have earned a raise."

Positive self-presentations can be used influentially in several situations. You can use self-enhancement when interviewing for a job; no one can sell your skills like you can. Self-enhancement can also be used to become more influential in an organization. For instance, a member of a committee may state, "I have successfully resolved a similar problem. This is my recommendation . . . ."

EXAMPLES OF ASSERTIVE
STATEMENTS

It takes thought and practice to formulate assertive statements and recognize nonassertive and aggressive statements. Nonassertive and aggressive statements may dominate interaction simply because we respond out of old habits. To formulate assertive statements requires extra effort because the words are often "strangers" to our mouths. Sometimes you may not be assertive in a situation

Positive assertions:
- I like what you did.
- I think Pat deserves a promotion.
- I like the way you handled that.
- What is your fee?
- I am a competent nurse and a good problem solver.

Negative assertions:
- I am annoyed that you want me to make an exception for you.
- I feel put down with comments like that.
- I don't agree with you.
- I am not satisfied with this work. I want it corrected.

Limit-setting statements:
- I would like to think further about that before deciding what to do.
- I prefer that you not make commitments for me.
- I don't doubt your concern, but I want to make my own decision.
- That is not a priority for me; I choose not to do it.

Figure 8.3
Examples of Assertive Statements

because you cannot formulate the statement quickly enough. You are left thinking, "Well, next time I will say . . .." This may happen because you have not heard many assertive statements and are not yet fluent in expressing your rights. In Figure 8.3 some examples are presented of positive assertions, negative assertions, and limit-setting statements. Remember, however, that the nonverbal message must be in harmony with the verbal message to communicate a clear message and that a great deal about the specific situation is being assumed.

NONVERBAL COMPONENTS OF ASSERTIVE COMMUNICATION

The verbal components of assertive, nonassertive, and aggressive behavior have been discussed to this point. However, as already noted, nonverbal behavior is vital in communicating effectively. The nurse may effectively deliver an assertive message to the patient who has repeatedly refused a bedbath by stating in an even, firm tone of voice while looking into the patient's eyes, "Mr. James, I understand that you have refused a bath. You need to have a bath now to keep your skin healthy." Consider the impact of the assertion had the nurse avoided eye contact and had spoken softly.

Research has shown that the following nonverbal behaviors may be important assertive behaviors: the duration of looking at the other person, the duration and loudness of speech, and the affect in speech (Eisler, Miller, & Hersen, 1973). The nonverbal behaviors that convey self-confidence and strength were discussed previously and can be effectively used in affirming assertive verbal messages.

Three Final Words about Assertiveness

With this brief introduction to assertiveness must come three final words on the subject. First, adoption of assertive behavior represents a change for many people. You will find that the response of others to this change in your behavior will range from acceptance to puzzlement to rejection. It may prove helpful to develop a support system with friends who are aware of your efforts to become assertive. In this way you can share both the successes and blunders that you will no doubt encounter on your way to assertiveness. Be aware of the fact that your new assertiveness will change your relationship with some people! It is a change of philosophy and interaction patterns, so changes in relationships should be expected.

The second "final word" is related to your right to choose not to be assertive. Assertiveness is *not* appropriate in every situation. Moreover, assertiveness is a philosophy, and there may be situations where differing philosophies prevail. While the following example is not an ideal situation, it certainly does exist. Consider a strongly autocratic supervisor who may not allow some assertions. Your supervisor may accept your negative assertion ("I don't agree with you") in private, but not in front of others. You will thus have to consider the consequences of assertiveness in certain situations like this one, and remember your right to choose *not* to be assertive in any given situation.

The third "final word" about assertiveness as a skill is that it requires more than didactic learning. As an interactive pattern of behavior, it must be learned in an interactive setting. Assertiveness training is now widely available from qualified trainers. For the person interested in assertiveness, the authoritative and most complete written resource is *The Assertive Option* by Particia Jakubowski and Arthur J. Lang. However, assertive training is incomplete without interactive training.

SUMMARY

As a source of power, personal effectiveness is perhaps the most individualized, most stylized, and most potent of all. The elements of personal effectiveness are highly variable and combinations are more than the sum of the parts; the variety and uniqueness of personal effectiveness is manifested in the intangible quality of some people called *charisma,* which is that special quality of leadership or influence that appeals to many.

Personal effectiveness is gained through wise use of dress, voice inflection, facial expressions, hand gestures, positioning, assertiveness, and positive self-presentation. The resulting success in task accomplishment and confidence will build the self-esteem necessary for being influenctial and creating change.

BIBLIOGRAPHY

Argyle, M.: *Bodily Communications.* New York, International Universities Press, 1975.

Barnlund, D.: *Interpersonal Communication: Survey and Studies.* Boston, Houghton Mifflin, 1968.

Dennis, H. D. & Knapp, M. L.: Three components of the actor's nonverbal response: power, immediacy, and responsiveness. *Empirical Research in Theatre,* Summer. 44–52, 1974.

Eisler, R. M., Miller, P. M., & Hersen, M.: Components of assertive behavior. *Journal of Clinical Psychology 29*:295–299, 1973.

Fast, J.: *Body Language.* New York, M. Evans, 1970.

Galassi, M. & Galassi, M.D.: Assertion: a critical review. *Psychotherapy: Theory, Research, and Practice 15*:16–29, 1978.

Gibson, J. L., Ivancevich, J. M., & Donnelly, J. H.: *Organizations: Behavior, Structure and Process,* 3rd ed. Dallas, Business Publications, 1979.

Greenleaf, N. P.: The politics of self-esteem. *Nursing Digest 6*:1–8, 1978.

Harnden, G. M.: The power of positive self-reporting: responses of superiors to subordinate's self-presentation. *Dissertation Abstracts International 39*:4822–A, 1979.

Heide, W. S.: Nursing and women's liberation: a parallel. *American Journal of Nursing 73*:824–827, 1973.

Jakubowski-Spector, P.: Facilitating the growth of women through assertive training. *The Counseling Psychologist 4*:75–86, 1973.

Jakubowski, P. & Lange, A. J.: *The Assertive Option: Your Rights and Responsibilities.* Champaign, Illinois, Research Press, 1978.

Manderino, M. A.: Effects of a group assertive training procedure on undergraduate women. *Communicating Nursing Research 8*:140–147, 1975.

Mehrabian, A.: *Nonverbal Communications.* Chicago, Aldine/ Atherton, 1972.

Minnigerode, F. A., Kayser-Jones, J. S. & Garcia, G.: Masculinity and femininity in nursing. *Nursing Research* 27:299–302, 1978.

Molloy, J. T.: *The Woman's Dress for Success Book*. New York, Warner Books, 1977.

Muhlenkamp, A. F. & Parsons, J. L.: Characteristics of nurses: an overview of recent research published in a nursing research periodical. *Journal of Vocational Behavior* 2:261–273, 1972.

Reynolds, P. D.: Leaders never quit: talking, silence and influence in interpersonal groups. Paper presented at the 1980 Meeting of the American Sociological Association, 1980.

RECOMMENDED READINGS

Chenevert, Melodie: *Special Techniques of Assertiveness Training for Women in the Health Professions*. St. Louis, Moxby, 1978.
This delightfully clever, humorous, and insightful little book will have a motivating effect on the reader to become assertive. It exposes clearly the many barriers to assertiveness which are experienced by women in the health professions.

Jakubowski, Patricia & Lange, Arthur, J.: *The Assertive Option: Your Rights and Responsibilities*. Champaign, Ill., Research Press, 1978.
This is probably the most comprehensive self-help book on assertiveness. It will assist the reader in identifying personal rights, discriminating among assertive, nonassertive, and aggressive responses, changing the houghts that are barriers to assertiveness, and practicing assertive behaviors. Do not end your study of assertiveness until you have read it.

Molloy, John T.: *The Woman's Dress for Success Book. New York*, Warner Books, 1977.
The suggestions made for dress in this valuable resource are based on nine years of research. It is a difinitive source on how to use clothing effectively and is *must* reading for every nurse serious about succeeding. This author also wrote a similar book on men's dress: *Dress for Success*. New York, Warner Books, 1976.

DECISION MAKING, TIME MANAGEMENT, AND POWER

RAE WYNELLE LANGFORD

Decision making and time management are two skills that can serve as pivotal points in obtaining and maintaining power and in developing our abilities. They are closely linked in that effective time management requires effective decision-making processes, while effective implementation of decisions requires effective time management. Hence, the development of both techniques simultaneously will contribute to an overall increase in personal effectiveness and subsequent power development. The development and effective use of these techniques are valuable to the head nurse, staff nurse, and administrator. Indeed, they are valuable for all professionals who wish to enhance their power base through increasing personal competencies.

DECISION MAKING

The very act of living requires making many decisions each day. Certainly the practice of nursing involves continuous decisions that must be made. Yet, the decision-making process varies widely from person to person. Some people rely on trial and error, some on common sense, others appeal to outside authority, while some choose to allow others to make decisions for them. Only a few employ a process approach and these people are candidates for developing and maintaining a personal power base. The key to developing an effective decision-making style is to examine the factors that underlie a process approach to decision making, and to choose and put into practice those elements that best suit your individual style and personality.

Decisions

A decision is a judgment or a choice between or among possible alternatives. There is rarely a black and white

Factors

Decision Complexity

	SIMPLE		COMPLEX
Alternatives	1 to 3 —————————————→ ∞		
	Clearly defined		Vague, highly divergent
Information	Accessible Clear/Little Conflict Low Volume		Inaccessible, Conflicting, High Volume
Risks	None	Minimal Moderate	Great
Values/Perceptions	Clear No conflicts	Muddled	High conflict
Number of people involved	1 or 2 —————————————→ ∞		

Decision Line

Figure 9.1
Factors that influence decision complexity

250

choice between right and wrong but rather a choice among several courses of action where two or more of the alternatives would probably produce the desired effect. Decisions range from very simple and routine ones—for example, whether to make patient rounds and then pour 9 a.m. medications or to pour the medications and then make rounds, to the very complex ones—for example, how to introduce and implement a new patient care system.

A number of factors influence the complexity of a decision and must be considered when designing an effective decision-making approach. Figure 9.1 diagrams these factors, which may work singly or may interact to increase or decrease decision complexity. In order to assess the complexity of a decision, first examine the alternatives available: How many are there? Are they vague or clear-cut? Second, determine what information is needed. Is it easily accessible? A third factor to examine is the risks involved: Are they minimal or are they unpredictable or high? Values and perceptions are a fourth factor that also affects the decision's complexity. What perceptions and values are involved? Are perceptions muddled? Do conflicting values appear? The fifth factor to be examined is the number of people who will be involved in and affected by the decision (Figure 9.1). An examination of these five factors will lead to a conclusion about the simplicity or complexity of the decision-making task at hand.

If a decision is simple or routine in nature, then it is most efficient, effective, and advisable to make it, implement it, and move on. As easy as this sounds, one of the major problems for many nurses is the inability to make and implement routine decisions. This indecisiveness often stems from a lack of willingness to take even minimal risks as well as a lack of confidence in one's abilities. Instead of making a simple or routine decision, many nurses wait for someone else to make the decision and to tell them what to do. While this approach often decreases the burden of responsibility, it also reinforces dependent functioning, decreases feelings of confidence, and increases feelings of frustration and powerlessness.

It seems ironic that one of the major reasons for job dissatisfaction cited by nurses is the inability to practice nursing the way they would like to because of imposed restraints by the system or by physicians. Yet, many of these very same nurses refuse to accept the responsibility for routine daily decisions in the course of their jobs. One way for nurses to increase their power base and thus increase opportunities for input into the larger system is by accepting responsibility for the decisions that they must routinely make in their work settings. As confidence and skills increase through practical experience with everyday decisions, the more complex decisions become easier to approach and master.

Decision-making Process

Many elements are involved in the process of decision making, some of which are overt and some covert. The overt elements give rise to decision-making models and to variously described systematic step-wise decision-making systems. Most discussions of decision making focus on the overt elements. The covert elements which are, of course, less obvious are often not discussed in analyses of the decision-making process. Yet, it is these covert factors that often play a far greater role than the overt factors in the eventual success or failure of a decision.

Overt Factors

The overt factors in making a decision are largely mechanical steps or systems of thought that allow one to organize the process. These steps give rise to decision-making models that provide a systematic way to collect data, outline alternatives, and make choices. Bernhard and Walsh, in their book *Leadership: The Key to Professionalization of Nursing* (1981), present five such decision-making models. Each model has been used and tested by nurse leaders and is described in detail. Practical illustrations demonstrate the usefulness of the model in nursing, and each model outlines a step-by-step process to follow in order to arrive at a decision.

All decision-making models possess certain common characteristics: first, a systematic, step-wise process for making decisions, and second, similar elements within these steps, regardless of the model. In addition, all models include a data collection phase wherein information needed to make the decision is gathered. There is always a step in which the parameters of the situation are defined, then another step that generates feasible alternates or solutions, as well as several steps that involve the selection and implementation of one alternative. Finally, many models include an evaluation process that views the success or failure of the alternative that was selected and implemented.

A personal model for decision making can be developed. To do this, a variety of models should be analyzed for effectiveness and degree of accommodation to personal style. Key elements from several models may then be chosen and combined to create a new, individualized decision-making model. An example of such a model is as follows: (1) When confronted with a decision, identify the desired outcome or end result. (2) Analyze the situation for those factors that will facilitate the desired outcome and those factors that serve as barriers. (3) Generate alternatives that take advantage of the facilitating factors and overcome the barriers. (4) The risk and costs to the decision maker should then be weighed against the willingness to take the risk or pay the cost. (5) Select and implement the alternative. (6) Evaluate the outcome of the decision as well as the process of making the decision. If the desired result has not been obtained, the process is again applied. If there are obvious inefficiencies within the model, a revision of the process may be considered.

There are advantages in using such a systematic approach in making decisions. The elements noted above force the person to consider the goal sought, to collect needed data, to outline feasible alternatives or solutions, and to choose, implement, and evaluate the best choice. A systematic approach is also quite useful when a group is involved in making a decision since it provides a standard format for the process and allows easy visualization of the process.

Certain factors need to be considered when deciding whether to use a model and, if so, which model to use. First, the use of a decision-making model requires time and thought. Obviously, if there is ample time available and if the decision is a fairly complex one, it is best to use a model. Second, most models outline a certain style of reasoning in which the person begins with the goal or problem, then generates alternatives, and selects a final choice. This approach is a form of deductive reasoning, which means reasoning that starts with the whole and moves to the particular. By comparison, inductive reasoning means starting with specific facts and coming to a general conclusion. Many persons who use inductive reasoning as their primary thought process may find a model which employs deductive reasoning to be frustrating or useless. Nurses are generally taught to reason inductively, using the nursing process. In addition, the problem or goal may not be readily definable and alternatives may be vague, overlapping, or so numerous as to defy listing. Enormous time and energy may be invested in attempting to define the problem or in clarifying alternatives when such a definition or clarification is improbable or unnecessary. Third, although decisions are defined as judgments, hence subjective in nature, the majority of models do not refer to use of the subjective factors involved in the process. Thus, many decisions arrived at by using an objective, orderly process are failures because they have not taken into account the subjective or covert influences.

Decision-making models and other systematic thought processes should be viewed as tools. If one such tool proves useful in making certain decisions, then it should be used. If it does not prove useful, it becomes burdensome and adds to the frustration of arriving at a decision rather than relieving it.

Covert Factors

The many covert factors that play a role in decision making are not as apparent as overt factors and are therefore harder to analyze with regard to one's own decision-making style. Nonetheless, they are important. Such elements include the decision maker's values, level of self-esteem, defined roles and functions, control motivations, and the amount of structure required by that person to make decisions.

VALUES

Values underlie all decisions and actions. Regardless of how objectively one sets the criteria for decision making, every decision is ultimately based on the decision maker's value system. Values possess intrinsic worth. For example, if you decide to include family members in teaching a patient about his care, this decision will reflect your valuing of the family as an integral part of care. If you decide that taking routine vital signs must be done before spending time with an anxious presurgical patient, you are illustrating the value you place on carrying out the daily routine. If one is unaware of the values upon which decisions are based, then a key element in the process is absent. If values are not examined, then actions may not be understood or may appear to be irrational.

Values develop through interaction with the environment. Kohlberg's explanation of the stages of moral development aids in understanding how values develop. The following charts Kohlberg's levels and stages of moral development.

KOHLBERG'S LEVELS AND STAGES OF MORAL DEVELOPMENT

Preconventional Level. At this level, the person is responsive to cultural rules, labels of good and bad, right and wrong, but views these rules in terms of punishment/reward or favor exchange orientation.

Stage 1: "Punishment-obedience" stage. The consequences of the action determine goodness or badness. The values at this stage are avoidance of punishment and deference to authority.

Stage 2: "Instrumental-relativist" stage. Right is determined by what satisfies one's own needs and occasionally the needs of others. Elements of fair play exist, but only in terms of a "you scratch my back, I'll scratch yours" orientation.

Conventional Level. The predominant value here is conformity and loyalty to personal expectations and social order. There is active support of the individual family, group, or nation.

Stage 3: "Good boy-nice girl" stage. Good is defined by what pleases and is approved of by others. The individual earns approval by being good or nice.

Stage 4: "Law and order" stage. Right is defined by "doing one's duty," by keeping the law for its own sake, and by respecting authority.

Postconventional Level. Here there is an effort to define moral values that have application apart from the persons or groups that hold these values.

Stage 5: "Social-contract legalistic" stage. Right is defined in terms of general individual rights that have been agreed on by society as a whole. There is an emphasis on legal rights, but with consideration of changing the law for greater social utility.

Stage 6: "Universal ethical-principle" stage. Right is defined by decision of conscience in accord with self-chosen ethical principles that appeal to "logical comprehensiveness, universality, and consistency." These are the principles of justice, equality, and respect for humans as individuals.

(Adapted from Kohlberg, L., Moral and Religious Education and the Public Schools, in *Religion and Public Education* ed. T. R. Sizer.

In the stage commonly called "the good boy-nice girl" stage, the person's values are derived from those actions that please or help others and that are approved by them. Thus, both the values and the decisions made are based on earning approval from others. If we wish to earn approval from the hospital administration system, for example, we will make decisions based on the needs and wants of the administration. If approval from patients and their families is what we seek, then our decisions will be based on their needs and wants. An example of conflict here would be in deciding whether to uphold visiting hours (system want) when a family wishes to stay with the patient (family want).

In the "law and order" stage, values are derived from maintaining the rules and regulations. This basis for decision making shows a strong orientation toward authority and maintenance of order. The key here, in terms of decision making, is who or what is viewed as authority and which set of rules and standards are upheld. Very different decisions will result from viewing the patient as authority than from viewing the physician as authority.

The next stage is what is known as the "social contract" or "individual rights" stage. In this stage, values revolve around the welfare and protection of all people's rights, which is often described as seeking the "greatest good for the greatest number." Here, there is an awareness that human beings hold a variety of values and that these values often conflict. Decisions are based on seeking a solution that is right for most people. At this stage, decisions may be difficult because no single solution will ever satisfy all concerned parties. Compromises are often made that balance system needs with patient needs. In this stage, many people are also involved in attempting to change the system for the betterment of the patient and the staff.

Because people are in constant interaction with their environment, the development of values is a lifelong process. A person may move from one stage to another or change orientation within a particular stage as new input is received or organized in new ways. It is extremely important, however, to be aware of where we stand and what we value so that we are able to determine how these factors influence the decisions we make. We can become aware of our personal values through values clarification activities.

Activity
Examine what you value both personally and professionally, by making a list of each. The book *Values Clarification: A Handbook of Practical Strategies for Teacher and Students* by Simon, Howe, and Kirschebaum (1972), which contains values clarification exercises, may be helpful in this listing process. (See also Chapter 10 for a discussion of value clarification.)

Are your personal and professional values congruent? Are your professional values congruent with the values of others in the profession as well as with those of the system in which you work? How do these values influence the course of the decisions you make? Can you think of examples where a conflict in values hindered your decision-making process?

SELF-ESTEEM

Self-esteem and confidence also play a part in the way that decisions are made. If people are comfortable with who they are and what their purpose is, then they are more likely to risk failure or success in making decisions. It should be noted, however, that many people with a low sense of self-esteem often invite failure by taking gigantic risks, with the negative consequences far outweighing the potential benefits. Confidence in the ability to make decisions also determines the risk that one is willing to assume. Past experience plays a large role in this situation. If one has a history of making successful decisions and of learning from mistakes, one can build confidence in one's decision-making abilities. It is very important in this building process to work within a system that is tolerant of error and that encourages growth and learning from failures as well as success.

Activity
Ask yourself the following questions. How confident are you in your abilities? Are you willing to take risks? Are the risks in line with the benefits? Do you view mistakes as a way to grow or as an indication of failure? How are your decisions affected by the way you view yourself and your abilities?

ROLES AND FUNCTIONS

The roles and functions that are assumed within a given system also influence decisions. If you view yourself in the role of patient advocate, for example, the decisions you make are likely to be quite different from those who view themselves as advocates of the system. If you see one of your primary functions as listening and comforting, your approach to patients will be different than if you consider one of your primary functions to be that of giving information and dispensing treatment.

Activity
Make a list of those roles and functions that you perform on the job. Which ones do you view as most important? In what ways do they influence the ways that you make decisions? Are you satisfied with the role and functions that you have chosen as your priorities?

The decisions people make are also affected by whether they are primarily derived from a task-oriented or a people-centered approach. These different bases for decisions hold both for the people involved in the decision-making process and for those who are affected by the decisions. If one is highly task oriented, then getting the task done or accomplishing a goal will take precedence over consideration of the people affected by such action. Those with a high people orientation will consider the wishes and needs of the people affected, perhaps even to the detriment of achieving the goal or task. By the same token, a highly task-oriented person seldom involves others in the decision-making process. Rather, a decision is reached and pressed on others for action. However, a highly people-centered person may involve large numbers of people in the process of making the decision and will often refuse to act until some kind of consensus is reached.

Nurses often find themselves in conflict as a result of their orientation. Many nurses enter the profession in order to care for people. This people-centered approach results in conflict when nurses find themselves in a system that is highly task oriented. Obviously, some sort of balance in needed to arrive at optimum decisions. If nurses value both the people involved and the task, they can employ a decision-making process that seeks the best compromise. A compromise will allow for both accomplishment of the goal and consideration of the people affected without sacrificing one for the other.

Activity
Consider whether you operate from a task- or people-oriented approach. For which approach are you rewarded in the organization in which you work? How has the orientation of the organization influenced the way in which you make decisions? If you operate primarily from one orientation or the other, how might you find a better balance?

CONTROL MOTIVATION

The way in which we view and use control also affects our decisions. In his social learning theory, Rotter (1974) expounds the concept of internal versus external locus of control. Internally controlled people believe that they can act to alter outcomes in their lives. Externally controlled people believe that outcomes are largely a matter of change or luck. Those with an internal locus of control are more likely to take an active part in ongoing decision processes. Those with an external locus of control are more likely to allow others to make decisions, to make no decision (other than the decision not to decide), or to postpone making decisions until the very last minute and to trust luck to pull them through.

The amount of control one needs also affects the decision-making process. A person with a great need for control may make and attempt to implement all decisions independently of other people, or to make and press that decision on others. This is the person who constantly checks and rechecks every phase of the process and who often gets so bogged down in the collection of voluminous data and the generation of multiple alternatives that the process becomes overwhelming. A person with less need for control operates more effectively in arriving at and implementing group decisions. This person usually wlecomes differing opinion as it generates new perspectives and a wider range of alternatives.

The amount of control needed is often related to self-esteem. A high or excessively low need for control indicates poor self-esteem and little trust in the ability of others. A person who is able to loosen the control reigns is often more secure in self-esteem and is better able to trust the abilities of others. Balanced control—neither too much nor too little—leads not only to more optimum decisions but also to an increased sense of power.

Activity
Ask yourself how much control you generally exercise? Do you trust your abilities and those of others? Do you leave matters to chance or fate?

STRUCTURE

Finally, it is important to examine how much structure or freedom one needs to feel comfortable in making decisions. A person who is accustomed to or needs guidelines and boundaries within which to make a decision may feel totally overwhelmed when given endless freedom and unlimited time. Another person who functions quite effectively when given an endless range of choices and freedom may feel hampered and frustrated by superimposed guidelines and directives.

It is important for the nurse to determine how much

structure is comfortable and will promote the making of optimum decisions. Once this is determined, it is possible to negotiate with others for more or less structure and guidance. It is also possible for people to set up their own structure to aid in the decision-making process.

Activity
Consider the amount of guidance you feel comfortable with. Are you getting it? Are you getting too much? Do you set up guidelines and structures for yourself, for others?

Deciding on the Best Approach

Analysis of both the overt and covert elements involved in making a decision will result in a better understanding of one's own decisions as well as those of others. Once an understanding of the elements involved is gained, the choice and use of those elements will increase decision-making capabilities. Since many of the elements involved in making a decision are subjective in nature, there is no one style or model of decision making that suits everyone. Thus, your task will be to evolve an individual style that best suits your personality and work setting. As nurses put their own style into practice and gain confidence in its use, they will discover that they have the capacity to act. Hence, nurses will gather power and use their unique abilities and talents to their fullest.

TIME MANAGEMENT

All nurses have wished more than once for just a little extra time to do what had to be done. A commonly voiced response of nurses to new job demands or expanded roles is, "There just isn't enough time!" How many times have the following situations occurred: sitting down to begin chart-ing and paperwork chores fifteen to thirty minutes after the shift is over; wishing a few extra minutes could be spared for patient teaching or simply to sit with a patient in distress; needing more frequent contact with other mem-bers of the health care team? If any of these are routine occurrences in your practice, effective use of time may be the problem.

The following sections speak to the concept of time, the philosophy of time management and to time-management techniques and common time wasters. This information will allow for the development of effective strategies for managing time, thus increasing your sense of power.

Time

Time is viewed as a very important commodity in Ameri-can culture. Consider the number of ways that our lives are run by the clock, the calendar, or that all-important date book. Many of us live on a schedule. We get up, go to bed, eat meals, go to work and even play at certain fixed times. We view our lives in terms of past, present, or future time orientations. We have clocks and watches that tell us the time is 10:17 and 32 seconds. We form value judgments about people who are constantly late, or early, to meetings or social engagements. In short, we exist in a time-oriented society.

Time is one resource that can only be spent. It will not stand still; it cannot be stored or reused. Once spent, it is irretrievable. For many individuals, time is not only pre-cious but increasingly scarce. Thus, in this mechanized, computerized, and complex society, management of this precious resource has become an increasingly needed and often underused skill.

Time Management: A Philosophy

What is time management? Very simply, it is a philosophi-cal approach for deriving maximum benefit from minimum time investments. Unfortunately, the word time management often evokes images of endless schedules, lists, and mechanistic tools. Hence, many people begin to feel like slaves to the very timesaving techniques that they have instituted. However, time management need not be overly time-consuming or rigidly organized. In fact, excessively rigid and detailed time-management programs are self-defeating (Smith & Besnette, 1978).

A successful time-management program is predicated on a philosophy that views time as a limited resource to be used to its fullest, rather than a collection of controlling devices that map out each minute of the day. Successful time management becomes a continuous positive reinforcer for itself (Smith & Besnette, 1978). As a person learns to control and maximize the time available, the positive benefits accrued act as a stimulus for that person to continue managing time effectively.

Effective time management occurs not as a result of mere mechanics, but as a result of viewing time use in a different psychological and philosophical light. Managing time really means managing self. Certain simple techniques are great aids for effective time use, but only if time is seen from a certain perspective. The first step in effective time management is to stop and consider how you view time and whether you desire to use your time to its fullest potential. In short, what is your philosophy about time and its use?

If you have decided that time is precious and that you wish to derive maximum benefit from your time investments, then the next few pages contain ideas to help you achieve that goal. Keep in mind that the techniques presented are suggestions. Try them out. If they work for you, use them; if not, discard them. Tailor your own time-management program. Design it to fit your own needs.

Evaluation of Time Use

A time-management program is best approached by first evaluating the current use of the time available. This analysis will provide insight into current time-use habits and routines. It will also allow identification of areas where time is routinely wasted or poorly used.

There are a number of effective methods for analyzing time use. Jackson and Hayden (1974) provide a questionnaire format that can be easily adapted for nurses and nursing. Alec Mackenzie (1972) also offers an excellent process for measuring time use in his book *The Time Trap*. His method involves setting goals and priorities along a time line the day before the evaluation day. A follow-up log is then kept for the day that the priorities were set. Here, the person keeps track of actual tasks accomplished and the time used in accomplishing them. A comparison can then be made between what was planned and what actually occurred.

These tools are helpful, or a new one may be devised. For example, the events of a particular day could be recalled to account for the time from rising to bedtime. This method may be used to pinpoint when time is wasted. The tool chosen to make that initial evaluation of time use may also be used periodically to evaluate the effectiveness of time management technique.

Time Wasters and Time-Management Techniques

There are a number of habits that "fritter away" and waste time. Three of the most common in nursing seem to be procrastination, indecision, and operating in a constant crisis mode.

PROCRASTINATION

The chief motivation for procrastination is usually fear— fear of failure, fear of rejection, or fear of embarrassment. People tend to put off those tasks that they perceive as unpleasant or awkward. These tasks may range from making a phone call to the laboratory about a blood sample that was not drawn, to answering the call light of a demanding patient, to arranging a conference with the head nurse about unsatisfactory work assignments. There are numerous elements in the everyday work setting that cause uneasy feelings resulting in procrastination.

Activity
In order to tackle the tendency to procrastinate, you must first examine those things that you routinely put off until the last minute. Armed with such a list, you can then analyze your fears. What are you afraid of? Is the fear real or is it exaggerated? A good way to check this out is to fantasize about the worst thing that could happen. In the case of the phone call to the laboratory, for example, you might decide that the worst that could happen might be that the technician would be gruff or refuse to return to draw the sample.

Spend a minute and list three things that you have put off or delayed doing in the past week. Ask yourself, "What is the worst thing that could happen if I do these tasks?" Often the answer boils down to momentary embarrassment or discomfort. Or, you may discover no fear at all; rather, you have just gotten into a habit of putting things off until the last minute. However, if there is a fear that remains, the next step is to imagine yourself actually doing the task. Picture yourself performing it with smooth confidence and a calm manner. This type of mental imaging often gives you a feeling of control and strengthens your belief in your abilities to handle the situation.

BREAK THE HABIT OF PROCRASTINATION

If you find that procrastination has become a way of life, you might try one or more of the following suggestions to help you break the habit:

Doing It First
One very direct approach is to identify the most unpleasant task of the day and do it immediately. This not only cuts off deadly delaying tactics; it also quickly disposes of

the most unpleasant item of the day. An added advantage is that having successfully faced and accomplished the unpleasant early in the day, you can face the rest of the day with confidence and a sense of control. You have, in effect, set a positive tone for the day. So start right now. Make a decision about which task you are dreading the most and do it immediately.

Bite-size Pieces
There is an old elephant joke that asks, "How do you eat a two-ton elephant?" The answer, of course, is "one bite at a time." This line of logic works well if the task is large and seems overwhelming, another prime reason for procrastination. If you find yourself putting off a major task, try breaking it up into several smaller and more manageable steps. Then resolve to carry out the first step immediately. You may want to list each identified step and post the list in a conspicuous place. Then, as each step is finished, cross it off the list. This strategy not only makes a seemingly overwhelming task manageable, but provides a source of growing staisfaction as more and more steps on the list are crossed off. So tackle that elephant one bite at a time when you are next faced with a big job that seems impossible.

Gain-loss Columns
A third approach is to tally up what you gain and what you lose when you delay accomplishment of a certain task or chore. To use this tactic, simply grab a piece of paper and draw a gain column and a loss column. Then, list what you have to gain by procrastination of the task under the gain column and what you have to lose under the loss column. Quite frequently, the only reasons in the gain column will be items like avoiding embarrassment or avoiding an argument. The loss column often contains items such as time loss, guilt feelings, inability to think of anything else, the fact that the task must still be done, and so forth. This approach quickly and graphically illustrates the general disadvantages of procrastination.

Whatever combination of ideas you choose to help you break the procrastination habit, you will find that with a little persistence, a new set of timesaving habits will soon replace the impulse to "put it off."

INDECISION

Nurses are required to make on-the-spot decisions every day in the course of their work. Failure to make those decisions promptly and to proceed onward is a major time waster. It also makes others hesitant to grant control or power over larger issues. Indecision takes the form of agonizing over the decision-making process, vacillating between choices, or being afraid of making a mistake. In fact, the biggest mistake made is the very act of indecision. While some decisions involving major change require time and thought, many decisions are daily, routine occurrences where a real advantage is gained by decisive action that insures uninterrupted job functioning. For any situation, there are several alternatives that could lead to successful results, not just one "right" way. Act decisively on any one of those several alternatives, and you will maintain a smooth flow of action.

CRISIS MENTALITY

Many nurses operate in a crisis mode; that is, no decisions are made until a crisis arises demanding that some action be taken. When this mode is in operation, all response is *reaction* oriented rather than *action* oriented. Soon a vicious cycle is created in which all decisions are provoked by crises, routines are disrupted, and feelings of powerlessness ensue, which reinforce reactive behavior. As one becomes enmeshed in the cycle of pressure, frustration and anger build until there is a feeling of being trapped in a hopeless maze. This state feels much like being in a pressure cooker, with no steam value for relief. If you find yourself faced with an endless series of crises, then you may be operating in a reaction-oriented crisis mode.

There are many causes of crisis, which include improper planning, muddled communications, failure to anticipate, lack of priority setting, and failure to delegate and follow through after delegation. Indecisiveness and procrastination also play major roles in generating crises because they reinforce a reaction-oriented mode of operation.

Planning, Anticipating, Prioritizing

Planning for and anticipation of events can avert many crises. Plans, of course, need not be formal or "chiseled in stone." However, a game plan is always helpful whether playing football or working an eight-hour shift. One easy method of planning is to briefly review and jot down the tasks that need to be done for that particular day. Once this is accomplished, the items can be ranked in priority. The setting of priorities may be done according to urgency or importance (Bliss, 1976). Most people tend to set priorities according to urgency; that is, when a task absolutely must be done. What must be done immediately is done and everything else is delayed. But soon, tasks are accomplished only when they must be done to meet a deadline, and consequently important tasks do not receive enough thought and planning.

If, however, tasks are scheculed first by importance and then by urgency, a new plan emerges. Bliss (1976) suggests a strategy for setting up priorities that can prove to be quite effective. He suggests starting with a list of things to be done for the day (the daily game plan). Then each item is reviewed in light of its importance by placing a check next to the items that contribute to the accomplishment of established short- and long-range goals. Each checked item is scrutinized for how soon it must be done and how long it will take. Then, with consideration of all these factors (importance, time needed, and urgency), the items are numbered in the order that they will be done. The unchecked items are then ordered by priority. This strategy offers a balanced system of planning work to be done.

Communication, Delegation, Follow-through

The well-known verse, "the best laid schemes o' mice an' men gang aft agley" is food for thought at this point. Planning and setting priorities are ineffective if certain ideas are not shared with others in the setting. Clear, concise communication and delegation are essential in the work environment. Muddled messages and mixed messages about who is to do what are monstrous time wasters and feed into a cycle of confusion and reactive behavior. If you find that others seldom understand what you say or that you have difficulty getting your ideas heard or accepted, then your communication skills may be lacking. These skills can be improved and developed through self-help books or workshops.

When it comes to delegating tasks, too many people feel they have more power to control if they do it all themselves. Or they nuture the idea that the only way to get things done right is to do it themselves. This is not only poor time management; it also stifles growth and responsibility in subordinates. Failure to delegate tasks also inhibits teamwork and encourages a crisis operation mode as the daily routine becomes unmanageable for one person.

Successful delegation entails involving others in such a manner as to fully use their talents and abilities. It requires that trusting relationships be fostered so that sufficient authority is delegated to another for decision making. Proper delegation thus fosters the sharing of power and control. Ultimately, this shared power approach generates more power for the delegator because subordinates—given sufficient power to operate effectively—reinvest power and entrust it with the one who delegates.

Follow-through after delegating a task is a *must* to insure success. It promotes smoother operations, leaves less room for the occurrence of a crisis, and gives the subordinate an operating frame of reference. Yet, follow-through does not imply constantly looking over a subordinate's shoulder; rather it means setting a frame for the task and planning a time for evaluation of the task at completion. This evaluation period once again calls for clear and open communication about whether the task was completed satisfactorily.

If these suggestions are used, crisis situations will occur with less frequency and more time for other things will be generated. In addition, when real crisis situations occur, the effective time manager will feel more in control and ready to cope with them.

Miscellaneous Tips

This section contains a few selected tidbits to round out your time-management program.

Remember that time management may be used in home life as well as at work. For example, delegating some household chores to other family members not only frees time, but also builds responsibility and a sense of control for children and spouses.

Many people have difficulty in turning down requests and must learn the art of saying "no." (See Chapter 8 for a discussion of how to say "no" assertively without guilt.) Unless requests that do not contribute to your priorities, pleasure, or well-being can be firmly declined, all the time that you have carefully saved through time management will be consumed by others.

In managing personal and professional time, it is important to consider personal needs for rest and recreation. Rest is vital to efficient and effective functioning. Work time must include scheduled breaks in a place conducive to relaxation. Fun, exercise, and proper nutrition can receive the attention of the nurse who has effectively managed time, and these are primary contributors to mental and physical well-being.

SUMMARY

Effective decision making and time management are two skills that go hand in hand in developing a broader power base. Each increases our capacity to act, which is the very key to power. In addition, both of these concepts offer much promise in the field of research. To date, much of the research on decision making has focused on the analysis and evaluation of the effectiveness of various decision-making skills. More research is needed about the influence of covert factors upon the decision-making process. Research on time management has dealt primarily with time and motion studies or with the evaluation of highly elaborate and complicated systems designed to measure efficient time use. More research is needed to examine factors that interfere with effective time use and ways to decrease the influence of these factors. Studies on procrastination, crisis operation, and indecision as time wasters may provide valuable insight about effective time management.

Further research can make it possible to develop effective decision-making and time-management skills with greater precision and ease. All of these will lend to an increased power base and to a fuller development of talents and abilities.

BIBLIOGRAPHY

Bernhard, L. & Walsh, M.: *Leadership: The Key to the Professionalization of Nursing.* New York, McGraw-Hill, 1981.

Bliss, E. C.: *Getting Things Done, The ABC's of Time Management.* New York, Charles Scribner's Sons, 1976.

Jackson, J. A. & Hayden, R. L.: Rationing the scarcest resource: a manager's time. *Personnel Journal* Oct.:753, 1974.

Kohlberg, L.: Stages and aging in moral development. *Gerontologist* Winter: 497–502, 1973.

Mackenzie, R.A.: *The Time Trap.* New York, McGraw-Hill, 1972.

Rotter, J. B. & Liverant, S.: Social learning theory. In Washburne N. F. (ed.): *Decisions, Value, and Groups.* New York, Macmillan, 1974.

Simon, S. B., Howe, L. W., & Kirschenbaum, H.: *Values Clarification: A Handbook of Practical Strategies for Teacher and Students.* New York, Hart, 1972.

Smith, H. L. & Besnette, F. H.: Effective time management: the forgotten administrative and nursing supervisor art. *Hospital Topics* Jan/Feb:32–37, 1978.

RECOMMENDED READINGS

Decision Making

Bernhard, L. & Walsh, M.: *Leadership: The Key to the Professionalization of Nursing.* New York, McGraw-Hill, 1981.

This short paperback offers a variety of strategies to enhance the effectiveness of leadership skills. The chapter on decision making presents and evaluates five decision-making models. Each model outlines a step-by-step process and is accompanied by a practical illustration demonstrating the model's usefulness.

Garofalo Ford, J. A., Trygstad-Durland, L. N., & Crew Melms, B.: *Applied Decision Making for Nurses.* St. Louis, C. V. Mosby, 1979.

This short self-study paperback illustrates practical uses of both covert and overt elements of the decision-making process. It is geared to nurses and nursing decisions.

Steele, S. M. & Harmon, V. M.: *Values Clarification in Nursing.* New York, Appleton-Century-Crofts, 1979.

This slim paperback presents the process of values clarification for nurses. Included are case studies and a chapter on values clarification exercises. A concise explanation of Kohlberg's theory of moral development is also incorporated. It should prove helpful in allowing the reader to explore his or her own value systems to aid in the decision-making process.

Time Management

Bliss, E. C.: *Getting Things Done, The ABC's of Time Management.* New York, Chalres Scribner's Sons, 1976.

This slim volume provides a humorous and helpful approach to time management. It offers numerous insightful suggestions for eliminating time-wasting activities.

Mackenzie, R. A.: *The Time Trap.* New York, McGraw-Hill, 1972.

This is a helpful primer on time management. It contains a number of practical illustrations to improve the use of your time. Included are methods for setting goals and priorities, as well as for evaluation of progress made in learning to use time effectively.

10

PERSONAL POWER AND THE NATURE OF NURSING

HARRIET L. SANDERS

This chapter examines a unique issue of power—that is, the very nature of nursing and its contribution to, or detraction from, the nurse's power and influence. The topics of interest here are (1) the outcomes of nursing education, both positive and negative, and (2) the ever-present stress that seems to permeate nursing, be it clincial, educational, or administrative.

The evolution of today's nursing education is, in many ways, a success story. Programs have moved with great speed from apprenticeships to academically based degrees, which, of course, has added to the nurse's expert power. Nursing education, however, has produced several situations that detract from power. The variety of educational requirements for entry level into practice discussed in Chapter 2 is partially due to the rapid evolution of educational programs. In the wake of rapid changes in education, nurses prepared at various entry levels (associate degree, diploma, and bachelor's degree) are unclear about similarities and differences in their competencies. The resulting negative impact of this situation has already been addressed in Chapter 2. A second detraction from power produced by the evolution of nursing education is the phenomenon of *reality shock.* This phenomenon results from the conflict that occurs when students are socialized to hold one value system during education and then, upon graduation, find themselves in a work setting that holds a quite different value system (Kramer, 1974). The difficult transition from school to work setting *can* be managed and its obstruction to power reduced if the nurse is aware of the phenomenon of reality shock and has a clear understanding of the value systems that are in conflict. Once the barrier of reality shock is removed, the nurse has access to one of the most potent sources of power derived from education: expertise.

Another barrier to power related to the nature of nursing is the stress that is present in all aspects of nursing practice. Several factors contribute to this stress. Clearly, nursing is a profession that provides services to people, and most often these services are of a nature that is essential to recovery from illness. The competencies of the nurse are therefore usually vital to the welfare or health of another, thus making the responsibilities of practice weigh heavily on the practitioner. The stress that results can decrease the nurse's professional and personal impact.

In the following sections, the nature of nursing is discussed as it acts as a power-enhancing factor and as it acts as a power-inhibiting factor. Specifically, the topics discussed are (1) education, expertise, and power; (2) reality shock, values and power; and (3) stress.

EDUCATION, EXPERTISE, AND POWER

A factor not fully recognized or used by many nurses who attempt to influence the system is that the nurse occupies a special role in health care delivery and possesses unique expertise and perspective of the totality of care. The holistic approach and 24-hour care provided by nurses are vital aspects of this role. By comparison, other members of the health care team have a relatively fragmented knowledge of the patient and the care required. However, the nurse has the ability to put together all the elements of the care required to benefit the whole person, thus making the nurse's role potentially powerful as a member of the health care team and as a patient advocate.

In addition to the nurse's 24-hour, holistic care, a second source of expert power stemming from education is the nursing process. The nurse's expertise derives from the use of a problem-solving approach based on scientific knowledge; that is, the nursing process. With this process and knowledge of basic scientific principles, the nurse can function in a variety of diverse situations. This flexibility renders the nurse valuable in many settings, ranging from wellness clinics to acute care settings to hospices. From all these bases, nurses have the potential to develop an influential voice in health care.

Another power-enhancing factor that originally evolved from education is the growth of nursing research. A body of distinct nursing knowledge is being developed through nursing research. "Research can help to clarify underlying theories and concepts related to nursing, each step leading toward an identification of a nursing science" (Abdellah & Levine, 1965). As the science of nursing is developed, the status of the profession will be enhanced. In this way, research contributes to the nurse's expert power base. Moreover, the importance of research-based nursing practice is evident today in the research activities now being based in clinical settings.

The acquisition of advanced education is also a means of attaining expert power. "A person gains expert power through knowledge, skills, and information" (Marriner, 1980). French and Raven (1968) have asserted that the strength of expert power depends on the degree of knowledge that others perceive the person to have. This power is limited to the specific area in which the expertise lies. Therefore, the path to expert power is open to nurses who are willing to attain expertise through education as well as clinical experience. The ability to apply high-level theoretical concepts to the clinical area would increase the scope of the nurse's expertise to expand theoretical and clinical application. In addition, advanced education opens the door to job opportunities and positions with power that were unavailable before. These are positions of authority that carry some measure of legitimate power. A higher level of power can be attained if the nurse is seen as possessing expert power, thereby increasing the scope of her or his influence. Advanced degrees attached to your name lends additional legitimacy to your opinions while your experience in an area of specialization gives credence to your ideas and plans. Advanced preparation also qualifies the nurse to conduct research and contribute to theory development.

With the evolution of nursing education, the expert power base of the professional has been increased. This expertise has several aspects: (1) the holistic approach of nursing is supported by applying a nursing process that is based on science and research; and (2) advanced education directly adds to expert power and indirectly adds to it by increasing research activities.

REALITY SHOCK, VALUES, AND POWER

The education of nurses has contributed to their power and influence. However, one aspect of the education process has indirectly distracted from power. This aspect is reality shock.* Reality shock is ". . . the phenomenon and specific shock like reactions of new workers when they find themselves in a work situation for which they have spent several years preparing and for which they thought they were going to be prepared, and then suddenly find out they are not" (Kramer, 1974).

Causes of Reality Shock

Several types of conflicts cause Reality shock. The major conflict that occurs during the nurse's transition from education to work is the professional-bureaucratic conflict (Kramer, 1974). To understand this conflict it is necessary to understand the evolution of bureaucracy as a system of work organization.

---

*Much of this discussion is based on the concepts developed by Marlene Kramer and Claudia Schmalenberg.

Bureaucracy evolved as a result of the standardization and interchangeability of parts in the production of goods. This "assembly line" approach was developed to increase productivity, with the result that it led to a part-task division of labor. As we know, on an automobile assembly line, one worker assembles hoods while another bolts on wheels. At the same time, this approach required a supervisory role since it was necessary for one person to have knowledge of the whole process. As this bureaucratic approach proved very effective for the industrial production of goods, it was believed that it could also be applied to the production of services. Thus functional nursing was born. Then, because the bureaucratic concept was inherently unworkable with human services, the human relations approach emerged. However, the part-task system of work organization is still prominent in the delivery of health care, especially in hospital settings. For example, one nurse may take the vital signs of all the patients while another administers the medications for the whole unit.

In contrast, work organization within a profession is arranged in a whole-task system which enables the professional to provide more complete services. This approach necessitates a broader base of knowledge and, therefore, a long preparation time. The control for accomplishing the task does not come from a supervisor but rather from a sense of professional accountability. In nursing, a whole-task orientation would mean that the nurse provides comprehensive, individualized care to the patient and family. Primary nursing is an example of nursing care delivered in a whole-task system.

Conflict occurs because the nurse's educational preparation is oriented to the whole-task approach and accompanying values while the nurse's work in the health care organization is oriented to the part-task approach and bureaucratic values. As the nurse moves from the preparation phase to the work phase, a professional-bureaucratic conflict arises between the two disparate sets of values.

In addition to the professional-bureaucratic conflict, two other factors contribute to reality shock: backstage reality and different feedback systems. Backstage reality is that reality which the student nurse seldom, if ever, sees before graduation. Some time after employment the new nurse discovers that the things that go on every day do not match—and may even violate—the principles or values learned in school. One instance of this reality is that the nurse may administer a drug about which he or she knows little. The new nurse finds this shocking because the school standard dictated that the actions of a drug must be understood by the nurse before administering it.

The differing feedback systems that exist in school and work also contribute to reality shock. In school, the feedback from instructors was predictable, balanced between positive and negative, direct, and usually patient centered; for example, "Your organization was good, sterile technique was good, but you need to provide more explanation to the patient." In the work setting, feedback is somewhat different. It is unpredictable, mostly negative, indirect, global, and often disguised. Consequently, in the work setting, the nurse's attitude toward feedback is likely to be "no news is good news." Further, professional ideals are often unrewarded in the work setting so that the new nurse is left feeling unsure of progress and adequacy of performance.

These three factors—professional-bureaucratic conflict, backstage reality, and differing feedback systems—make the transition from school to work a difficult one. The reaction of the new nurse to these conflicts is the phenomenon called reality shock.

Phases of Reality Shock

Reality shock is a recognized sociological phenomenon that occurs in many practice professions, nursing included. Kramer (1974) defines reality shock as "the startling discovery and reaction to the discovery that school-bred values conflict with work-world values." The neophyte nurse is frustrated because all that was learned in school is not seen in actual practice.

Four phases of the phenomenon of reality shock have been identified by Kramer (1974). These phases are (1) honeymoon, (2) shock and rejection, (3) recovery, and (4) resolution. In the honeymoon phase, the graduate is experiencing many positive aspects of employment. The nurse is receiving a paycheck and can now be self-supporting. The new nurse is also being socially integrated into the unit staff. This is a time when the new graduate can take advantage of the opportunity to master skills. It is also a time when she or he can develop relationships with co-workers and establish some social power. During this phase, the new graduate has boundless enthusiasm for the job. It is a period of high-energy levels and a positively distorted perception.

This enthusiasm wanes in the shock phase. During this phase, the nurse discovers conflicting values and methods of functioning. Frustration and anger abound; perceptions are negatively distorted. Some reactions include "Didn't these nurses learn anything in school?" or "Why didn't my instructors prepare me for this?" The graduate experiences a loss of satisfaction as a result of high-level goals and a decreased level of achievement. The high energy of the honeymoon phase has now been replaced by fatigue and depression.

The recovery phase is marked by the return of the graduate's ability to find humor in the case at hand (Schmalenberg & Kramer, 1979); the new nurse is now able to view the job more realistically. During this period, the new graduate is able to start reassessing the situation in the hope of resolving it.

The last phase is that of resolution. There are several directions that resolution can take. One of these is job-hopping. Here, the graduate moves from job to job seeking the "perfect hospital," not realizing that it does not exist. Another type of resolution is to go back to school in an attempt to remove the perceived deficiencies. This type of resolution is referred to as the "lateral arabesque" (Kramer & Schmalenberg, 1977). The nurse may even attempt to resolve conflict by limiting involvement in the job. There, the prevailing attitude is "It's just a job; I'm not going to let it get to me!" Two more methods of dealing with this conflict are to turn the conflict inward and "burn-out" or to quit the profession altogether (Kramer & Schmalenberg, 1977). The nurse who has "burned-out" develops a negative attitude. None of these types of resolutions are constructive for the nurse or the patients.

The successful resolution of reality shock is biculturalism (Kramer, 1974). The bicultural nurse is able to function in the "culture" of the new work world while retaining the values learned in the "culture" of school. These nurses are able to make a valuable contribution to health care.

Making the Most of Reality Shock

While the occurrence of reality shock is a hindrance to power, its effects can be lessened. Measures can be taken that will make the transition less traumatic for the new nurse and the resolution more positive. Kramer and Schmalenberg have identified conflict as "the cutting edge of growth" (1976). Indeed, conflict presents an opportunity for constructive resolution. An obvious example of this is the "survivor" of reality shock. A survivor is the one who has resolved the conflicts inherent in transition and is now bicultural. Indeed, a new graduate who adequately prepares to face the approaching reality shock usually emerges with an increased sense of confidence and authority. Those survivors of realtiy shock who have been adequately forewarned resolve the conflicts earlier. The sooner the nurse gains self-confidence in his or her abilities, the sooner professional knowledge can be applied. Nurses go through the process of resolving these conflicts without ever realizing the intrinsic power available. Yet, the ability to function in both subcultures—to be bi-cultural—is a source of power and influence.

This influence may exist both on a personal as well as a group level. The comments and suggestions that have come out of various reality shock seminars could be presented in a constructive manner to nursing service administrators, thereby helping to lessen the severity of reality shock for other new graduates. These comments and statements are profitable information for the institution since many nurses use coping mechanisms during the resolution phase that are not constructive, with the result that they sometimes leave the institution before becoming productive staff members. The hospital can protect its investment in neophyte nurses if it can effectively assist them through the resolution of reality shock.

Each of the phases of reality shock presents an opportunity for the new nurse to grow. How can the experience be a positive one? The following are suggested ways of coping with each phase to make the outcome more positive.

The honeymoon phase is a time of high energy and positive outlook. During this time, channel energy into building the support system that you will need during the next phase. Offer help to coworkers and ask questions to find out what others think and value. Use your energy to master skills and the routine of the work setting. In four to five weeks, the competency you will have gained in performing skills will build self-confidence. And self-confidence in turn will help to cushion the negative perceptions of the shock phase that will follow.

The negative perceptions of the shock phase make it perhaps the most difficult with which to deal. Physical exhaustion and the increased need for sleep leave little energy to focus on dealing with the anger present during this phase. However, dealing with this anger is of prime importance in order to move on to the next stage. The first step in resolving the conflict is to accept feelings of moral outrage, disappointment, and anger. Talking with a peer can also help, but the conscious selection of that person is important. The best person to choose is one who understands and who can listen without being judgmental or becoming defensive. This person must not be on the same unit. Moreover, it is important that the listener not suggest solutions at this time, as the resolution must be accomplished by the new graduate. Having someone who will listen may not make this phase less painful but it will make it easier to deal with. During this time, socialization seminars are valuable as an outlet for the seemingly overwhelming frustrations. One constructive use of the distorted negative perceptions is to record the criticisms you make. Write down all the things you see wrong and all of your recommendations for change—but *only* write them down! Save them to review at a later time when (a) your perspective is more accurate and balanced, and (b) you are more aware of the history of the unit and the multiple aspects of the problem. After your sense of balance is restored and you have gained some social acceptance and power, review the list and *selectively* share those ideas that still seem viable.

In the recovery phase, balanced perspective is restored. It is a time of growth and creative problem solving. Use the energy to resolve the conflicts and to establish an identity and value system in the organization. Values clarification activities are useful during this phase.

The conscious choice of biculturalism as a positive means of resolving conflicts will lead to your valuing both the professional and bureaucratic aspects of the health care organization. Some factors that should be considered are awareness of your strengths and accomplishments, self-confidence, expertise gained through education, and personal communication effectiveness such as assertiveness. Organizational awareness should include a knowledge of formal and informal sources of influence within the system. Once the transitional phase is resolved, the new graduate can move on to establish other sources of power and influence.

The following are questions that a new graduate may ask

himself or herself in order to help assess where the areas of conflict exist and to establish ways of resolving them.

- What experiences caused you to feel inadequate as a nurse?

- What was your reaction to these experiences?

- How could these experiences have been handled to make you feel less negative?

- What experiences made you feel you were functioning well in your new role?

- Why did these experiences cause you to feel this way?

- What can you do to convert the negative experiences to positive ones?

Decreasing Reality Shock

If "school-bred values" create such conflicts, then why are they perpetuated? These values or ideals have been established by the profession as its standard. Yet in practice, some of these ideals have slipped quietly by the wayside because they seemed inexpedient in accordance with the circumstances. Often the excuse for their disappearance is a lack of time or a lack of staff to do things the ideal or right way.

Even though reality shock is recognized as an unsatisfactory situation, it can be inadvertently perpetuated by nurses. Experienced nurses who are in powerful positions do not realize that they are merely adding to the shock state by encouraging the new nurse to "see it like it really is." Unfortunately, it only contributes to the powerless feelings held by new graduates at this time to be "let in" on the backstage reality.

What can be done about the phenomenon of reality shock to remove it as a barrier to power? The key to diminishing reality shock lies with those in nursing education as well as with those in nursing service. These two groups must endeavor to balance theory and practice. Until they decide on a common ground where theory can be put into practice in the clinical area, reality shock will continue to occur. There is evidence of efforts being made toward this end. An example of such an effort is to have clinical specialists function as adjunct faculty. Their background helps to make the students clinically competent (Habgood, 1981), and their involvement in nursing education creates a closer alignment between theory and practice.

While reality shock still occurs, educators owe it to their students to make them aware of their strengths. Nursing educators teach students to be adaptable and to rely on sound nursing principles in unfamiliar situations. While this approach is commendable, it contributes to the new graduate's feelings of inadequacy in the new job. The graduate is frustrated because he or she does not know how to perform certain specific tasks. Educators should make students aware that they cannot know all the required tasks at once, and build the student's self-esteem by explaining the wisdom of using nursing principles and its long-term advantages.

Experienced nurses need to be reminded periodically through continuing education about the basic principles they were taught. They must also be made aware of the ways in which they can help to reduce the reality shock experienced by the new graduate, a responsibility that is often ignored. One way that experienced nurses can assist new graduates to cope with shock is to be supportive of their efforts. They can also help the new graduate in making decisions when the situation is ambiguous or difficult. This kind of assistance will also help to build the new graduate's self-esteem.

Some hospitals today are organizing Reality Shock or Socialization Seminars for new graduates. These are groups consisting of a leader and an assemblage of new graduates. The leader of the seminar should be knowledgeable in the processes of reality shock, crisis intervention, and group dynamics (Schmalenberg & Kramer, 1979).

The purpose of the group is to explore the problems and crises experienced by the new nurses. Through peer support, the group is able to help nurses resolve the conflicts they are experiencing and partially relieve the frustration experienced at this time.

Another method that may also be effective is to assign the new graduate to an experienced nurse within a "buddy" system. This provides the opportunity for the graduate to receive input as to method of operation, skill mastery, and protocol from just one person, thereby reducing conflicting messages from other staff. This also allows the experienced nurse a greater opportunity to support the new nurse and to build his or her self-esteem.

Each of these methods gives new graduates a feeling that the institution cares about them and their future. After all, both the new graduate and the institution have the same goal—a competent practitioner.

Values

Since the conflict between school-bred values and values in the work setting are at the heart of this difficult transition phase, reality shock can be more easily resolved and personal control gained when new graduates examine and clarify their value systems. Beyond this transitional phase, our value system is where all decisions in life originate (Uustal, 1980).

"A value is an effective disposition toward a person, object, or idea. Values represent a way of life, and give direction to life" (Steele & Harmon, 1979). They can change as the person learns and grows. How does an individual clarify personal and professional values? The values clarification process involves choosing freely from available alternatives after considering the consequences of one's decision; being proud of the choice and publicly endorsing it; and incorporating the value into behavior on a consistent basis (Uustal, 1978). Nurses must make a conscious effort to clarify their personal values. We all learned in nursing school that the nurse should not impose personal value judgments on the patient. How can the nurse do this if his or her personal values have not been explored and clarified? Uustal (1978) has devised several strategies to help the nurse assess values relative to several pertinent nursing subjects.

It is important for the nurse to assess what values he or she holds and their relative strengths. At the same time, the nurse also should learn to recognize what values others hold and use this knowledge in planning care. For example, the recognition of patients' values will help avoid imposing one's own values on them. To the patient, nursing is an influential profession but this influence must be thoughtfully exercised.

One thing that nurses must learn to value is their knowledge. If the profession does not recognize and value their distinct body of knowledge, which is essential to delivering a high level of health care, then no one else will value it. Nurses, as a group, have chosen values that they prize among themselves. However, the profession has not been effective in publicly affirming these beliefs or in consistently acting in accordance with their values. But can an entire profession agree on, and stand behind, one set of values? Or is it the profession's responsibility to lay the foundation on which its practitioners base their individual values?

Later in this chapter we discuss stress. Misplaced or imposed values are a source of stress. If a nurse is the subject of imposed values that he or she does not regard as worthy, then a source of stress is created from the conflict. Values can also be misplaced. For instance, if a nurse believes that all patients should get well as a result of good nursing care, that value is misplaced—it is unrealistic. The reality exists that patients do not always get well. This situation would then be stressful to the nurse whose values were misplaced and impossible to uphold.

Each nurse must assess her or his personal beliefs about whether or not power is valuable (Uustal, 1980). In other words, the profession must believe in power before nurses can effectively gain and use it.

Value clarification, then becomes a means of becoming more effective in decision making. In examining the origin of decisions, one can consciously develop a value system. The resulting personal control and awareness will enhance one's acquisition and ethical use of power.

STRESS MANAGEMENT

As nurses, we learn how patients are stressed and how to help them deal with their stressors. But we do not learn much about how to deal with our own stress. In fact, until fairly recently, no one admitted that nurses were ever stressed. When people are able to adequately handle stress, they are viewed as being "on top" of the situation, which is a source of power. Therefore, stress management is a means of removing a barrier to power.

First, let us deal with what stress is and how to handle it. Stress, as defined by Selye (1956), is the "state manifested by a specific syndrome which consists of all nonspecifically induced changes within a biologic system." In other words, it is a response that is nonspecific to the demands, both physical and emotional, that are made on an organism. Stress is a normal occurrence and is necessary to survival and well-being. "However, when stress becomes prolonged or excessive in relation to an individual's adaptive capacities, changes might well occur" (Smith & Selye, 1979).

The response to stress can be either physical or emotional. Some of the physical responses to stress include anorexia or overeating, urinary frequency, insomnia, lethargy, muscular aches, headaches, tachycardia, and blushing. Psychological disruptions include disorientation, disorganization, frustration, depression, indecisiveness, irritability, and withdrawal (Scully, 1980). Each person reacts to stress in a different way and may exhibit any combination of these responses.

Sources of Stress

A multitude of factors specific to nursing can be stressful for the nurse, including places where nurses work, and stages in a nursing career. Figure 10.1 outlines some of these factors.

One major complaint in hospitals today is a lack of staffing. If the deficiency of staff is viewed by the nurses on a unit as being significant, the situation can be stressful (Scully, 1980). The nurses have little time for essential nursing functions due to a lack of staff, so they view their care as inadequate. This is damaging to their self-esteem and is additionally stressful (Scully, 1980). If this type of situation is not resolved, the nurses feel powerless and as this feeling of powerlessness increases, the quality of care decreases (Kramer, 1974).

The nature of nursing itself can be a source of stress. Nurses often consider it stressful when they have several challenging and time-consuming patients to care for. If they are not accustomed to setting priorities, the situation may be overwhelming. Moreover, if the nurse does not adapt well, any new situation may be viewed as stressful.

Many nurses find it difficult to deal with the patient who is dying, and the family of the patient. This situation arouses many personal feelings about death and dying. It is potentially stressful, as the nurse often identifies with either the patient or the family. The inevitability of one's own death is also made clear and may be stressful if the nurse has not dealt with this. When the nurse is able to handle the stress of death and dying, it puts her or him in a position of power due to the ability to use knowledge and skills for the benefit of the patient and family.

Nature of Nursing
   Staffing deficiencies
   Difficult patient load
   Death and dying
   Varying types of staff

Places of Increased Stress
   Intensive Care Units
   Emergency Room

Times of Increased Stress
   New graduate
   Promotion
   Changing jobs

Figure 10.1
Stressors in Nursing.

New graduates, as well as nurses accustomed to all-professional staffs, may find it difficult to work with various types of staff members. Nurses may have difficulty relating to staff who are the age of their parents. For example, "How can I give directions to someone who is old enough to be my mother?" Other nurses have never had to deal with racially mixed staffs. This situation may be awkward if the interaction within the group is strained. One of the most frustrating and, therefore, potentially stressful circumstances is that of dealing with an incompetent staff member. The more vital the position of the incompetent staff member, the more stressful it is for others. If the institution places a high value on seniority, regardless of capability, the situation is even worse.

Nurses who work in specialty areas such as an intensive care unit or an emergency room are usually subjected to a higher level of stress. According to research involving members of the American Association of Critical Care Nurses, there are seven major sources of stress in intensive care units (Stephen & Bailey, 1979). These include (1) interpersonal conflicts involving coworkers, administrative personnel, or physicians; (2) management aspects of the unit itself; (3) pressures of direct patient care; (4) inadequate knowledge and skills on the part of the nurses; (5) the physical environment of the unit; (6) life events such as personal or family problems; and (7) lack of administrative rewards such as pay and benefits. The patients in this area are critically ill and the nurses have a high level of responsibility placed upon them. These are significant factors in raising their stress level.

There are several periods in a nurse's career that are more stressful than others. Most authorities agree that a new graduate usually experiences some measure of reality shock since the person is in a new environment with unfamiliar people and unfamiliar hospital policies and procedures. At this stage, the new graduate is also unsure of his or her nursing abilities. For the first time, this nurse does not have an instructor to turn to for guidance and to answer questions about nursing care.

New graduates may also find the conversion in lifestyles difficult. One day they were students who had nights, weekends, and holidays to use as they wished; now they are "low on the staffing pole" and have to rotate shifts, work weekends, and holidays. This is a difficult change for some to adjust to, especially when families and friends do not cooperate. And the change is particularly stressful if the nurse views his or her life as being "out of sync" with the rest of the world. Others find the situation both physically and psychologically stressful because they are unable to adjust their circadian rhythms to evening and night shifts.

A great source of stress for new graduates is the unrealistic expectations that they set for themselves. They approach the job expecting to function as their role models do, not realizing that organized, efficient functioning only comes with experience. "Expecting too much of oneself can lead to burn-out faster than any other single stressor" (Scully, 1980).

Another stressful time for nurses may be when they are promoted to positions of authority with the resulting legitimate power. The new position may be stressful because of its increased responsibility and demands. This nurse not only has to account for personal actions but also for the actions of many other nurses. This nurse may also be faced with administrative duties and may feel incompetent functioning within a bureaucratic institution. Such sources of stress create a feeling of powerlessness at many levels of the managerial hierarchy.

Moving to a new institution can also be stressful. The policies and procedures are different. The nurse must establish a rapport with the nurses on the unit, physicians, and ancillary personnel. Available equipment may be different and this nurse must learn the physical layout of the institution. These factors are indeed stressful, but the amount of stress incurred will vary according to the individual.

The nurse who is in the process of being hired is in a position of temporary power. The job seeker is a sought-after person, especially if there is a nursing shortage in that area. An orientation program is the method that most institutions use to introduce the new nurse to their system. The power of this situation for the new nurse lies in his or her right to insist that certain aspects be covered in the orientation to better prepare him or her for the job, or that the orientation be extended if it was inadequate. This nurse also can influence changes in the orientation program.

Dealing with Stress

What can a nurse do to convert these stressful situations into sources of power? The first step in converting stress to power is a realistic self-appraisal. However, the individual must first recognize the stress. One way to do this is to assess your body state several times a day. Are your muscles tight? Is your pulse rapid? Are you finding it difficult to concentrate? Do you have a headache? These are physical signs of stress (Scully, 1980).

The next step is to notice when you are stressed. Is it

related to a particular situation? Does it always occur at a certain time of day? There have been several scales established to rate the stress induced by various changes in a person's life. The higher the rank on the scale, the more stress that change invokes (Holmes & Rahe, 1967; Johnson, 1981). The skill of assessing sources of stress and eliminating or defusing them thus becomes very valuable. Once the sources of stress are identified, a systematic approach may be taken to correct them.

One recognized method of relieving stress is to rid the body of excess energy through relaxation exercises. "It is physically impossible to be nervous in any part of your body if in that part you are completely relaxed" (Jacobson, 1978). Such relaxation exercises involve the progressive tensing and then relaxation of every part of the body. With practice, the exercises become very effective in providing total relaxation.

Another popular relaxation technique is for the person to focus all thoughts on slow, rhythmic breathing. When this concentration is total, the person can imagine air passing through every part of your body, bringing warmth and energy and releasing tension (Jasmin, Hill, & Smith, 1981).

An individual may also choose to "escape" from stressful surroundings, which involves taking quiet time alone to do something that is considered relaxing. It could be reading a novel, listening to music, or sitting in a hot tub (Scully, 1980). It is important to allow for these quiet times during stressful periods. Active exercise is also a method of relieving tension. Any active exercise the person enjoys would be effective (Scully, 1980).

All of these methods are effective in coping with stress. The knowledge of what situations are stressful to a person can be used to assist that person in either avoiding the stress-provoking situation or in preparing in advance to decrease the stress. People who are successful in using effective coping mechanisms to deal with stress possess a power that is often unrecognized.

What can a nurse do to resolve work-related stress that have been identified and, therefore, build a power base? If the sources of stress involve interpersonal conflicts or dissatisfaction with the management of the unit, group sessions can be encouraged. The problem-solving capabilities of the group can be used in resolving the existing conflicts. This process enhances the power of the group because it increases the group's ability to handle the environmental stresses. It also builds a power base for the facilitator of the group.

If the stressors involve direct patient care or inadequate knowledge or skills on the part of the nurse, then the solution is different. The nurse may seek assistance from whatever resource people are available in the institution to solve the existing problem. If the nurse is a new graduate or one who is returning to practice and feels inadequate in technical skills, opportunities that improve specific skills can be sought.

The physical environment of the unit can also be changed to reduce stressors; that is, it can be improved within the confines of the physical arrangement. The improvement of the immediate work area may increase the nurse's esteem and, therefore, power with cohorts. If construction or renovation is planned, the nurse can request a place on the planning committee, a position that would afford more power to change the environment.

Stress is a factor that is present in every aspect of our society. The methods used to cope with stress and thereby increase functional capacity in one area can often be used in other areas as well. Therefore, adaptive behavior that is learned by nurses can establish them as powerholders in more than one setting.

SUMMARY

The power available to the nurse can be both enhanced and limited by education, reality shock, or stress. Education provides the most direct route to acquiring expert power and enhances power in several ways. At the same time, the evolution of nursing education has increased the professional orientation of the nurse's preparation. This situation has produced disparate school and work value systems, resulting in the phenomenon of reality shock in the transition from school to work. In addition to reality shock, other stressors are present in nursing. Throughout this discussion, suggestions have been made about measures to take to increase power-enhancing factors and reduce power-inhibiting factors.

BIBLIOGRAPHY

Abdellah, F. G. & Levine, E.: *Better Patient Care Through Nursing Research.* London, Macmillan, 1965.

French, J. R. P., Jr. & Raven, B.: The bases of social power. In Cartwright, D. and Zander, A. F. (eds): *Group Dynamics,* 3rd ed. London, Travistock, 1968.

Habgood, M. K.: Preventing reality shock: one AD program's plan. *Nursing and Health Care 2,* 74–75, 1981.

Holmes, T. H. & Rahe, R. H.: The social readjustment rating scale. *Journal of Psychosomatic Research 11:*213–218, 1967.

Jacobson, E.; *You Must Relax.* 5th ed. New York, McGraw-Hill, 1978.

Jasmin, S. A., Hill, L., & Smith, N.: Keeping your delicate balance: the art of managing stress. *Nursing 81 6:*53–57, 1981.

Johnson, J. W.: More about stress and some management techniques. *Journal of School Health 1:*36–42, 1981.

Kramer, M.: *Reality Shock: Why Nurses Leave Nursing.* St. Louis, C. V. Mosby, 1974.

Kramer, M. & Schmalenberg, C. E.: Conflict: the cutting edge of growth. *Journal of Nursing Administration 6,* 19–25, 1976.

Kramer, M. & Schmalenberg, C.: *Path to Biculturalism.* Wakefield, Mass., Nursing Resources, 1977.

Marriner, A.: *Guide to Nursing Management.* St. Louis, C. V. Mosby, 1980.

Schmalenberg, C. & Kramer, M.: *Coping With Reality Shock: The Voices of Experience.* Wakefield, Mass., Nursing Resources, 1979.

Scully, R.: Stress in the Nurse. *American Journal of Nursing* 5:912–915, 1980.

Selye, H.: *The Stress of Life.* New York, McGraw-Hill, 1956.

Smith, M. & Selye, H.: Reducing the negative effects of stress. *American Journal of Nursing* 11:1953–1955, 1979.

Steele, S. M. & Harmon, V. M.: *Values Clarification in Nursing.* New York, Appleton-Century-Crofts, 1979.

Stephen, S. & Bailey, J.: Sources of stress and satisfaction in ICU nursing. *Focus* 11:26–32, 1979.

Uustal, D. B.: Values clarification in nursing: application to practice. *American Journal of Nursing* 12:2058–2063, 1978.

Uustal, D. B.: Exploring values in nursing, *AORN Journal 31:*183, 1980.

RECOMMENDED READINGS

Reality Shock and Values

Kramer, M. and Schmalenberg, C.: *Path to Biculturalism,* Wakefield, Massachusetts, Nursing Resources, 1977.

This work is based on the original work of Kramer and is a "must" for all new nurses. It describes what the graduate needs to know and do in order to become bicultural. The book contains programs to help the reader understand and utilize the material presented. The modules are structured to help the new nurse progress through each stage of Reality Shock.

Schorr, T.: Reality Shock: What It is How to Deal With It: *IMPRINT. 9,* 26–28, 1979.

Dr. Schorr briefly describes the process of Reality Shock and some methods of relieving it. This is a good introduction to the subject.

Steele, S. M. and Harmon, V. M.: *Values Clarification in Nursing,* New York, Appleton-Century-Crofts, 1979.

This is an excellent resource for any nurse who wishes to clarify personal and professional values. It provides helpful activities and relevant examples.

Uustal, D. B.: Values Clarification in Nursing: Application to Practice: *AJN, 12*:2058–2063, 1978.

Ms. Uustal describes the theory of values clarification. She applies this theory to nursing situations. She also outlines strategies to help the nurse clarify his or her own value system.

Stress

Jasmin, S. A., Hill, L. and Smith, N.: Keeping Your Delicate Balance: The Act of Managing Stress. *Nursing 81.* 5:53–57, 1981.

The authors describe stress and its effects on the human body. They present a stress inventory to assist the individual in assessing the significance of various stresses in their life. Methods of reducing stress in everyday life are delineated.

Scully, R.: Stress in the Nurse. *American Journal of Nursing.* 5, 912–915, 1980.

The author describes areas which are stressful to the nurse and methods of relieving this stress. The nursing experiences are graphic.

Selye, H.: *The Stress of Life,* New York, McGraw-Hill Book Co., 1956.

This is one of the original studies on the effects of stress. The stress concept is defined, described, and applied.

INDEX